the
country
wife

the country wife

ANNE GORMAN

BANTAM
SYDNEY AUCKLAND TORONTO NEW YORK LONDON

A Bantam book
Published by Random House Australia Pty Ltd
Level 3, 100 Pacific Highway, North Sydney NSW 2060
www.randomhouse.com.au

Penguin
Random House
RANDOM HOUSE BOOKS

First published by Bantam in 2015

Copyright © Anne Gorman 2015

The moral right of the author has been asserted.

All rights reserved. No part of this book may be reproduced or transmitted by any person or entity, including internet search engines or retailers, in any form or by any means, electronic or mechanical, including photocopying (except under the statutory exceptions provisions of the Australian *Copyright Act 1968*), recording, scanning or by any information storage and retrieval system without the prior written permission of Random House Australia.

Random House Books is part of the Penguin Random House group of companies whose addresses can be found at global.penguinrandomhouse.com.

National Library of Australia
Cataloguing-in-Publication Entry

Gorman, Anne, author.
The Country Wife/Anne Gorman.

ISBN 978 0 85798 506 4 (paperback)

Gorman, Anne, 1934–
Women – Australia – Biography.
Community leadership.
Leadership in women – Australia.

920.720994

Cover image © Susan Fox/Trevillion Images
Cover design by Christabella Designs
All internal photographs courtesy the author.
Internal design by Midland Typesetters, Australia
Typeset in 12.5/17 pt Minion by Midland Typesetters, Australia
Printed in Australia by Griffin Press, an accredited ISO AS/NZS 14001:2004
Environmental Management System printer

Random House Australia uses papers that are natural, renewable and recyclable products and made from wood grown in sustainable forests. The logging and manufacturing processes are expected to conform to the environmental regulations of the country of origin.

Dedicated to

James Bruce Gorman

and our children
Alexandra Margaret
Austin Bruce
Vanessa Mary
Henry George
Rebecca Jane

every one a pearl of great price

contents

Prologue: The Iron Gate — ix

BOOK ONE: BEGINNINGS
1. Legacies — 3
2. The Statue of Liberty — 9
3. My Oedipus — 16
4. Iva John Austin — 23
5. The Wrong Mother? — 28
6. World War II — 37
7. Evacuation — 44
8. Losing Myself — 52
9. Home, 1943–1945 — 57
10. Parallel Lives — 67
11. The Solution — 75
12. Kincoppal-Rose Bay — 80

BOOK TWO: A GIRL IN THE COUNTRY
13. Sydney University — 87
14. The Apple Pie Man — 99
15. Facing Reality — 110
16. Thomas Edward and Frankie — 118

17	Settling In	124
18	Giving Birth	132
19	Three Times Lucky	142
20	Four Little Australians	153
21	The Village	164
22	Expansion	171
23	Branching Out	181
24	The Dinner Party	190
25	A Pope, a Priest and a Bishop	195
26	The Labor Party	205

BOOK THREE: A WOMAN OF THE WORLD

27	The Horse without a Rider, 1965	213
28	The Surgeon without a Soul, 1967	218
29	Melbourne	224
30	Hope	229
31	The Deep End	236
32	Academia	247
33	An Out-of-body Experience	254
34	The Rhythm Interrupted	265
35	The Release	275
36	Catalysts	280

Epilogue	288
Acknowledgements	297
About the Author	301

prologue
the iron gate, 1967

I stood at the iron gate looking west across the old cow paddock to the dam beyond, the sun's rays casting long shadows over the thirsty earth. Normally, this sunset scene would have filled me with delight, but not tonight. Tonight, fear closed around my body like a vice as I began to face some awful possibilities. Right at this moment, too, the dusty sunset brought a portent of another disaster: unmistakable signs of drought.

Off in the distance, a freight train trundled along beside the highway, a sound that never failed to soothe me when I woke in terror as a child at boarding school in the Blue Mountains. Back then, it reminded me that out there, real people were going about their business, men were shunting trains and blowing whistles, so there was nothing to fear from my dreams. But this time, the threat was real and here and now.

Beyond the dam, the paddocks were packed to the edge of the firebreaks with tall green stands of wheat. There would be time, if the rains came now, to fill their heads with grain. For weeks, we had been watching the sky for the spring rains to arrive. In the ten years I had lived in this place, their delivery of abundance had never let us down. Why had they done so now, and precisely when we needed them most? Perhaps we had become too cocky in our expectations. *One thing you can rely on*, I thought wryly, *is that the sun comes up in the east and goes down in the west every single day and, well, that's about it.*

My eyes fell on the stone fence flanking the iron gate. What a fiasco that fence had turned out to be. In a moment of artistic madness, when I thought I could make a real practical contribution to the farming operation, the children and I had constructed that fence. We'd taken the ute far up into the hill paddock, where stones grow out of the ground as if planted there by some ancient farmer, harvested them and brought them home. Piece by piece, we stuck those stones together with the cement I mixed by hand. The first fence fell down. My husband, Bruce, said nothing and we started again, learning from our mistakes as much as a four-, five- and six-year-old could learn by watching their mother sweat its progress.

Here it was now, five years later, still proudly standing as a tribute to the longevity of all ill-conceived and ill-constructed fences. Doing its job of keeping our cow, Dawn Fraser, out of the garden but comically so, with its stones going this way and that, to the amusement of all who looked at it.

When I had put Bruce on the 5 am train to Melbourne the previous Friday, I had driven home from the station feeling relieved that we might at last be getting to the bottom of his mystery illness. The doctor had said he was to have an exploratory operation to investigate cysts in his abdomen. I'd had a cyst or two. Pretty harmless. That didn't sound so bad. Driving home, as I looked east to the hills, the translucent brilliance of the pink and purple sunrise, and the flocks of birds playing outrageously in the early morning light and dancing beside the car along the highway, seemed determined to assure me that everything would be all right. But when I spoke to the surgeon over the phone on Saturday night, he had put an end to my optimism.

'I don't want to discuss this now with you,' he said, 'but it's not good news.'

'What do you mean, "not good news"?' I said.

'Come to my rooms in Collins Street on Monday morning and I can tell you more then.'

That was the conversation – short, brutal and to the point. Only, perhaps, it did leave room for some doubt. Just a little? I was now in limbo and not a very hopeful limbo at that. 'Come to my rooms in Collins Street on Monday morning.' That was fifteen hours away.

When I was at university, or perhaps long before, I made a vow not to allow myself to suffer the way my mother had. I would organise things differently – for sure I would, for sure. My mother had lived in a different time. She had birthed thirteen children, grieved the loss of two and raised us on her own after our father died. But that was then and this was now. Nothing like that would happen to me in this age of advanced medical knowledge.

Funny, I thought, as I stood there at the entrance to the cow paddock, *how some things seemed destined to repeat themselves in families.* How stupid I had been to believe I could control my future. Here I was, a woman of thirty-three, with five children under eight, standing alone at the iron gate realising that the future I had looked forward to with enthusiasm might turn out very differently. And why had I let Bruce go off on the train by himself? My best friend.

Now, the only sign of the departing day was a thin strip of crimson edging the long rim of the western horizon, out there beyond the north–south rail line. The call of a curlew was the only refrain. My body shivered violently as the chill night air closed in around me.

Oblivious to my drama at the iron gate, the children were enthralled in their own drama: Mister Ed's one-upmanship against his master. The cold flicker of the television was the only light coming from the house. I was out here alone. Perhaps that was how it was going to be from now on.

I saw the lights of a car making its way down the three-mile lane leading off the highway. If it turned left, it would be heading for our place and it would be Debbie, our helper, returning after her weekend off. The trail of dust that stretched all the way down from the highway marked her progress to our property's entrance, at the beginning of the poplar drive. In a moment, the clickedy-clack of her car over the ramp into the garden would signal her arrival and she would be pulling up outside the house.

Funny how surreal these mundane things become at desperate moments. A car returning and its lights flicking from tree to tree, dust on the road, children watching television.

It was time to get the children fed, ready for bed, school tomorrow and the unknown journey ahead of me.

book one
beginnings

Two things are terrible in childhood: helplessness (being in other people's power) and apprehension – the apprehension that something is being concealed from us because it is too bad to be told.

– Elizabeth Bowen

1
legacies

My grandfather, known to all as Honest Tom Donovan, was a respected leader in the community of Molong, in western New South Wales. Catherine Dempsey, his wife, was a hard worker, a very fussy homemaker and a strict disciplinarian. My mother was born to these two souls in 1892, the ninth of eleven children. Both her parents came from prodigiously fertile families whose ancestors included the earliest Irish settlers in the colony, the first of them arriving in New South Wales in 1820, probably as convicts.

My grandfather, a large red-headed man, was the licensee of the Courthouse Hotel, which housed a constant stream of travellers who changed trains or horse-drawn vehicle to go east to Sydney or west to Forbes, Dubbo, Warren and other destinations on the western plains. And no doubt after their long journeys they arrived with reliable thirsts. He provided his family with a comfortable lifestyle, and each child was educated until the age of fifteen, at a time when barely two per cent of the population continued schooling after twelve.

Iva John Austin, my father – known as John and sometimes called Jack – was posted to Molong as a salesman for a tractor company that was cashing in on the revolution in automated farming. He set up his headquarters at Honest Tom's hotel and got to know his family, especially his beautiful daughter Christina. Iva went on to establish an automotive business in Mudgee, a hundred miles away in the fertile Cudgegong River valley north-west of Sydney. He returned to Molong in 1915 to claim Christina as his bride.

The newlyweds drove to Mudgee in a T-model Ford to set up a home and start a family: the first of the children, a girl called Philomena, arrived in January 1916 and the second daughter, Elizabeth (Betty), arrived in 1917. The third child, a son, Dudley, arrived in 1918, while John – also called Jack – was born a year later. During that period, they built a very modern house with ensuite bathroom and many other advanced features – the house still stands to this day.

The family grew apace and the business thrived, so much so that John and Christina also bought a home in Sydney so their children could get a good education. The home they purchased was large, had a tennis court, and sat on the corner of Serpentine Parade in Vaucluse, a stone's throw from the harbour. Mother employed a nanny for the younger children – by then Meg, Molly, Larry, Joan and Ken had arrived on the scene – and a maid for the house. Every second weekend, Father would drive or fly to Sydney to spend time with the family. But once the Depression struck in 1929, such luxury was out of the question and the family moved back to Mudgee, where they could augment their income by living off the land.

Like most families, mine had it tough during the years of the Depression. It must have been especially hard for Mother, who had a sense of her own gentility as the daughter of Honest Tom and Catherine Donovan.

Some people gave up on their appearance during the Depression – what the hell, knees out of a pair of pants, shoes worn down at soles and heels. This was not how our mother did things. Mass on Sunday was a public ritual, when every eye could see how well the family was surviving the hard times. So Saturday night was not a night to relax. Mother and the elder girls, Philomena and Betty, would stay up past midnight, their eyes heavy with sleep, to relentlessly patch and mend, patch and mend all the children's clothes.

If a dress could not be found for one of the girls that night, she would have to wear her school uniform to Mass, a humiliating experience. Even if you had to share your brother's shoes and go to Mass at a different time, that is what had to be done. Bare feet were okay at home but for school or Mass on Sunday, unthinkable.

Cutting, trimming and keeping the nits at bay from hair was something everyone in the family learned to do, but you didn't talk about it outside the four walls of home.

In 1928, Allan, the tenth baby was born. By then little Dudley, the third child, had tragically died as a toddler in the great flu epidemic of 1921.

Betty, the second of the ten, was to be the next casualty. Lively and full of fun, by 1933, at sixteen, she was Mother's greatest helper and companion, the one who organised games for the younger children, constantly busying herself with what needed to be done. Baby eleven was now on the way, and Betty's arms ached to hold the new infant. Always available after school to ease Mother's burden as her energy waned in the summer heat, Betty knew what to do to keep everyone happy. When there was a party, Betty made cakes and rostered jobs among the younger children. Phil, the eldest daughter, was a bookworm and preferred to play the role of Mary to Betty's Martha. Jesus may have loved Mary, but in this family it was the Martha who was the glue holding everything and everyone together.

Hope and opportunity lay ahead for Betty. She was leaving school and the family was moving back to Sydney. As before, the move was driven by our parents' desire to give their growing brood a better education so they could look forward to more prosperous futures.

There was, though, another imperative for our mother. She was pregnant again. In Mudgee, she was frequently stung by asides and even blatant comments about the size of her family. One landed dowager said, 'Christina, you will have to stop breeding like rabbits.' After that, Sydney seemed like a nirvana – a place that offered the freedom of anonymity.

To celebrate the milestone of Betty finishing school, Mother threw her a party. The menu included her favourite: a great big fruit cake. A day or so later, Betty complained of severe pains in her tummy, and Mother summoned the doctor.

'Don't worry,' he assured her, 'it's nothing really. Fruit cake does this to young people. She probably had too much.'

Phil, Betty's constant companion, agreed with the doctor: 'Oh, yes. She's such a guts, she had three pieces', and everyone laughed with relief.

But the pain didn't go away. Suddenly, an ambulance was at the door and Betty was carried out on a stretcher. Once in the small hospital, the doctor, sticking by his first diagnosis, administered a purging dose of castor oil. Within hours, she was dead from septicemia, the result of a ruptured appendix.

'She went oh so quickly. There was no time to say goodbye,' my sister Joan, who was nine years old when it happened, told me years later. Penicillin, which might have saved Betty, would not be discovered until eight years after she died, pressed into invention to save the wounded in the wake of World War II.

It was a very hot December day and far from a season of joy in the Austin household when Betty's funeral was held. Mother, beside herself with grief and eight months pregnant, did not attend. But there was no escaping the awful reality of it. Shrouded in dust, Betty's cortège passed along the road within sight of the house and then across the bridge on the edge of town to the Mudgee cemetery beyond. At that moment, Joan witnessed Mother falling back in her chair with a scream of anguish.

'Be careful, Christina,' a neighbour urged her. 'Think of the new baby.'

The older surviving siblings were stunned at Betty's death, while the younger ones were simply bewildered, failing to fully comprehend what had happened. But Phil was left with a profound sense of guilt. In the early hours of the morning, a few weeks after Betty's death, Mother woke to hear a noise in the kitchen. She found Phil on her hands and knees, tears streaming down her face, vigorously scrubbing the kitchen floor. A form of self-administered penance perhaps? Mother gathered her up into her arms. She knew too well the burden of guilt and although she carried it herself, she knew such agony was too much to be carried by one of her children.

'Come here, darling, it's not your fault. You are not to blame.' The sobbing lessened. 'I want you to help me with the new baby. You will be her special little mother. Go back to bed now and sleep. There's a lot to do before the baby comes. It might even be tomorrow.'

Some of the guilt Mother carried was for the burden of having committed a mortal sin. After Allan's birth in 1928, against the strong dictates of the Catholic Church, she used contraceptives. So six years had passed without another baby.

I can only speculate on the sense of freedom this must have given my parents. Dancing maybe, short trips away from the family, games of tennis or swimming, unworried sexual activity. A blissful interlude in their marriage. But there was a big downside. Other Catholics would have been watching and noting that she was not fronting up to communion at Sunday Mass. For her to be pregnant again, either the contraceptives let her down or she had stopped using them.

Betty's death must have seemed like divine retribution. A terrible price to pay for disobeying the rules of the Church. Those rules were constantly reinforced from the pulpit, with lurid details of the punishment that would follow the wickedness of eating meat on Friday; missing Mass on Sunday; masturbating, which would make you go blind; having sex outside marriage, and aborting the foetus if you got pregnant; fantasising about the opposite sex; kissing a boy or girl; or, worst of all, using contraceptives, thereby cutting off the source of supply to fill church pews and Catholic schools.

This was the context of my arrival into the world on 17 January 1934, under the sign of Capricorn, in the same hospital where Betty had died just a few weeks before.

Luckily for me, Phil took her duties with the new baby seriously. I thrived, putting on weight, walking and talking early amid the stimulation of all my elder brothers and sisters, who also took turns at taking care of me. No doubt the novelty wore off when two more girl babies arrived in quick succession, making a total of thirteen pregnancies in all for Mother.

2
the statue of liberty

The morning's timetable at our household was measured by the 8 am Catalina flying boat landing at Rose Bay, coming all the way from New Zealand. This was the signal for Joan, Larry, Ken and Allan to leave for school and the older children for work or study. Eventually, when I went to kindergarten, I would leave the house at that time, too.

My earliest memories of this home were of eleven children and two parents all squeezed into a house at the top of Victoria Road, Bellevue Hill, a cauldron of activity, where crises boiled over at unexpected moments. Larry, at fourteen, in order to experiment with what he had learned in science class, set up a science room under the garage and, mixing a brew of unknown substances, blew himself up. I watched as he was carried off to hospital in an ambulance to remove the glass embedded in his face and body. One day, Allan, accompanied by a Marist Brother, suddenly appeared at the front door with his arm in a sling, injured at school gymnastics. It was a broken collarbone.

Then there were the conflicts. Mother simply couldn't abide arguments among her many super-active children. Skirmishes for territory, possessions, differences of opinion and opportunities for attention were an inevitable part of family life with such a crowd in a time of scarcity. Nevertheless, she clung to the notion that one could rule by 'peace imposed at any price' and she kept trying.

There were many things Mother couldn't control, no matter how hard she tried. One of them was the well-worn path of dissension between Daddy and Jack. A favoured child in early life, Jack grew up with a giant sense of entitlement.

Jack was regarded as a bit of a villain by the rest of the family; his antics used to leave our father in deep despair, with our mother his only defender. When I was an adult, I heard the story about the time in Mudgee when he was around fifteen and working with our father during the school holidays. These were the Depression years; Daddy had been putting money away all year to pay Christmas bonuses to his staff and Jack discovered the money and stole it.

Our father was outraged and Jack ran home and hid from him. When our father came home from work, he eventually came out from his hiding place and Daddy started punching him hard. Jack hit back, and between the two of them they broke a glass door leading onto a sleep-out. They only stopped fighting when Mother went running in with a straw broom, put herself between them and started beating them both with its spiky end. Later that night, an announcement was made over dinner that Jack would be going to boarding school as soon as the school holidays were over.

'Otherwise,' Daddy told him, 'I cannot be responsible for what I might do to you.'

Then it was up to the Brothers at St Joseph's College,

famously unsparing of the rod, to teach Jack right from wrong. Quite a forlorn hope, as it turned out, since Jack distinguished himself by becoming a recidivist runaway.

At seventeen, he finished school and after months of trying unsuccessfully to find a job, Daddy found one for him.

When I was about three years old, I became aware of both Daddy's fury at Jack's behaviour and Mother's distress at their ensuing rows. One evening, Daddy had just come home from work and was greeting Mother. Carmel, my younger sister, and I were sitting at the kitchen table eating dinner. Suddenly, the tranquillity of this cosy little tableau was shattered when Jack walked in and arrogantly announced that he had quit his job. This was the last straw for our father. I thought he was going to explode. He started shouting at Jack and Jack shouted back.

'You're going back,' said Daddy, 'if they will take you.'

'No, I'm not,' said Jack.

Daddy began to shout louder. I sat there eating, trying to look small and, if possible, invisible. I was becoming more and more amazed and anxious. It was the only time I saw our father beside himself with rage and it frightened me.

'You have disgraced this family! I asked them to take you on as an apprentice. It was a big favour to me because you couldn't get a job anywhere else. They are my friends and we do a lot of business with them. I begged them to take you. I begged them, do you hear? Now you have humiliated me and the whole family … again.'

'I'm not going back to work there and you can't make me. I'm leaving. I'm going to the country to get a job, away from all of you,' said Jack.

Mother was, as usual, anxiously trying to keep the peace between them. At that point, she grabbed two-year-old Carmel and me each by an arm and dragged us out of the kitchen.

In my eyes, Daddy was always right and I thought it my duty to support him. Breaking free from Mother's grip, I stood my ground and said, 'You are a very naughty boy, Jack. Stop shouting at my daddy.'

Mother pulled me into the safety of the darkened hallway.

'See! See what you are doing to this family,' I heard Daddy say. 'Out of the mouths of babes. If you want to go, go and good riddance. You are no son of mine.'

The temperature in the house had reached boiling point. I heard a door bang and the house seemed to shake with relief. Abruptly, there was silence and no one dared to utter a sound. In the morning, Jack had disappeared and peace had returned for the time being, but not tranquillity.

There were other worries for Mother to deal with, the biggest of which was our father's health. He had begun to pass blood in his urine. Mother begged him to see the doctor but like many men of that time, he ignored her advice.

'Nothing wrong with me. I don't trust those quacks. I've never had a day's sickness in my life,' he said.

Fear, I realise now, must have been gripping him like a vice. Having moved the family back to Sydney, he had established a new textile business and, although it was going well, he had eleven children, including his recalcitrant eldest son, and an overworked wife to support. Mother gave him natural remedies and I saw lots of ginger ale in the kitchen cupboard and a fizzy powder. When I wanted some of that, I was told it was not for children, that it was medicine.

Among all the mayhem of life in a large family, I can remember precious moments when I had Mother all to myself. One day, a big box of apricots arrived in the kitchen. A tireless worker and intent on storing enough jam for the winter, Mother had soon chopped the fruit into small pieces and there it was, vigorously bubbling away on the stove and filling the house with its almondy aroma. I shadowed her around the kitchen.

'Can I try it? Can I help you put the jam in the jars?' I said, impatient for the process to be finished.

'When it's cooked and cool,' she replied. 'Here's a piece of bread. Just wait. Don't touch anything. I don't want you to get burned.'

Even with all the distractions she faced, I always felt Mother loved me. It was such a privilege to have all her attention in these few moments, when the younger two were having their midday sleeps and everyone else had left the house. To magnify these moments and gain more of her love, I would seize every opportunity to offer help, as if somehow that would make her happy and earn more of the attention that had to stretch across so many others.

When I was five, I started kindergarten at Holy Cross College on Edgecliff Road and went there in the mornings with my sister Joan, who was fourteen.

Arriving home one day, Joan and I found our mother sitting on a chair in the kitchen, her hair singed and her head and face covered with a wet towel. She was gasping for breath, while baby Christine and Carmel quietly played at her feet.

'What happened?' asked Joan.

With great difficulty, Mother explained, 'I lit the oven and it went out. When I tried to light it again, it blew up in my face. Ring your father urgently,' she gasped.

Joan ran to the telephone hanging on the wall in the hall. 'Come home quickly, Daddy' was her frightening plea to our father. 'Mummy has had an accident.'

He arrived shortly afterwards and rang the doctor, who ordered an ambulance. Up on the street, holding Christine and Carmel's hands, I watched a stretcher being lifted into an ambulance, our father sitting beside our mother in the back. Then they drove away.

A terrifying thought began to take hold. *Was everything I knew and loved about to come to an end?* Others in the family had accidents but not my mother. She was always strong and reliable, always there. I was suddenly aware of her vulnerability. Without her, what would we do? It was a frightful prospect.

My eldest sister, Phil, was a nurse at the hospital and was waiting for the ambulance to arrive that afternoon.

'Mother was still gasping for breath from the shock of the oven explosion. She hadn't been burned but it was feared she wouldn't last the night, because the doctors had found that she was suffering from double pneumonia,' Phil told me years later. 'This was virtually a death sentence before the days of penicillin. The odds were not good, not good at all, but she was tough. It took more than a bout of double pneumonia to kill her.'

'Oh, yes,' I agreed, 'she was tough.'

'But after a few days at death's door, she seemed to be getting better.'

'Then what happened?' I asked.

'We realised after a while, something was not right. I was there when Daddy questioned the doctor. "Look, she seems to be all right now but she doesn't recognise me. She just turns her head away. Something else seems to be happening. What's wrong, and what can we do?" he pleaded.

'"John, we are lucky she is still with us. Let's give it a bit more time," said the doctor.

'For days it remained a mystery, as Mother lay there in hospital, no longer sick but not well enough to go home, either.'

Phil remembered going into her room to give her a meal. 'She just glared at me and said nothing.'

One afternoon, after visiting hours were over and the nurses were busy preparing for the evening shift, Mother did an extraordinary thing. Dressed only in a flimsy nightdress, she climbed out of her hospital bed and, in her bare feet, walked down the iron and cedar staircase of the hospital to a wide landing guarded by a six-foot statue of the Virgin Mary. Then, with all the strength of a demented person, she picked up this white and blue plaster sentinel and flung it over the balustrade onto the marble floor below, where it shattered into a thousand pieces.

Pandemonium broke out in the hospital. The Reverend Mother was appalled at the desecration and the disruption this event had caused in her domain. No doubt she was wondering what else might be in my mother's sights – the big picture of the X-ray vision of the Sacred Heart in the foyer, or the statue of St Vincent de Paul near the entrance? She called my father and spoke to him in the way only a hospital matron can.

'I'm afraid we have had to take some strong action. I am sorry but your wife has had to be restrained in a straitjacket,' she told him. 'You couldn't manage her. She is not in her right mind. A danger to herself and everyone and everything in the hospital. I recommend we transfer her to Mount St Margaret's Mental Hospital immediately!'

3

my oedipus

Uppermost in my father's mind was what to do with his children now that his wife had gone out of her mind. Certainly, he faced a dilemma. Perhaps he could hold back one of his elder daughters from school or training. But even if he kept everyone together at home, who would have the kind of strength Mother brought to her maternal tasks, especially with three very young children and three extremely active adolescent boys, not to mention a recalcitrant eldest son? Besides, he had realised his own health was failing and he had a factory to run – the means of our financial security. It might have been a toss-up between a boarding school and an orphanage. Fortunately, the boarding school won.

I must have blocked out the memories of packing up and moving from that house at Bellevue Hill, with its view of Rose Bay on one side and Bondi Beach on the other – the house I loved so much, along with the people and all the activity that went on there.

My first memory of the upheaval is of sitting in a chair in a parlour with Daddy, surrounded by suitcases. Joan, fifteen;

Carmel, three; and Christine, two, were there as well and we were waiting for the Reverend Mother.

Many times during my life, a smell has triggered the memory of the first moment in that convent. Now I know it is a combination of beeswax and carbolic and, when a nun came within range, something else to do with nuns' unwashed bodies. Indefinable but appalling!

'Where is my mummy? She always smells nice,' I would say to Joan early in our stay there.

At that, she would look the other way and assure me that Mother would be coming to visit us 'soon'.

I thought again of that ambulance driving away up Victoria Road with my mother on board. Why wasn't she coming back to rescue us from the brown-clad witches, the nuns? Where was she now when we needed her most? Where was everyone else – my other sisters, brothers and my dearest daddy?

'Will we be going back to Bellevue Hill, Joan?' I would ask. 'Back to school at Holy Cross College?'

Then she would answer, 'Maybe we'll have a new place.'

This made me more anxious because it implied that the place of stability I knew as home might not be there any more. I wanted reassurance. I wanted to be given back stability. I wanted family.

'I don't want a new place, I want to go to our own home at Bellevue Hill,' I would say emphatically.

Home was comforting, secure – a place I could rely on and know my way around. But this convent was not like that. Here were tall ceilings, long dark polished corridors, hideous crucifixes and pictures of long-dead saints, admonishing us, the living, to repent of our sins. Then there were the steep flights of stairs leading to dormitories and unseen other places. Who knew what might be lurking behind closed doors, down other dim, hardly glimpsed labyrinthine corridors, their floors polished so highly that they were slippery and dangerous to a child's hurrying foot. It was out of scale. Out of time, out of place. I never adjusted to it and have hated all places like that since, or anywhere that looks or smells the same.

Daddy's idea was to keep everyone in the family as close to one another as possible. That is why he chose St Joseph's Convent. It was close, just up the hill, to where our brothers Larry, Ken and Allan were staying, at St Joseph's College at Hunters Hill. But it was a long way from home, across two bridges and in unfamiliar territory.

Hungry for family, we would listen out for the unmistakable crunch, crunch of many marching feet, the sound of boys walking in unison down to the Lane Cove River. At that moment, Joan and I would run to the upstairs windows to wave to our brothers as they marched by with the other boys, beach towels nonchalantly slung over their shoulders.

The fertile minds of the dear Sisters must have run riot. What occasion of mortal sin might waving to boys lead us into? The solution they came up with was first to lock up the windows on that side of the school and, when that didn't work, to paste them over with brown paper. What our father had expected was that both schools would make an effort to keep the family in contact with one another by organising weekly visits and arranging for us to attend one another's sporting and special events. But it wasn't to be. We might as well have been two thousand miles away, not just down the hill from our brothers.

Every week we thought our stay at that school at Hunters Hill would come to an end. 'This will be over soon – maybe even tomorrow!' I would tell my two younger sisters, though my words were largely wasted on Christine, who was still learning to speak. But month after month it continued.

Some Sunday mornings, when the nuns were saying their prayers and Joan had gone out for the day – she had more privileges, being older; I don't remember where she went or with whom – we three would be locked in one of the upstairs dormitories for a couple of hours. I used to think, *What if there's a fire, what if we are forgotten and just left here?* My reaction was to figure out a way we could escape. First, I examined what lay outside under the window sill. We were too high up to climb down but a brick ledge running along beneath the window offered a possible means of escape. If I climbed out onto that ledge, I could slide along, then reach another window leading into an unlocked room nearby. From there I could run around and unlock our door and let my two sisters out. Once I had worked that out, I relaxed. My earliest instincts were always to stay ahead of the game, however unrealistic my plans might seem in hindsight.

Another fantasy revolved around being rescued by our father. Sleeping Beauty, Rapunzel and Snow White had been rescued; why not us? From our upstairs vantage point, we could see the Iron Cove Bridge spanning the upper reaches of the Lane Cove River. On Sundays, I was sure I could see Daddy's white car making its way across that bridge, the sun glinting on its windscreen. Maybe today he would be coming to take us home.

'Is that one his?' Carmel would ask as we watched together.

'No, it will be the next one; that one is too small,' I would tell her with great authority and her little head would nod in agreement.

We were sometimes rewarded, when he came on Sunday afternoon to take us out for a drive and to buy us an ice-cream.

One hot afternoon, as a special treat, he took us to a place called The House of David, where there were ponies, led by men with long hair and beards. It was the first time I ever rode a horse and I loved it.

Then, for some unknown reason, our father stopped coming and no one told us why.

The endless days went by. Carmel, Christine and I slept in a dormitory with Joan, so we would see her in the morning and sometimes during the day around lunchtime. She was in the senior school, while Carmel and I were with the juniors. During school time, an old nun called Sister Agnes was Christine's special guardian. She mothered her, making frilly dresses for her and trying to teach her to play the piano. But I fear Christine was often left in her cot with no one coming to fetch her. I often crept up to see if she was all right, running to find a nun if I thought she needed attention.

Eventually, I gave up my scrutiny of the bridge and settled into a reluctant state of resignation. No one was coming to rescue us and there was no use hoping. I got on with learning new things, including how to read and write and sing new songs. When I was at a loose end, I would play on a piano outside the refectory but I had no idea how to make sense of the notes. I was ready for tuition but alas none was forthcoming.

In their own way, the nuns tried hard to be good to us. But their ideas of caring for children in distress were grounded in ignorance and a lack of awareness of the impacts of family upheaval on young children. It must have been difficult for them to look after us during school holidays, when all the other children had gone home to their mothers and fathers and we had to find ways of filling those empty days with nothing much to do. Our childhoods were slipping away from under us and would never be reclaimed.

When I turned six, it was time to make my first communion. As I woke on the big day, I could see my white dress and tulle veil hanging beside my bed and said to Carmel, who was just waking up in the bed beside me, 'Today is the day Daddy will come; he wouldn't miss my first communion.' This was by way of reassurance. If I said this out loud and often enough I believed it must happen.

I was excited and also anxious. Anxious at the instructions given by the nuns, who admonished us not to touch the small white host with our teeth (it was, after all, the body of Christ). Excited because I knew absolutely that my daddy would be there for the celebrations. In my white dress with pink roses embroidered on the bodice, echoed by a circle of tiny pink roses holding the white tulle veil in place on my head, I knew I looked my best for him.

Shortly before Mass, Joan took me aside. 'Darling, he isn't coming. But I tell you what! He has sent a bunch of pink carnations just for you.'

'Where are they?' I asked.

'They're on the altar,' she replied.

I bit my lip trying to hide an agony of disappointment. All during the Mass, I kept my eyes fixed on the altar: on either side, twelve candles flickered in two brass candlesticks. A large gold crucifix towered in a niche above it all, while the priest stood with his back turned away from us, resplendent in a cream vestment with a big gold and red cross embroidered on the back.

A forest of pink carnations sat among it all – in vases on the altar, on the floor and close to the rail where we would come up to make our first communion. *Maybe I can stretch out my hand and touch one*, I thought, but when the time came they were too far away. Which ones were mine – the ones Daddy had sent me? If I knew, I would feel better that he had remembered this big day and maybe I would be able to hold them and take one up to my dormitory, put it under my pillow and breathe in the very essence of my daddy's presence. Even so, I knew pink carnations were no real substitute for him, and the nagging disappointment went on and on, leaving no room for thoughts of Jesus and the momentous idea of eating his body for the first time.

After Mass was over, I sought out a place to cry in private. That is where Joan found me.

'Come on,' she said, 'you're missing the first communion feast. There's ice-cream and cake. Everyone's waiting.'

Meekly, I followed her to the big hall crowded with parents and their children, still in their veils and white dresses. I could see the sun streaming into the hall from the windows high up near the ceiling. A million tiny specks danced their way up and down the stairway to heaven, making the place hot and steamy. Margaret, my best friend, ran up to me and said, 'Mum and Daddy are taking us out for the day. Sorry, I won't be able to play with you.' The room began to move sideways. I tried to focus on the brightly coloured food spread out on the table. Red and green iced cakes, jellies of all shapes and sizes, bread spread with hundreds and thousands, and glasses of milk and orange cordial. We wouldn't be going out unless one of my parents came, and I knew they wouldn't be coming. The room was getting stuffier and I was finding it hard to breathe.

'Eat up,' said Joan. To please her, I took a cake and then a plate of jelly, and forced it all down onto my fasting and nervous tummy. Without warning, I was overcome with nausea, sending it all up again onto the floor and over my beautiful new dress. Someone cleaned me down and then lifted me up and I was carried off to bed with a racking headache, and I slept the sleep of kind oblivion for the rest of the day.

4

iva john austin

After Mother's nervous breakdown, Daddy's choices were limited, and I had to learn to live with them – all of us did. Could he have told me what was going on? Maybe not, but if I'd at least received an explanation for why he sent us to boarding school, it might have been better than living in the dark. What I always craved was simply to understand.

Perhaps as a consequence of these early traumas, I discovered at six something that followed me through my entire life: a vague notion that everything would always be all right and that I had the strength to make it so.

Where did that resilience come from and why does it endure in many members of my family? I know I inherited some of it from Mother but also from Daddy, and perhaps even further back than that.

Daddy's mother, Isabella Rich, had died when he was eight, and at fifteen he left his family in Launceston, Tasmania, to escape the proverbial wicked stepmother, whom his father married when he was ten. From then on, he found his own way in the world, working in engineering shops, learning on the job as he went. By the time he was twenty-two, he already had a thriving automotive business in the prosperous district of Mudgee.

That was when he wrote to his father to tell him the news of his impending marriage to Christina Ellen Donovan. Steeped in Protestantism and outraged at Iva John's intention to marry a Catholic, my grandfather sent his wedding present in the form of a venomous letter. At that point, Daddy converted to Catholicism and severed all contact with his father for the rest of his life. That is why I never met this grandfather, although he died at ninety-three.

My father was a self-taught engineer who saw opportunities where others' eyes were closed to them. At a time when many said the car would never take on, he launched Austin's Garage, a business selling Fords, then Oldsmobiles, Chevrolets, tractors and Australia's new invention, the Mackay combine harvester. He marketed them at field days, where he ensured the machines were majestically displayed in a paddock for all to see, touch and feel. Crowding around these wonders, potential buyers or simply the curious were introduced to their amazing possibilities by a group of enthusiastic company representatives. This kind of marketing was an innovative endeavour.

In 1920, when Daddy was in his late twenties and World War I was well over, he extended the reach of his business to encompass aviation. Following the Armistice, many people were stuck in the notion that planes were instruments of war, and since the world had just seen the war to end all wars, there would be no more use for them. As a result, planes were going cheap, and this presented my father with an opportunity to be part of another new world, the world of faster transportation.

Daddy bought a plane and began by running a passenger and freight air service between Mudgee and Sydney, one of the first of its kind in Australia. At field days and on the weekends, he offered joy flights for ten shillings to those brave enough to view the world from the air for the first time. The first pilot he interviewed was a veteran from the war called Charles Kingsford Smith, whom he considered a risk taker. Instead he employed a pilot who would eventually become one of the founders of Qantas.

Another of my father's innovative ideas was the introduction of a time payment system for farmers to buy the latest cars and harvesting equipment, an idea he borrowed from Henry Ford on reading the *Saturday Evening Post.* When the Depression hit, that initiative, which had proved so lucrative and successful in good times, became his Achilles heel, because farmers couldn't make their repayments. That was the point at which Daddy salvaged enough of what was left of his business, packed up the family and moved to Sydney, starting a small textile business in Alexandria, then the heart of the city's industrial centre.

From a very early age, I knew I had a special place in Daddy's heart. Many joyful memories of being cuddled to sleep in his bed and the absolute joy of his love remain in my memory. Sometimes, too, he would arrive home from work carrying a treat for me. My eyes would light up as I saw him place a paper bag on the sideboard.

'Is that for me?' I'd ask.

At that he would nod, smile and say, 'Why don't you take a look?'

Screaming with delight, I would open the bag and say, 'A meringue! Oh, you remembered!' and then I would throw myself into his waiting arms amid his laughter. Mother would shake her head in mild disapproval but would be laughing, too.

It was a great game for a three- or four-year-old and one I never grew tired of. He would sneak me butterscotch or butter menthols and if one of my brothers or sisters had a birthday he would bring me home a present, too.

One of my earliest memories was listening to the wireless, memorising songs and then singing them back word for word. I only had to hear something once or twice before I could sing it right through. The song Daddy loved the most was 'Danny Boy'. I would begin with:

'O Danny boy, the pipes, the pipes are calling.'

With his rich tenor, he would softly join me in singing:

'From glen to glen, and down the mountain side.'

And on we would go to the end, while the audience of my brothers and sisters looked on, sometimes complaining that I was too much 'Daddy's little darling'. I knew I was special to him, even though in this big family there was much competition for love and affection. Later in life, this gave me a sound capacity for love and trust no matter what the circumstances.

After the disappointment of my first communion, my optimism – or was it my resignation? – was rewarded. Daddy sent for me and I was collected from boarding school one Sunday morning by my eldest brother, Jack. Now in his early twenties and a reformed character, Jack had just come home from the country and had learned to drive while he was away.

I had expected Jack to take us to our home at Bellevue Hill but this was a strange place and we were going up in a lift. Jack was talking to someone.

'How's your father?' the stranger asked.

Jack repeated a prediction Daddy had made about the war and added, 'He says he's glad he won't be here to see it.'

As the stranger nodded, looking suitably grim, I pulled Jack's arm. 'What do you mean, Jack?' I asked. 'Where is he going that "he won't be here to see it"?'

Then the lift door opened and we were ushered into the flat by my eldest sister, Phil, who was dressed in a white nurse's uniform.

Daddy was propped up in a double bed surrounded by a half-circle of windows. Outside the window, I could see the treetops kissing the window just above the sill.

'Sing to me,' he said.

By now, the nuns had expanded my repertoire to songs such as 'Cockles and Mussels, Alive Alive O', 'Mother McCrea' and 'Ave Maria'.

'I want you to sing our song, darling, not any of those,' he said. 'You know, the one we sang together.'

As the adults melted out of sight and we were left alone, I confidently stepped forward to give full voice to my six-year-old falsetto.

'Oh Danny boy, the pipes, the pipes are calling
From glen to glen, and down the mountain side.'
Daddy began to weep silently. But I went on.
'But come ye back when summer's in the meadow
Or when the valley's hushed and white with snow.'
And on I went till the end:
'Oh Danny boy, oh Danny boy, I love you so.'

And then, as I saw his tears flowing freely, I climbed onto his bed and hugged and kissed him, weeping, too, though I didn't exactly know why.

Two hands then pulled me away. 'Don't upset your father, dear.'

And that was the last time I ever saw him.

5
the wrong mother?

I didn't recognise the person quietly sitting in the parlour of the boarding school waiting to see us. She looked different, very different; thin and pale and very quiet, not the plump rosy-cheeked person I remembered from a year before. Joan was standing beside her chair smiling. Christine ran up and hugged her. Carmel was more reticent and hung back. I hung back, too.

'Who is she?' I whispered to Joan, not quite believing it could be her. But the woman just smiled and nodded, so I knew it must be her.

'She says she is my mother but I'm not sure,' I said to one of the nuns, as we walked down the corridor, away from the parlour.

She reassured me, 'Yes, it is your mother. She has been sick and is better now. That's why she looks a bit different. She is going to take you home soon.'

Well, that is a mercy, I thought. Even if she was the wrong mother, at least we would be getting out of here. At last I would see my darling daddy again and know where I belonged.

A few days later, we packed our bags and said goodbye to the nuns, hoping never to see them again. When we arrived at the apartment, I ran to the sunroom, ready to sing again. It was empty. The bed was gone.

'Where's my daddy?' I demanded.

'Oh, darling,' said Ken, one of my brothers, 'he's gone to heaven.'

Vaguely, I knew what that might mean but I was not ready to accept it.

'Where is heaven?'

'It's up there, in the sky,' he said, pointing upwards. 'Look, he's died, sweetheart, and we had to bury him in the ground.'

'Why do people have to be buried in the ground to go there?' I asked, incensed. 'It doesn't make sense to me.'

'Well, he just closed his eyes and couldn't open them again.'

'That's ridiculous. Why couldn't you keep his eyes open? I could have kept his eyes open. Why did you let my daddy die?' I protested.

I believed that if I'd been there, he would not have left me. I could have made him live. I cried, oh how I cried, but I didn't want people to see me crying. I took refuge in the bathroom.

Then I heard Phil calling, 'Where's Annie?' and I had to show myself again.

'Come along,' said Ken and, as if to console us, 'lunch is waiting at our new home, called Rosemont, where you will be sleeping in your own beds.'

That magic word 'home'! I dried my tears.

Our home from now on was a large rented apartment on Edgecliff Road. This lovely sunny apartment with spacious rooms, a wonderful view of the harbour and the luxury of carpets was where we landed, after all the trauma, and where our mother brought the family back together again.

Molly, twenty, was training to be a secretary at a business college in the city and would soon announce her engagement to a sailor, whom Mother didn't like because he was not a Catholic and, in her assessment, Molly was marrying beneath herself. Meg, twenty-one, was working as a governess in the country, engaged to a country boy, Hector, now resplendently outfitted in a blue air force uniform. Mother liked Hector. He was a charmer and knew exactly how to please her with flattery and flowers. Jack had taken a flat at Double Bay and would one day soon marry Leonie, a school teacher and a welcome addition to the family. The other boys – Larry, Ken and Allan – were still boarding at St Joseph's, but when they came home for holidays, the place was crowded, with makeshift beds in every spare corner.

Until our father's death, Mother had never driven a car. In most families, men assumed the right to be the sole driver. One day, a blue Studebaker arrived at our front door and I went downstairs to inspect it. I wondered who would drive this car. The question was soon answered when Mother went off to take driving lessons. From then on, around the dinner table in the evening, her exploits on the road became the topic of amused conversation. One day, she drove the car up onto the footpath, which triggered hilarity among my brothers. But she took it all in good heart, knowing, I am sure, their little jokes would be short-lived once she got the hang of it. And she did get the hang of it. Within six weeks, she was driving to and from the textile factory Daddy left her as the means of our family's survival, and taking us into the city and out onto country roads.

Not only did Mother have to endure the nervousness of being a new driver and the jokes of her sons but, since there were so few women drivers on the road, she was the butt of much male abuse. Seated in the front of the car beside her, I felt angry on my mother's behalf when men gratuitously flung insults like 'bloody woman driver' from their moving vehicles. I took it on myself to lean out of the car window and poke my tongue out at them. 'Don't do that,' Mother would say. 'It just encourages them!' But I couldn't see how that could be. They needed no encouragement from me!

Women eventually had the last laugh, especially when we saw newsreels of the future Queen of England, Princess Elizabeth, in military uniform, driving a truck or bent over an engine, spanner in hand. Women were taking over the road and keeping the economy moving while the men, off at the war, had other enemies to shout at now.

Since the start of World War II and more so now, with the threat of a Japanese invasion, the suburbs had become markedly emptier. Some people went inland, including to the mountains. Some put their houses on the market or just locked up and left them empty. As a result, properties in the Eastern Suburbs around the harbour were going cheap. One hundred pounds could buy a substantial home. 'This is the time to buy,' I heard people say.

I tried to persuade Mother to take advantage of the situation, and she did come close. I remember going with her to inspect a house at The Crescent, Vaucluse, where the lawn ran down to the harbour and there were plenty of bedrooms and spaces to play in. While I sat in the car, she discussed the price with the eager man selling the property, and I closed my eyes and prayed, 'Make her say yes, God. Make her buy this for us.' At home, I heard her telling Phil she liked the house and wanted to buy it, but for reasons unknown it never happened.

The original Vaucluse house in Serpentine Parade had been sold at a big loss when my parents moved back to Mudgee during the Depression. The memory of that loss had preyed on Father's mind, and before he died he extracted a promise from Mother not to invest in real estate again. But years later, she did buy the apartment in the Rosemont building, in Woollahra, which remains in family ownership to this day.

From the first night I slept in the Edgecliff Road apartment, more tears had to be shed for my daddy, and I cried them quietly in the privacy of the night for months, until there were no more tears to shed and getting on with life was the only option.

One of the great sadnesses was the fact that no one mentioned our father much after that. There was a kind of conspiracy between everyone that to do so would make Mother sad. Whenever she spoke about him, she was hesitant. Once, she commissioned an artist to paint his portrait based on photographs. I liked it, but she hated it. 'It's not him. He didn't capture him properly,' she declared.

I don't think anything could ever have done justice to the man she loved. The portrait was put in the hall cupboard and I don't know what happened to it after that.

But this was really the thing. I loved my father and knew I was special to him. Yet no matter what I told my friends about him, like how clever he was or that he once owned a plane, it didn't impress them. Once people were dead, it seemed, they were dead. He was no longer a living presence. I was fatherless and that was that.

A sense of stability began to grow … except … except for a lingering doubt. Mother was now the only bulwark against the threat of being left an orphan. Her racking cough, a legacy of three bouts of pneumonia, haunted me throughout my childhood and I often wondered if she would make it to the time when I was independent enough to look after myself and my two younger sisters. What would happen if she didn't make it? Would we be put into a boarding school again or even an orphanage?

Absence from her for a year at five years old had been enough to bend the fragile reed of intimacy between us. My dealings with Mother were often tinged with wariness on my part. Looking back, I appreciate that she was so busy with day-to-day concerns that there was simply no time for expressions of sentiment. Not that she gave effusively of her hugs and kisses anyway. Facing the task of coralling this unruly bunch, Mother did the best she could to establish a sense of control, especially keeping her children on the Catholic 'straight and narrow'. She insisted on Mass on Sunday, a meatless Friday, rosary in the evening, regular novenas and confessions of one's sins.

At Mass at St Joseph's, right next to our parish school on Albert Street, Mother would sit with me, Carmel and Christine on the side-facing aisles, which gave her a good view of where other family members were sitting or kneeling. After Mass, we would buy a block of ice-cream to go with the dessert of fruit salad and hurry home to put it in the fridge and then we would get the big lamb roast and baked vegetables into the oven. Carmel, Christine and I would have shelled the peas the night before. Around twelve, the house would start to fill up with family members and often we'd set the big cedar table with extra places for visitors.

When it was just family, Mother would often raise the issue of her Mass observations, saying something like, 'Larry and Ken, I didn't see you at Mass this morning.'

They would reply, 'Oh, we were right down the back in the entry alcove. We had to stand up. The church was full and there were no places left.'

Then Mother might say, 'I won't have you joining the one knee brigade', using her term for the despised group of people who always came late, loitered down the back and escaped before the end of Mass.

Continuing her interrogation, she would say, 'Well, why didn't I see you at communion?'

They would look surprised, mumble something like 'We were there – didn't you see us?' and start to clear the plates.

Her suspicions were then aroused. Not going to communion meant they might be in the state of mortal sin, and the following weekend she would take them both to confession.

After that, the older members of the household, including my brothers, started going to Mass at St Canice's Church at Rushcutters Bay, close to Kings Cross. It was the society church of the day and the one Phil and other nurses from St Vincent's Hospital, as well as many servicemen and -women, attended. Mother took to interrogating Phil about their attendance.

No one knew much about psychology in those days, and Mother never wanted to talk about her year at the mental hospital, except to say how much she hated the straitjacket, the shock treatment and being locked up for hours in her room with no escape.

From my perspective all these years later, it's not surprising Mother had a nervous breakdown. This was, after all, a woman who had given birth to thirteen children, ten of them in just ten years. She had lost two along the way in tragic circumstances. She saw her lapse into mortal sin – the use of contraceptives – as something she had to be punished for, and I believe she spent the rest of her life atoning for it.

I am reminded of A. D. Laing's definition of insanity, 'a sane reaction to an insane situation'. No wonder she took revenge on the Virgin Mary, that 'purest of creatures, sweet mother, sweet maid', in the words of the hymn; Mary was only ever asked to have one child – and had a virgin birth at that!

Back then, locking Mother up for a year, maybe forever, was the only solution for the nuns.

In any case, her return to sanity was a miracle. From the time she made the decision to come back to us, she was for me a magnificent, resilient role model. I was not yet old enough to understand what it takes for someone to make a recovery the way Mother did. However, what was being embedded in my understanding was the fact that optimism, survival and recovery are three notches on the same belt. Linked to this notion was the idea that miracles are part of the warp and weft of life. Perhaps the stories of Jesus' miracles led me to expect miracles to happen in my world. But, still, I could hardly believe my mother was back.

It would be years before I learned the role our father's illness and death had played in Mother's recovery. When I was older, Phil told me that soon after her visit to see us at the boarding school – when I had suspected that she was the wrong mother – she came out of hospital for the day. As everyone sat around the table for lunch discussing the war, Mother suddenly stood up, cleared the dishes and, without saying a word, threw them out the window. This had the effect of making everyone walk on eggshells around her.

Seeing Father in his sick bed in the sunroom had not been enough for Mother to register the awful truth. Given her still-fragile state, my elder brothers and sisters were concerned about whether to tell her that our father was dying.

The doctor said, 'The shock might be too much. It could trigger another collapse.'

The nuns from St Vincent's thought the family should pray for guidance. Friends of the family had offered other opinions.

Eventually, Phil, all of twenty-three years old, told her: 'Mummy, Daddy is going to die soon. I think you should know that he only has a few weeks or even days to live.'

Suddenly, the fog was lifted from our mother's eyes and from that time on, everything became clear to her. According to my sister, Mother immediately said, 'I'm not going back to hospital. We have a lot to do. There are arrangements to be made.'

She spoke to Father about the business and learned as much as she could about how best to run things. Jack was now a responsible adult and, under our father's guidance, was managing things at the factory at Alexandria. It was a tribute to Father's relationship with his employees that they stood by him during that time and ensured the business kept running.

How did our mother endure? Was resilience in her genes or learned through the circumstances of life? I know for sure that it was a quality she encouraged in her children. She had a compelling goal, of course. She told me once that the responsibility of paying fees for seven children still at school was enough to keep her going.

Little things she said come back to me after all these years, like, 'Don't cry; tomorrow is another day. This will look different tomorrow.' And it always did.

One day, she found me hiding behind the curtains crying at some disappointment and she said, 'If you get upset about small things, you'll never be able to cope with big things when they come along.'

And, of course, she was right. I knew she was right, so I remembered it and took it on board.

6
world war II

The Japanese had bombed the US fleet in Hawaii and then gone on to invade the Philippines, northern Malaya and Hong Kong. Although I had no idea where those places were, everyone said this was a calamity and would have 'big consequences'.

Undeterred, Mother had rented a huge old weatherboard house overlooking the ocean at Terrigal beach. We would have Christmas there and stay until the end of January – a chance for the whole family to spend a bonding time together.

Terrigal was an unspoiled beachside village, not the overdeveloped busy place it is now with a luxury high-rise hotel and apartments. Back then, a fish and chip shop, a greengrocer, a small grocery store and a butcher supplied the inhabitants with everything they needed. On our way there, Mother filled the already overburdened car with fruit, eggs and honey from roadside stalls dotting the highway. The full impact of food rationing was not yet being felt, especially once we got out of the city.

Soon after arriving, I was horrified to see that the ocean and the beach were unprotected. In every direction, I could see miles of deserted beaches and no sign of a defence force – an open invitation to the enemy. What if an armada of Japanese boats landed on Terrigal beach in the middle of the night, murdering us all in our beds?

A makeshift dinner table big enough to accommodate the whole family had been rigged up, supported by trestles at either end. Sitting there one night at dinner, I volunteered my worries to the group.

'What if we are invaded? That beach doesn't have any barbed wire on it,' I said. (I had seen that in one of the newsreels at the pictures.) 'What will stop them coming to Terrigal, and if they do, how will we kill them? I think we should all have guns.'

Nervous laughter and raised eyebrows around the table.

'Don't worry, darling,' said one of my brothers. 'We will protect you!' More laughter.

I couldn't see how my brothers, who were mere youths, would be up to that assignment. I knew they were not taking me seriously. I must have looked worried, because Mother intervened.

'I want this conversation to stop immediately. Larry and Ken, stop. Do you hear me? Stop. Anne, darling, it's all right, we are safe here. No one is going to invade us. After all, we have the army to defend us, so don't worry.'

I hoped I could trust Mother. Then again, I *had* to trust her – what other choice did I have? She was my mother, after all. She wouldn't tell me lies. So I got on with enjoying the holidays. The endless hot days. Freedom, oh freedom, to run and play at will, without adult interference, for the first time since we left Bellevue Hill for the boarding school. There was too much going on for anyone to worry about what I was doing – and what I was doing was giving myself the opportunity to be alone with my imagination, the sea, the beach and the headland, where from the top of the cliff I watched the waves breaking against the rocks below.

That holiday was the beginning of my lifelong romance with the Australian coastline and one of the happiest times of my childhood. War or no war, there was a great feeling of joy and relief as we all got to know one another again. Family friends and family members came and went but there were rarely fewer than seven or eight of us in the house at any one time. At weekends, when everyone came up from Sydney, we all piled into the cars and attended Mass at the boarding house near the beach, taking up most of the available space on its verandah. When we got bored we could always watch the activity on the beach or assess the surfability of the waves below. Always a topic of discussion.

At night, I watched my elder brothers and sisters jitterbugging to the music of a wind-up gramophone. Nights were long now because the government had introduced daylight saving to preserve electricity for the war effort. I stayed up well beyond my bedtime, because going to bed when the sun was still shining was unthinkable. So I took part in the most exciting thing in the world: my brothers tossed me round and I danced until, flushed-faced and excited, I was packed off to bed, departing oh so reluctantly. How happy I was and how lucky to have such a wonderful family.

During those holidays I turned eight and Mother made a big cake with candles, the first proper birthday I had celebrated since Bellevue Hill. Now, at last, I felt that growing up might be worth the effort after all.

For a widow of fifty-one years, getting this displaced family back together again and building it into some sense of cohesion was not an easy task. In spite of all her efforts, Mother never quite achieved it. A new family culture had to be developed, because since her breakdown and our father's death, everyone had changed and had not only become more self-reliant, but determinedly so in some cases. Resuming full parental authority over the older family members was beyond Mother now. Nevertheless, she did try hard to control them, especially when it came to forcing the issue of the practice of our Catholic faith.

The fact was, Mother wanted all of us to go to heaven and probably imagined that if she played her cards right, we'd all be there as a family, preferably having been to confession the night before. I had no doubt I would be among that celestial group, and somehow that holiday by the sea reinforced my belief that I would be.

But there was another side to it all. Although Terrigal was isolated, we still got the newspapers every day. Since I didn't want adult decisions to take me by surprise any more, I put my antennae out to avoid any more sudden shocks, but I was also naturally curious. I could read and I knew what the headlines said. I kept asking questions when I saw headlines such as 'Japanese Subs Sunk Off New Guinea'. 'Does that mean we are winning or losing?' I'd ask. But no one seemed to know, or if they did, they were not prepared to tell me.

Immediately after we came home from Terrigal, some terrible things happened in the Pacific. On Sunday nights, we gathered around the big rosewood veneer wireless in the lounge room to listen to the Lux Radio Theatre (I washed my face assiduously with Lux soap until Phil told me that it caused ageing), and it was on that wireless that I heard Singapore had fallen to the Japanese. Abandoned by the British government, whose focus was the fight in Europe and the Middle East, most of our soldiers had been trapped. Thousands were taken prisoner and many others hideously murdered. Then Japan went on to take the Netherlands East Indies, Dutch Borneo, Sulawesi and Sumatra in a hundred days of conquest, sinking the Australian frigate HMAS *Perth* in the process, with the loss of 466 lives.

The people of Sydney panicked as they began to understand the fate that could await them. In our household, I was suddenly aware of a certain tension and whisperings behind closed doors.

One of Philomena's patients at the hospital was a Chinese rubber plantation owner, a Mr Robb, from Singapore. He was suffering from a skin disease and had come to Sydney for treatment before the fall of Singapore and was not able to get back. Mother invited him to dinner, a large very fat man with a ruddy face. I found it hard to take my eyes off the many gold rings on his fingers.

He said to my mother, 'I can't get in touch with anyone. The Japs have taken over my house and I am not sure if my wife and children are all right.' Immediately, I was packed off to bed but I lingered long enough to hear other snippets of conversation such as: 'Communications were lost ... my English manager ... murdered ... Chinese staff as well ... I have to go back ... hoping to get on a ship.' One of my brothers, who always liked to further my education, told me Mr Robb's manager had been decapitated by the Japanese. A horrible image to take to bed.

The pictures of the Japanese on awnings and lamp posts everywhere told us they were evil slitty-eyed monsters. The only thing I knew about them was their cheap imported toys with 'made in Japan' stamped on the underside. Those toys almost always broke after their first use, breaking our hearts at the same time. The doll's hospital didn't seem to know how to bring my china doll back to life when its open-and-shut blue eyes fell inside its skull, rendering it lifeless. I found it hard to love my dolly after that or the Japanese for that matter.

A few days after Mr Robb's visit, my brothers Ken and Larry said, 'Mum, we want to sign up.'

Mother was adamantly opposed. 'You are too young, Larry. You are seventeen, and Ken, you are just sixteen. You are going back to school.'

As I was not supposed to hear any of these discussions, I hid behind a door or looked out the window at the harbour, pretending not to listen. These were the best ways of finding out what was actually going on. I had to know. My ears were burning, not simply with curiosity, but with fear of what might happen next. By now I had acquired the nickname 'big ears' and sometimes, even worse, 'stickybeak', but it didn't stop me. There was too much at stake. I was wise to the vagaries of the unexpected decisions adults make when the going gets tough.

Despite the war, our family prospered. The textile business Father had set up manufactured carpet underfelt and cotton waste. Both products could be made using the same machines, with some adjustments. Cotton waste was created by feeding cotton cloth and rags into the machines, to produce multi-layered bales of tangled absorbent fibres ideal for cleaning oil and other substances off machines and for polishing furniture. The war created a huge demand for cotton waste, which was indispensable for the maintenance of army, navy and air force machines. The underfelt business relied on jute imports from India, and the war had cut off that supply, so the decision was made to turn all the machines over to cotton waste production.

With guaranteed military contracts, a steady stream of profit from the business was assured. A new car was purchased, new furniture and antiques appeared, and Mother took us to David Jones to buy new dresses every winter and summer.

Jack was helping Mother run this essential business. Since he was considered to be a more valuable asset to his country at home rather than abroad, he wasn't called up. By now he had a wife and baby to support and he bought a car of his own.

Having recovered her senses, here was our mother, the Managing Director of the Australian Cotton Manufacturing Company, at fifty-one, driving herself to work every day and negotiating contracts with the military. Women, married or single, old or young, were being conscripted into workplaces hitherto exclusively a male domain. To help achieve this personnel redistribution, a bureaucracy called the Manpower Office was established to ensure everyone who could work did work. The unemployment and dole queues, which dominated the 1930s, were a distant memory. People had money in their pockets but not much to spend it on.

In Sydney, there was a movement to arm the population. People trained as guerrillas, air-raid shelters were built and mass evacuations to the mountains took place. Children, especially, were being sent away from the coast to protect them from the unthinkable.

Would we be among those to be shipped out? Please, God, make my mother look the other way!

7

evacuation

But Mother didn't look the other way.

With every mile that passed, my heart sank further into my solar plexus, finally lodging as a dead weight in my feet. We had been driving for a long time, climbing the windy roads up through the Blue Mountains towards Katoomba, a hundred miles west of Sydney. Finally, the Oldsmobile swept through imposing iron gates and we beheld, in the centre of the lawn, that all too familiar signature of convents everywhere, an all-white statue of the Virgin Mary. I knew only too well what that statue meant and was in despair at the sight of it.

'Here we are at last!' Mother said too brightly.

Looking up at the building, I recognised another version of what we had left behind at Hunters Hill. Heavy sandstone walls, a witch's tower rising from the roof of the second floor, adorned by a crucifix, and large black metal locks and hinges on tall front doors, all sending a message of impenetrability. *No hope left now*, I thought as I peered through the car's windows. *Oh, my God. As bad as before, maybe even worse!*

Anchored by that lead weight, I found it impossible to budge. Mother remonstrated with me: 'Anne, darling, get out of the car. Give a good example to your sisters.' This was a frequent admonishment, as if I had to be the standard-bearer on all critical occasions.

Even as we left Rosemont, I had argued against this move but Mother didn't listen. In any case, Joan was already here because she had asthma and it was thought it would be cured by the mountain air.

No wonder my mother is cheerful, I thought, *she's getting rid of us again.*

The front door opened and the Reverend Mother swept out. 'Good morning, Mrs Austin. Oh, here are our little charges,' she said, mustering the sweetest smile.

I didn't trust that for a minute. She was swathed in a black habit, rosary beads hanging limply from a leather belt at her waist. The only signs that there was a human being under it all were a white face and two hands sticking out. She cut a formidable figure, but now I was eight she was less intimidating to me than the nuns at Hunters Hill had been. How dare she look so cheery. If only she knew how I was feeling.

Even now, I was hoping Mummy might change her mind and see the sense of the many arguments I put to her before we left Sydney. The fear of the Japanese was nothing to what I suspected lay ahead of us at this convent.

Joan arrived at the front door. It was now March and she'd been studying for her leaving certificate at Mount St Mary's Convent since the beginning of the school year. With her arrival, I realised the game was up. I could resist Mother but not Joan, my friend and guardian. It wasn't fair to leave her here alone; we had to keep her company.

Jack unloaded the bags from the boot, and as if by magic two young nuns came out, picked them up and vanished inside. I wanted desperately to run after them and get the luggage back. I heard the Reverend Mother whisper to Mother, anticipating the possibility of a difficult parting.

'Better not stay. It's best if you just go quickly now,' she said. My mother nodded.

'Say goodbye to your mother and brother, dears,' urged another nun and I could see that authority had been passed.

We followed her instructions and then, from the front door, forlornly waved as the car moved off, all hope gone as the tail-light disappeared out the gate and onto the road along which we so recently came.

Joan took my hand and I took Carmel's, throwing my head back, hoping the tears would defy gravity. Joan had little Christine, now four, by the other hand. Christine looked bewildered and I realised she had no idea what was happening.

The familiar smell of beeswax greeted us as we went up the polished wood-panelled stairs to our dormitory and unpacked our clothes into lockers beside our beds. Like the statue outside in the garden, the dormitory, a long enclosed verandah with windows running along one side, was reminiscent of those days at Hunters Hill. The difference was that the beds were crammed closer together because the authorities had directed the nuns to triple their number of occupants. As we were to discover, the school was groaning as a result of this directive, with the Sisters of Charity doing their best to hold it all together. It was, after all, the war and they were, perhaps, saving us from death.

The first night, I wet my bed and vomited all over the bedclothes. A ghostly figure in a white nightgown hovered over me. She was wearing a nightcap with strings hanging down the back. Through my sick haze, I realised that this strange apparition was a nun without her habit. It dawned on me that beneath that heavy garment dwelled a real person. I could even imagine her naked in the bath. Not so fearful, really; just like me. That thought effectively kept my fear of the nuns at bay.

I shared this realisation with Carmel: 'Whenever you feel frightened by a nun, just imagine her without any clothes on or sitting on the toilet and you won't feel so scared.' She nodded approvingly.

The overcrowding of the school had some unpleasant consequences. Once a week, Carmel, Christine and I sequentially shared the same bathwater with unlucky Joan, who stepped into it last. Since this was the primary ablution for the week, she made us promise not to pee in the bathwater which, I recall, took some doing.

The line-up to receive a spoonful of cod liver oil with a dash of sugar was one of the most hated weekly rituals but we were told it was important to keep everyone healthy.

Another problem: the dreaded head lice. In the worst cases, heads were shaved – fortunately, not mine or my sisters', but we all had our hair washed in stinking kerosene and fine-tooth combing became a regular painful exercise.

Then the sewerage system failed and its water spilled out over the concrete yard where we played. Our balls rolled into it, but we picked them up anyway, shook them dry and went on playing.

It is a cold, cold place that town Katoomba, perched as it is on the edge of the vast Blue Mountains escarpment. There was never enough warmth or protection from the mist and fog as they crept through and around everything, even on some summer days. I hate the cold and my hands became covered in painful chilblains. I made sure Mother saw them when she came to visit, telling her they would not clear up until we left Katoomba. As if to prove my point, the chilblains disappeared during the school holidays, when we all came home to visit, imminent Japanese invasion or no imminent Japanese invasion.

Some weekends, Mother travelled up to see us and took us out for the day. Sometimes she brought Philomena and one of her friends and they stayed at the Carrington Hotel or the Hydro Majestic.

I longed to be in that warm Sydney coastal plain where they had come from. Our outings included visits and picnics to the lookout above the Megalong Valley. Sometimes Mother even took us for afternoon tea at the Paragon Café in Katoomba's main street, famous for its beautifully boxed biscuit assortments. The biggest treat of all was afternoon tea at the Carrington Hotel, a baroque wonder-filled building with plaster statues and an imposing curved staircase at the entrance. The nymphs and fountains that adorned the hotel caused my imagination to run riot with the romantic possibilities of a world that used to be.

On other days, there were picnics at Echo Point. We looked down into the valley far below and thought about the stories told to us at school about people who ventured into its shadowy depths, some of them never to return. The floor of the valley was often covered in a heavy carpet of mist, burying any poor souls who might be lost there. No search could be mounted until the sun rose high, when suddenly the mist would be transformed into deep gullies and enormous gum trees. It was a place of mystery and sadness and sometimes I wondered if the lost souls heard us as our laughter carried across the gorges from our playground.

The Echo Point lookout was built to frame the magnificence of the Three Sisters, tall ragged rock towers guarding the valley floor. 'The Three Sisters, just like you three,' Mother said, as she winked at Joan, while Carmel, Christine and I laughed weakly at their little joke. Privately, I thought we were more like three orphaned waifs, far from home, lonely and nervous about our future.

Just outside the entrance to our dormitory, a solid wooden staircase led up to the tower, a place I had never dared to think of exploring. Perhaps to prevent us from going there, we were told that it was the haunt of the convent's ghost, a nun who died in tragic circumstances.

On a morning in late spring, I woke to see the sun struggling to reach my bed through a hazy mist. It was going to be a fine day. As I took my pyjama top off to get dressed, I suddenly became the centre of attention. 'Ooh!' the other children said. 'Ooh!' Looking down, I saw a chest covered with red blobs. Panic erupted and a nun appeared from somewhere. She took one look then announced, 'I think it's chickenpox, dear.'

And with that I was put back to bed and everyone else was summarily dismissed from our dormitory.

Later in the morning, it was quarantine time; in an effort to avoid an epidemic, I was sent off to the tower. Terrifying as that was, by then I was too sick to put up much of an argument.

The ghost's tower turned out to be a large room with windows on all sides. As I arrived, a couple of senior girls who called this place home were hurriedly folding their bedclothes and moving out, not too pleased at this unplanned rearrangement. When they saw me pathetically clutching my dolly, my face by now splotched with blisters, they softened and went quietly.

'You'll be all right,' one of them said. 'It's lovely up here.'

'What about the ghost?' I asked.

'Oh, she left when she knew you were coming,' she said, laughing. 'Don't worry, that's just a lie. There's no such ghost. Whoever told you that was telling fibs.'

'I knew that all the time,' I said, cracking hardy, hoping they'd believe me.

In time I was joined by other girls with chickenpox, including Judith Hurford, whose father owned the newsagency in Double Bay near where we lived at Edgecliff. Judith and I had taken to each other soon after we arrived and had become best friends, spending all of our spare time together.

Judith was not like me. At eight, I had grown tall, with lanky legs and straight black hair. Once people used to say, 'She's a pretty little thing,' but no one said that any more. Judith was pretty and had long brown curls falling in waves around her shoulders. I loved her.

As Judith, the other quarantined girls and I recovered from our chickenpox, we formed a kind of special group, playing games and telling stories. We were visited by friends, who stood at the entrance to the tower room so they would not become infected. In time, the witch's tower became too small to accommodate any more chickenpox cases. Since we were in recovery, we reluctantly returned to our old beds. Oh, well! Nothing lasts forever.

Back in the dormitory, I often wet the bed because the toilets were a long way away and all the lights were turned off. Joan asked the nuns to leave a light on. They had to make a choice: was avoiding wet beds a more important priority than the likelihood of being targeted from the air by a Japanese bomb? Fortunately, the Japanese didn't win this argument, and one light stayed on and there were no more wet beds.

One day, there came a terrible blow. My friend Judith tossed her chestnut curls over one shoulder, turned her back on me, linked arms with another girl and said, 'Go away. You are not my friend any more.'

The sting of that betrayal cut me like a knife. What had I done to cause her change of heart?

The next day, Judith was taken ill and I was told she was in bed upstairs in the dormitory. The girl she had linked arms with came to me with a message: 'Judith wants to see you,' she announced. 'She said please, please can you go up now.'

'Okay,' I answered and disappeared into the building as if to go and visit Judith. But I didn't go. Judith needed to be taught a lesson. *I'll go tomorrow*, I thought.

But tomorrow was too late. In the night, they took Judith to the Katoomba hospital. Although I begged the nuns to let me visit her, they said she was too sick. Then the terrible news came: she had died there in that hospital. Gone, just like that. No one told me how she died or from what disease. It seemed to be a secret. We prayed for her in class and comforted her little sister Helen, who was the same age as Christine and looked bewildered. The nuns consoled us with: 'Judith has gone straight to heaven. She is so lucky to be amongst the angels.'

But I didn't think so. I just knew I had let her down. I didn't say a word to anyone about my neglect. It would be a secret between me and my dead friend. What was it in me that ignored Judith's plea? That question haunted me for a long time as I wrestled with the shame of it. How could I be so unkind and unforgiving?

As I grew up, I knew I must move on from childhood mistakes and regrets. I decided that all I could do was to forgive myself and try to never make a mistake like that one again.

8
losing myself

I am asleep, trapped in a recurring nightmare. A tangle of interweaving multicoloured lines converge upon each other and then hold me fast in their long tentacles.

A dull humming sound is buried deep within the swirling lines, gradually sucking me into a vortex. *I am swallowed up. I am nothing. No one is here to save me and I cannot save myself.* The lines grow denser, like treacle, and I am trapped, unable to move as the lines criss-cross each other, forming and reforming as the humming sound gets louder.

Waking in a terrified sweat, I found the night deeply silent. Out of that silence, the reassuring swish of a solitary car scattered rain across the road. Lying in Mother's bed, I felt her stir beside me. I cuddled closer to the warmth of her body, pushing the fearful recurring dream further and further away, beyond the power to terrify me. *I am safe here in bed with her. I am safe … I am safe. There is nothing to fear … unless I go to sleep again …*

Sometimes the lines in the dream were brightly coloured, sometimes dull, and sometimes they transmuted into black and white print like the newspaper. Perhaps I was now dead or would die one night in this dream? I woke terrified each time, frightened to speak of it. In any case, I had no idea how to describe the dream to anyone. How could I describe the fear without recognisable symbols such as tigers, lions or witches? This was something far more terrifying – the loss of me, my very essence because of strange, indescribable and nameless forces.

We were home for the two-week May school holidays. It was 1942, and by now the war against the Germans was well advanced in Europe. The Japanese were being ruthless in their Pacific advance. Nothing about our lives was certain. At the Saturday matinee in Double Bay, we watched the Cinesound newsreels of the aftermath of the Japanese attack on Pearl Harbor and then saw pictures of the blitz in London. We knew what it would mean for us if the Japanese invaded. They had bombed Darwin; they were getting closer every day. Then, days later, 'There they are!' everyone yelled. 'The Yanks are here! The Yanks are here.'

The fear that had been spreading like a virus through Sydney instantly gave way to celebrations. Flags were draped from windows, American flags at that. People sounded their horns in the street. Running to the bedroom window, with its sweeping views, I saw what all the noise was about. A huge aircraft carrier was steaming down the harbour, surrounded by hundreds of little boats creating a flotilla of welcome for the US fleet, or what was left of it after the Japanese attack on Pearl Harbor. I could see from our window a line of white-clad sailors standing to attention on its decks. Soon it would dock at Woolloomooloo.

A few days later, at the local picture show, we saw the newsreels of the fleet's arrival. The triumphant caption on the screen read, 'Australia welcomes Yanks with open arms.' And open arms it was, literally. Young women in red lipstick and short skirts, their hair piled up on top of their heads, swarmed the dock to greet the fleet. They screamed with excitement at the sailors in their gleaming whites, who waved in reply across the ships' rails. The girls, hoping for a date for the night, jumped up and down, returning the salutes and invitations from men they had never seen before. Soon Potts Point and Kings Cross were swarming with sailors, and those 'brazen hussies', as Mother called the young women. Rescue from the Japanese seemed certain now that General MacArthur had arrived with his troops.

One night, right at the end of the holidays, I woke to hear the blare of an air-raid siren. 'Wake up, wake up. Put on your dressing gown,' Mother said. Half asleep, for a moment I couldn't remember where I was.

'Come quickly,' said Mother, wrapping my dressing gown around me while my elder sisters busied themselves with Christine and Carmel. 'We have to go downstairs to the garage.'

I staggered out and pressed the button at the lift outside our front door, then suddenly remembered we had to walk down the stairs. That was the drill we had learned. The garage in the basement of the building was the air-raid shelter, and the siren was the signal to take refuge; as soon as we heard it, the lift was a no-no.

I felt reassured as we went quickly down the three floors to the basement, peering outside onto the street as we went. So far, so good. No bombs falling yet. I wondered what we would do if a bomb did fall. Would we be buried under six floors of rubble? I kept this thought to myself. Didn't want to scare my younger sisters.

A full moon was shining in a cloudless sky. Hundreds of searchlights criss-crossed the sky, competing with the moon's brilliance, searching, searching for the alien intruder. We heard a plane overhead. Maybe it was the enemy.

I was pleased to meet up with the neighbours in the garage, all dressed in their nightclothes. We were in this together. Normally, Mother tended to keep her distance from the other tenants, a legacy of her time in Mudgee. Here the neighbours needn't know your business. I wished we fraternised more. I've always loved the light-hearted friendly chitchat of neighbourly encounters.

A two-year-old boy, son of an officer in General MacArthur's army who was renting on the floor below us, begged his daddy to take him outside to see the moon again.

'Don't go,' I said, anxious for their safety. 'They might drop a bomb on you.'

Everyone laughed and the pair went outside anyway.

I learned later that three small Japanese subs had slipped into the harbour, sending torpedoes towards the US naval vessels. After their daring air strike in Hawaii, the Japanese believed they could polish off the last of the US fleet holed up in Sydney Harbour. The Japanese midget subs and their occupants were doomed from the beginning and all died in the attempt; they missed their mark but hit an Australian depot ship, with the loss of twenty-one Allied lives. The Japanese mother submarines, waiting off the coast, shelled the Eastern Suburbs; a volley of fire struck a house just over the hill from us at Rose Bay. Although no one was injured, it was uncomfortably close to us on Edgecliff Road. Eastern Suburbs real estate prices would plummet further, panic would take hold in Sydney and Mother would feel justified in sending us away, as well as not investing in a harbourside house for us to live in.

Our American neighbour came back to tell us the plane we heard overhead was one of ours. There was a discussion.

Should we return to our beds? Mother made the decision to go upstairs, in spite of my objection. Tucked up again at 2 am, I heard the all-clear siren sound and drifted off to sleep, relieved the danger was gone for the time being.

But not in my dream. Would it come again tonight? Could I bear it? Soon we would be back in the mountains again and I would have no one to cuddle up to when I woke in fright. Then what?

Since my father's death and my mother's return home, I had begun to realise one immutable fact: the only thing I could rely on was me. But in the dream, even that assurance was taken from me, and it was all the more terrifying because of that.

9
home 1943–45

We had been at the Blue Mountains boarding school for nine months and were back in Sydney for the 1942 Christmas holidays.

'I'm going to keep the little mites home now,' said Mother to someone on the phone. 'They hate boarding school and now the US fleet is here, I think the danger of invasion is over. In any case, Joan is going to repeat her Leaving Certificate this year at Holy Cross College.'

It paid to be an eavesdropper, otherwise how would I have known about miracles? Just as well I took my 'stickybeak' duties seriously in this family. Knowing how good I was at it, I decided to be a spy when I grew up, fantasising myself into the role of a French Resistance member, blowing up German munitions and escaping unscathed to do more damage. All this was a legacy of the films we saw at Double Bay on Saturday afternoons.

When I overheard Mother's conversation on the phone, I was overwhelmed with joy and relief. No more dark cold nights. No more chilblains in winter. No more overcooked slushy food. When bad dreams arrived, my mother or my sisters would be there for me to stretch out and touch. I couldn't contain my joy and told my younger sisters the news. At last, we would enjoy a normal life again with people who really cared for us. With that realisation, we danced around the bedroom singing.

The most abiding sense of security during those years came from the large front bedroom Carmel, Christine and I shared with our mother. Until we were older and the boys left home, each of us three took turns sleeping with Mother in the double bed. The other two would sleep together in a three-quarter bed on the other side of the room. Although this arrangement was born of necessity, as we were cramped into a smaller space than before, I believe we each achieved a much needed re-bonding with Mother because of it.

The downside was our constant awareness of the state of Mother's lungs. Her occasional coughing fits were a reminder that she might not be long for this world. Finally we adjusted to it and accepted it as part of the way things were and would always be. I kept hoping she would live until we were old enough to survive by ourselves. I never discussed this with my sisters. To speak of it might make my fear a reality.

We returned to St Joseph's, Edgecliff, a parish Catholic school around the corner in Albert Street, next door to the Catholic church. Although we were not rich, I became aware that we were better off than most of the other girls at school. Little things seemed to set us apart: trees lined our street; our mother bought antiques; we had carpets on the floor, and a car; we listened to good music on the ABC; and, although my elder brothers didn't read it, we subscribed to the broadsheet *Sydney Morning Herald*, not the trashy evening papers the *Sun* and the *Daily Mirror* or 'that scurrilous rag', as Mother called it, *The Truth*.

Edgecliff Road was the high-status side of the school boundary, while Great Thorn Street, near our butcher's shop, was not. I had a friend called Sheila, who lived opposite Mr Judd's butcher shop in a terrace house. There was a piano and her mother took in pupils; the house was dark; outside in the yard, there was a dunny; the furniture was old (but not antique); and brown lino covered the floor.

Maureen was another friend. She lived in a grey-brick flat on the corner of New South Head Road and William Street, Double Bay, and invited me home one afternoon after school. Before I could come in, though, she had to check if her mother was home and ask her permission to let me in. She never got that far. Receiving a beating for being late home from school, Maureen emerged with a shopping list and showed me the red welts on her legs. As we walked to the shops together, I learned her 'uncle' was in the flat – an 'uncle' who often came to stay (her father was away at the war) and whose nasty habit, she confided in me, was to visit her in the middle of the night and do 'things' to her that she hated. It shocked me to the core that a grown-up relative would behave like that. In my heart, I knew he was not really an uncle but Maureen's mother's boyfriend.

After I told Mother, she said, 'Is that the kind of friend you really need?' and I decided it would be best to confine myself to friendships 'closer to home'. A year later, Maureen and her mother moved to Queensland, where her father was stationed. Although she said she would write, after one letter and my reply, I never heard from her again.

'Closer to home' meant that my sisters Carmel and Christine and I became best friends with the two Myers children, who lived a few doors down from us on Edgecliff Road. We all walked home from school together and I often met Jan, the eldest, who would walk with me when I was sent on short shopping errands for our household. Dr Myers was Jewish, while Mrs Myers was a Catholic. Those differences didn't mean much to me because it was never a cause for comment in our family.

Hardship and discrimination against Irish immigrants were not far from the collective memory of Mother's generation, and many Catholics remembered being foisted with a sense of inferiority from the day they landed in Australia. In our household, Sir Henry Parkes, the five times Premier of New South Wales, was regarded not as the beloved father of Federation but as the father of discrimination. Mother spoke of him with bitterness because he denied Catholic schools the same funding as public schools. The Catholic Church hit back, insisting Catholics attend their own schools under pain of mortal sin, thus entrenching the very thing Parkes, with his vision of an integrated society, sought to prevent.

By now, Catholics had long become used to funding their own schools, but they had never given up their resentment at being targets of discrimination. Catholic schools struggled to attract good teachers, which led in many instances to substandard schools, such as the one we went to on Albert Street, Edgecliff.

The Edgecliff neighbourhood was our territory, including an acre of vacant land called Quambi Place, just off Albert Street, a stone's throw from our school. The site was populated by huge Moreton Bay fig trees, which created a mysterious canopy, like the fairy bowers we read about in our story books. Their outstretched arms of thick, long, low trunks were an invitation to play house inside their abundant depths. To me, they were living presences watching over us while we precariously pretended to be trapeze artists, climbing all the way out on their branches, allowing our imagination to run riot. Then we were transformed into princesses waiting for our wandering knights, Deanna Durbin singing to an enraptured audience or Greek goddesses weaving magic spells. No wonder Enid Blyton wrote *The Faraway Tree*.

But one thing we would never have found in an Enid Blyton book was the man who came by with lollies one day. He was being oh so nice to us but when he unexpectedly unbuttoned his fly and showed us his penis, we knew there was nothing nice about him. We ran home immediately to breathlessly report this to our mother.

Subsequently, for a time, Quambi Place became restricted territory and instead we played in an open space between the apartment blocks or on Rosemont Avenue, beneath a cathedral-like canopy of old plane trees which, during autumn, covered the ground with mountains of dead foliage.

Hearing our laughter, Mary, an only child who lived in the adjoining apartment building, would come down to play. The thing that impressed us most about Mary was her wardrobe. We never saw her in the same dress twice. One day, when her parents were out, she took us up to her flat and showed us her wardrobe, lined with dresses for every occasion. She also had many dolls and all the paraphernalia that went with them. We were in awe because we had one best dress each and what our mother called 'play clothes', hand-me-downs or last year's worn-out dresses; one doll each; and a doll's house we had to share. Somehow, we understood not to ask for more than that, knowing 'there is a war on' – the catchcry of the day.

During dinner one night, we waxed lyrical about Mary's wardrobe and her dolls.

'Mary's father is into … you know … You can get anything from him. Clothing coupons, cigarettes and Scotch especially. Anything! Anything you want,' said Ken.

Mother looked distinctly uncomfortable but we were all ears and wanted to know more.

'How do people get "into … you know"? Why isn't Mary's father in uniform?' I asked.

My brothers laughed uproariously and at that point Mother put a stop to the conversation.

Later, in private, I asked Larry, who at eighteen was studying engineering and working part-time in our factory, 'Well, why isn't Mary's father at the war? Why isn't he in uniform?'

'Kiddo,' he said, 'Mr Stephens is what we call the "Ways and Means Man". He knows how to keep out of trouble and get anything you need. He has friends in the right places, you might say.'

At that he stopped. 'Now listen, kiddo, don't talk about this. Don't tell Mummy I told you. It's a secret between us, okay? Don't tell your friends or Carmel or Chris. They won't understand. And we don't want to get a visit from the Stephens across the way. Understand?'

'Okay,' I said.

No matter what euphemisms were used to describe it, I knew that Larry was talking about 'black marketeering', something Mother hated and would never be part of but which, for some reason, my brothers knew more about. No wonder Mary had so many clothes. No wonder she lived in a great deal more luxury than we did. No wonder the Stephens went places and did things we could never dream of.

Carmel, Christine and I were allowed to go to one of the two local picture theatres on Saturday afternoons, often in the company of the Myers children. The theatres, called Hoyts and Vogue, were situated within three hundred yards of each other on New South Head Road, Double Bay. We were given two shillings each, which paid for our entry and left enough for an ice-cream at interval. All the week before, we studied the showings at both theatres and finally agreed on which one to attend.

This was the highlight of our week. From newsreels and double bills, we caught up on the war, the world, romance and adventure. We were served up a steady diet of war movies in which 'our boys', and sometimes girls, always won. But war movies were not our favourites. Rather, it was 'olden day' movies, with women in crinoline dresses and gallant men who fell in love with them, or musicals. There they were, our singing heroes, Jeanette MacDonald calling to Nelson Eddy across the chasm of the Canadian Rocky Mountains; and there we were on our way home, singing, 'When I'm calling you oo oo oo, you will answer true oo oo oo,' still feeling the profundity of loss and reunion.

To be punished by not being allowed to go to the pictures was the worst thing that could happen because it robbed us of our imaginary world for a whole week. But it didn't happen very often, because our movie-going gave our mother and adult siblings at least three hours' respite from having to worry about keeping an eye on the three of us.

Carmel, Christine and I knew about the war yet there was a strange unreality about it. Day to day, we children lived in the present but the rest of the family were caught up in the future. These two sets of lives were being played out within the one household, like parallel universes. My two younger sisters and I gave up trying to make sense of it all, forgetting the dangers we were in as we played, went to school and immersed ourselves in our own fantasies. Meanwhile, Australian men went to war, were killed or returned wounded; other men and women kept the wheels of industry moving; people dealt with rationing, while others bought things on the thriving black market; women emerged from domesticity to replace men in the workforce, and the unmarried among them urgently seized the opportunity for romance with men in military uniform.

They could take their pick of Australian, American and British uniforms – there they were on the streets, at Mass on Sunday, on trams and buses and in the city. We learned how to recognise the differences between them. The American troops had better tailored uniforms and more cash than our Australian servicemen, and they brought with them chewing gum, silk stockings and perfume. It was hardly a level playing field for 'our boys' when it came to competing for Australian girlfriends.

With two very beautiful sisters, Joan and Phil, our household became a magnet for the Yanks, the Poms and Australians in uniform. Some days, we came home from school to see military caps and batons and occasionally a fancy leather belt outfit called a Sam Brown on the Chinese marble chair in the hall. The chair was possibly too precious to have such items slung over it. I had been with Mother when she bought it from an antiques dealer. It was wide enough for two children to sit on side by side, and we did, pressing our backs against the shiny mother-of-pearl inlays of birds, flowers and bamboo stalks, which provided a lyrical contrast to its solid black marble frame. Sitting on that chair, though, was forbidden; according to Mother, it might give us kidney failure, something we had recently learned had killed our father. We sat on it anyway, when no one was watching.

The three of us would study the configuration of the military caps against the mother of pearl, we would smell cigarette smoke and hear gramophone music – what was it today, 'In the Mood' or 'Begin the Beguine'? – then laughter and deep male voices coming from the lounge room. Alas, we had to keep out of the way. We would be ushered into the bedroom to change out of our school uniforms, have a snack in the kitchen and go downstairs to play for as long as possible.

Later, we might cross paths with one of the outgoing Americans. They sounded exactly like the movie stars of Saturday afternoon fame and they spoke to us as if we were grown-ups. I wanted them to stay around forever. They would romance my sisters and then go, sometimes leaving broken hearts behind.

When Phil's American airman boyfriend was killed over the Pacific, many tears followed and her bedroom door was closed to us for days.

It was widely agreed that Mr Judd on Great Thorn Street had the best meat in the Eastern Suburbs. Mother was very specific about the cuts she ordered from him. Mr Judd could always be counted on for a joke or a compliment. He was, I discovered from my brothers, exercising his 'chiacking right', a right unofficially adopted by butchers, whose job it is to maintain frivolous relationships with their customers. Indeed, I've never met a grumpy butcher. Mr Judd would often say things to me like, 'How are you today, Miss Beautiful Brown Eyes? How many hearts have you broken today?' and I would laugh and try to think of a witty remark in response, something I rarely managed.

This was the era when the milk and bread were delivered every day to a servery outside the kitchen door, and the fruit man and the egg and butter man trudged up the back stairs to sell Mother their produce face to face.

One evening, from my vantage point three floors up, I watched the old Chinese fruit man's horse and cart go clopping down the street in front of our flats. It was cold, getting dark; the street lights had just come on and a light drizzle made the bitumen glow in the half-light of evening. How sad he looked. I wondered where he went home to at the end of the day.

The next morning, as I walked to the end of the street, I saw his cart lying overturned at a bend in the road. Fruit and vegetables had been squashed on the road by overnight traffic. Standing there crying, I wondered if a car had hit him. Did someone think he was Japanese and deliberately do him harm? No one knew, or no one was prepared to tell me.

For a long time, a deep sadness overwhelmed me every time I thought about it. I was sad not only for him and his loved ones. I was aware of something precious disappearing from our lives, something that had been a reliable fixture. And I was right. I never saw him or his horse and cart again, nor did anyone come to replace his business in our suburb.

10

parallel lives

One of the phrases I heard a lot as I was growing up was, 'What a wonderful big family.' Another was, 'Large families are so good for a child's character' – mostly opined by nuns and priests who never had one. They were wrong. My mother was a wonderful woman but the 'big family' ideal was far from the truth. The bigger the family, the more likely it is that there will be bullies or stealth operators who perpetrate evil deeds on younger victims under the guise of brother or sisterly love.

Carmel, Christine and I were often left in the care of our elder brothers and sisters, especially during school holidays. When he was home from boarding school, Allan, the youngest of my brothers and six years my senior, was one of those left to watch over us.

I am not sure when it began. Perhaps even when I was eight. It sticks in my childhood memory as something that went on for years, becoming a source of constant anxiety whenever he was home from boarding school. My mother, so immersed in holding the family together and running the business, had little time to pick up on subtle clues. We were growing, we were healthy enough, and we seemed cheerful and a little naughty. What was there to worry about?

This is the way it often was. Allan would whisper to my two younger sisters, 'I need to tell Anne something. Why don't you two go off and play?'

'Oh, no,' I would say.

'Oh, yes,' he would say. 'Come in here now, it's important. I want to tell you a secret.'

Sometimes he even bribed my two sisters or promised to do something for them. There was no escape; he would get me alone.

'Look, just come over here for a minute, only for a minute,' he would say.

'What are you doing, Allan?'

And then I would find my skirt being lifted and something hard being shoved between my legs.

'I don't like this, Allan. Stop it.' And then I would be running outside to escape into the company of my two younger sisters.

The times I dreaded the most were when Carmel and Christine were taken out by one of my elder siblings and I was left alone with Allan. How could I say, 'Hey, everyone, don't leave me here with him. I know what's going to happen.'?

On those occasions, now that he had me all to himself, he became more audacious and my despair grew. It was then I found myself being squashed in a cupboard or dragged under a bed, and sometimes he tried to take my pants off, his 'thing' becoming warm and sticky. There was little chance of escape but I fought him to keep my pants on. It was agony, but I always succeeded.

I spent a lot of time thinking up ways to avoid him. I often said to myself that if Mother knew what he got up in her absence, she would at the very least make other arrangements. But she didn't know, and I didn't know how to tell her.

It was amazing that no one twigged to what was going on. I was elated when he went back to school. But still I told no one, not even my best friend, Jan Myers.

When I was nearly ten, impressed by the beauty of the Central Coast and obviously forgetting her promise to our father, Mother bought a small farm six miles from Gosford on the shores of Brisbane Waters, at a place called Green Point. Our farm consisted of ten glorious acres, a forest of gum trees, a horse, a cow, chooks and a vegetable garden plus it had its own little private beach and a motor launch. From then on, we went there during school holidays and many weekends, laboriously trundling over the winding roads in our car, which had patched, worn and uncertain tyres and a coke burner on the back to augment our meagre supply of petrol. Other motorists tried to beat the petrol shortage in different ways; the most popular was a kind of gas balloon that inflated on the top of the car and made it look as if the car was flying. There was much talk around our dinner table about which of them was better; for some reason, Mother preferred the heavy contraption of the coke burner.

To get to Green Point, we had to cross the Hawkesbury River. There was a railway bridge, but the only way for cars was a punt service which took about ten cars at a time and crossed the river by way of a motorised cable that winched it to the other side. Mostly, the wait was about half an hour but at busy times like Easter and Christmas, you could wait for hours for your turn to come.

One Easter we were picked up from school early – around 2 pm. It was Holy Thursday afternoon and we got to the punt only to discover ourselves in a long queue with an all-night wait ahead of us. Until dawn, we wriggled, complained and whinged in the back seat, until an enterprising man knocked on Mother's window selling fresh bread in a basket. Gratefully, we were allowed get out of the car; Mother found butter and jam in the boot, and our lives were saved till it was finally our turn to bump our way onto the punt.

Then the magic came. 'See how God rewards us for waiting, darlings,' Mother said. 'Look at the sunrise, children!'

And there it was, bathing the river in pink and orange Easter brilliance, while the train crossing the railway bridge further down the river flashed back yellow fire across the water's rippling surface.

Then we arrived. Freedom at last! Our sprawling weatherboard farmhouse was surrounded on all sides by a twelve-foot verandah. Three of the six bedrooms converged on a living room adjoining an enormous kitchen. The kitchen, a favourite place, sported a big wooden table, an enamel sink on one wall and a cast-iron wood stove on the other. Sitting next to it was a small green electric stove with a kookaburra on the oven door. Through the trees there were views of the river, a huge expanse of water sparkling in the sunlight. That Easter, by night it glowed softly under a full moon.

Twice a week – three times in the summer holidays – we bought huge blocks of ice from the local iceworks to keep meat, butter and milk cold in the Coolgardie safe. I helped Mother construct this safe out of a packing case and heavy grey canvas from our factory. At Rosemont, we had a refrigerator, but buying a new refrigerator for the farm was out of the question since all manufacturing was now devoted to the war effort.

Beyond the passionfruit vine walkway was an outhouse toilet consisting of a deep smelly pit dug by my brothers, with a wooden seat on top of a canlike structure, one of the most uncomfortable aspects of Green Point life. As often as not, we used newspaper as toilet paper, another one of our modest contributions to the war effort.

Mother, as it turned out, had advanced horticultural skills and knew exactly what to do on a farm. Her childhood years growing up at Molong and then the necessity of making ends meet during the Depression at Mudgee now paid off for all of us. She hitched the horse up to a homemade sled and we all gathered old cow and horse manure from around the property and helped her unload it onto the vegetable garden. The result of this toil was a harvest of beans, strawberries, lettuce, carrots and passionfruit by the bucket-load. The jersey cow provided cream and butter – two rationed commodities. A neighbour, Stan, who walked with a limp and was too old and disabled to go to war, ran a small dairy next door. He looked after our place during our absences and helped Mother with milking and other heavier chores.

Mother brought the surplus vegetables, fruit, eggs, butter and cream back to Sydney and bartered them for sugar, meat and clothing coupons to outfit the family and buy things like sheets and towels for her newly wedded daughters, Molly and Meg, who were living in flats of their own, their husbands off at the war.

I loved the holidays at Green Point and learned to ride a horse, fall off and get back on again. As well, I roamed, swam, read books and dreamt of great deeds while sitting on the edge of the beach as the trees whispered gentle encouragement. The best time was the Christmas holidays, when the whole family – including Jack, his wife, Leonie, and their babies – came to stay. All of us would go to Mass at Gosford, then Mother would cook a big roast with baked vegetables and our own greens from the garden. Excitedly, we would await the second course of plum pudding, filled with three- and sixpence pieces, now simmering away on the stove. After a big wash-up, one of our brothers might drive us to the surf beach at Terrigal, a rare treat in those days of petrol rationing.

To me, the farm was a symbol of transition, for it was there I learned to catch a wave, make friends with animals and come to terms with my fear of spiders, ticks and snakes.

Before I turned ten, more worrying than snakes and spiders was Allan, the one spoiler of those halcyon days. Now he was sixteen, he was old enough to go off with friends during the holidays, but he would sometimes come to the farm. Whenever his impending arrival was announced, I could think of nothing else but how to avoid his attention. Sometimes the fates worked against me. One day, Mother went into Gosford to shop for groceries, taking my two younger sisters with her and leaving Allan and me in charge of the house.

'Mummy, I want to come, too,' I said, desperate not to be left alone with him.

'No, darling. Please, I want you to stay and look after the phone. We have the family coming up and you need to take a message if they ring. If the phone doesn't answer they may think we aren't here.'

'Can't Allan do it?'

'Allan's job is to inspect the lobster pots out on the water,' replied Mother.

I wanted to tell her 'I don't want to be left alone with him' but if I did, she would ask me why and I wouldn't be able to think of anything. Obviously, she wasn't picking up the right signals. Stan, our neighbour, was digging in the garden outside. At least that was some protection.

Undeterred, as soon as Mother's car got onto the road and out of sight, Allan started to badger me. 'You have to come with me to check the lobster pots. I can't manage them and row the boat at the same time. I also need to check other things on the launch and can't do that by myself either.' On and on he went, insisting I come with him.

'No, no, I must stay here to answer the phone. I will get into trouble, Allan. You heard what Mummy said. I have to be here.'

'I need you, Anne. I simply can't manage on my own. You have to come with me. Come on, sweetie, it won't take long', and on and on. Same old story, and I knew how it might end. But I thought, *We won't be long. I will be safe in the small dinghy; he can't do anything out there on the water.*

When we finished inspecting the last trap, he rowed over to the launch. 'I have to see to something on board,' he said.

The launch was my elder brothers' pride and joy. They used it to go roaming across the water, for fishing and for visiting their school friends who lived on the opposite shore at Woy Woy.

I didn't want to get out of the dinghy onto the launch. I told him to check what he needed to check and I would stay in the dinghy.

'Allan,' I added, 'we have to get back before Mummy comes home.'

But he wouldn't take no for an answer and at great risk of capsizing the dinghy, he dragged me on board and in a flash was lying on top of me moving rhythmically back and forth while I screamed loudly. The look on his face was weird and frightening. I was struggling, terrified, miserable and angry, mostly at myself for being tricked once again, and then I began to yell with all my might, 'Help, someone. Help me. Stop, Allan, stop at once. Help, help', even though I knew there was no possibility of being heard by anyone.

Could I jump overboard and swim for shore? Would I be eaten by a shark on the way? Was I a strong enough swimmer to make it?

As if to read my mind, or maybe because he had got what he wanted, he climbed off me and dropped onto the floor panting. In this struggle, he had tried to remove my underpants but I fiercely resisted. To save clothing coupons, Mother had made our pants from very stout calico cloth, not included in the lists of rationed material. So, although they were a bit wet and sticky, he hadn't gone beyond that formidable barrier. I hated these homemade underpants but was now grateful for Mother's inadvertent protection, even though she would never know it.

When we got back to shore, I jumped into the water, clothes and all, to wash away the stink of him and the feel of his body on top of mine. Then I washed the clothes before Mummy came back.

At last, I knew I must take action and be strong. This had to stop. I couldn't risk another encounter like that one on the boat. It was time to face up and resolve the confusing dilemmas and overwhelming obstacles confronting me.

First, there was the horror of the acts themselves, repugnant in the extreme. But second, if this was ever to become known, I might be seen as complicit in my brother's wickedness. Third, I didn't have the language to describe what was happening. It was well past the time when I should have told someone, and my lack of action meant I might be blamed or, worse still, be in danger of losing my immortal soul. That meant ending up in hell. Mother's possible judgement was one thing. Eternal damnation was quite another.

11
the solution

I had to find the courage to save myself from the present and the possibility of burning in hell forever if I died. The prayer we said every night as children was 'Now I lay me down to sleep, I pray the Lord my soul to keep. If I should die before I wake, I pray the Lord my soul to take.' Well, what a daily reminder that was of the ever-present possibility that I might not be here in the morning.

There *was* another thing holding me back. And that was what Mother might do to Allan.

It was weird, really. I always pitied Allan, because he was the most vulnerable member of the family, a kind of scapegoat and the butt of my elder brothers' jokes. He was to be ignored on most occasions but on others to be ridiculed. The bigger boys called him 'squirt' because he was the most undersized of all the boys in the family, not very smart and, I believe, the most emotionally neglected. He was, after all, the tenth child to be born in as many years. He lived much of his life in a fantasy world, confiding in me that he would one day be a great piano player, even though he had had just one or two lessons.

Still to this day, I wonder if Mother could have coped with the knowledge of what he was up to. Somehow, I must have sensed that shocking events might push her over the edge again.

I didn't know how to protect Allan and Mother from themselves as well as protecting myself from both of them. What might Mother do to Allan if I spoke up? Then, too, what might Mother do to me? Would she think I was partly to blame and reject me as a result? I'd had enough rejection for one short life. There was nothing for it but to solve the problem for myself.

The nuns at school taught the religion of sin, fear and damnation. They repeatedly told us that if we went to confession with a sin on our soul and didn't tell that sin, then that was another sin on top of the untold one. Worse still, if we did tell a sin and did it again, we were doubly damned. So every time I went to confession, I was clocking up a mounting debt. Exactly like compounding interest, it was becoming bigger and bigger as the months went by. What to do?

Every Friday morning, our class was marched into the church next door to the school to go to confession. There we sat in rows, on hard wooden pews, waiting for our turn to enter the confessional. No escape. A nun sat at the end of the pew watching us, in the unlikely event one of us decided to run away, play up or refuse to go in. White as snow, each of us emerged from the airless cubicle washed clean with the Rinso of salvation. Except me, who would lie to the priest.

'Bless me, Father, for I have sinned. It is a week since my last confession.'

Desperate to think of something plausible to tell him, I would say, 'I have missed my evening prayers twice. I shouted at a girl in class who took my pencils. I disobeyed my mother once.'

'Is that all, my child?'

'Yes, Father,' I would lie, adding another sin to the compounding debit side of the ledger.

'For your penance, say three Hail Marys. Go in peace.'

'Thank you, Father.' But peace I did not go in.

After what happened on the boat, I made the decision to tell the priest, and now I faced another dilemma. What were the right words to say? 'My brother pokes his thing between my legs. I hate it and him for doing it.' Was that the right language? I didn't think so.

At school, I had heard one of the nuns mention the words 'impure acts and impure thoughts'. She described those acts as touching private parts or, even worse, letting a boy touch our private parts. That was it, I realised. That was it! Impure acts and private parts.

Now that I had the tools at my disposal, I could get it over with. It was a big mountain to climb but a better one than any of the alternatives. School was about to go back but I wasn't going to risk confession in the class line-up. The priest might have had me in there for ages and then what would the class or, worse still, the 'guard dog' at the end of the pew think about that? So I took myself off to Saturday evening confessions at the Edgecliff church, where a few adult souls were lined up waiting to be forgiven for their sins. Young men, older women. I was in good company. I was only nine going on ten. Hopefully they had worse sins to tell than I did.

'Bless me, Father, for I have sinned,' I said as I knelt down inside the dark cubicle. 'It is a month since my last confession. I have been guilty of impure acts.'

Suddenly this elderly Franciscan monk came closer to the dark grill separating us from each other.

'Who have you done these impure acts with, my child?' he asked.

'My brother, Father.'

'This is very serious.'

'Yes, Father.'

'It could be reported to the police.'

Dumbfounded, I felt my knees begin to give way under me. I thought I was going to be sick. Ah, but what about the seal of the confessional? No one else would ever know. *Keep going, this ordeal is nearly over*, I told myself.

'Yes, Father.'

'Do you repent?' he asked.

'Yes, Father.'

'Do you resolve never to do these impure acts again? You know it's a mortal sin, don't you?'

Keep going, I said to myself.

'Yes, Father.'

He let me off with a rosary for penance. Not as good as three Hail Marys but not bad either, all things considered.

Free at last, I resolved to do my penance with the family when we said the rosary at night. I was not going to stick around the church in case the priest recognised me when he came out of the confessional. I skipped home deeply relieved. Just to make sure the penance stuck, I said several extra rosaries as insurance in case the family one didn't carry enough weight with God.

Next time Allan tried to lure me away, I shouted at him, 'Go away. Don't touch me. I am going to tell if you do.'

He knew I meant it and didn't try again.

But that wasn't the end of his activities. During the next school holidays, I found Allan, having given up on me, taking Carmel's hand and leading her into the darkened back bedroom. I took her other hand and pulled her away from him.

'You are not going in there with him,' I said. 'And, Allan, keep away from my sisters. If I see you touching them, I will tell.'

From then on, my vigilance knew no bounds.

About a year later, it was confirmation time and I was ready to be initiated into more knowledge of my religion by the Reverend Mother, who took us for a lesson in Christian doctrine. A rotund woman whose ruddy face was criss-crossed by a tangle of intersecting red and blue veins, she rocked back and forth from the balls of her feet onto her heels, always with a cane in hand. *She must have been trained as a trapeze artist*, I thought one day, suppressing a smile, before paying attention because today's lesson was about mortal sin.

'Missing Mass on Sunday is a mortal sin,' she said.

I knew that.

'Eating meat on Friday is a mortal sin.'

I knew that, too. We always had fish on Fridays.

'Killing someone is a mortal sin. Impure acts are mortal sins.'

Now I really began to take notice.

The Reverend Mother went on to tell us about the three ways to know for sure if you have committed a mortal sin:

'Full knowledge of the guilt.

'Full consent of the will.

'A grave matter. Like killing someone.'

I breathed a sigh of relief. Mine was not a mortal sin after all. There was no way I had full consent – or any consent – of the will. What a relief! What a relief! What a relief!

The black shadow hanging over me was lifted. All I was left with was pity and a kind of compassion for Allan.

12
kincoppal-rose bay

When I turned twelve, Mother enrolled me as a boarder at the Convent of the Sacred Heart Rose Bay, now called Kincoppal-Rose Bay. More than once, she told me how I came to be there.

'When we moved back to Sydney,' she said, 'your father and I would occasionally go to see a film at the Wintergarten picture theatre at Rose Bay and then take a walk along the Rose Bay waterfront. He would look up at that school surrounded by its own bushland, dominating the bay and commanding a magnificent view of the Harbour Bridge. Then he would say, "That's where I'd like Annie to go to school."'

And so it was.

During my childhood, I prayed for anything and everything. That's what you did when you were raised a Catholic: you constantly asked God to intervene in your life, giving strict instructions about how you wanted your life to be. But when I prayed for a good husband when I grew up, what a good husband was, I hardly knew. After our father's death, our household was dominated by women. I knew women were strong.

How that accorded with the current marriage culture in films and magazines didn't quite fit with my exact experience.

Besides, I did wonder whether this lanky girl with straight brown hair would actually find a husband. Who could love me like my father had loved me? Who could love me like the heroes loved the girls in films and books? They were all universally beautiful.

The convent was one alternative. Maybe I could learn to love Jesus and Mary … enough. Yet it didn't have the same attraction as romance and family life.

For years, I watched other girls make the momentous decision to become nuns. Down the aisle they came in full bridal regalia, their hair still long and beautiful, about to take their vows of poverty, chastity and obedience. People of this world one moment but then, with vows said at the altar, they exited only to return in the grey habit of a postulant, hair cut short and head covered with a small white veil.

This school was the primary source of recruitment for those postulants. We all knew that. And we all knew we were under surveillance as possible recruits. I, for one, thought long and hard about it. I decided that if I made the choice to join the order, it would be agony for me as well as them. I was not ready to 'die to self', which was what they used to say was necessary. I had too much energy and mischief inside me to be a renunciant. And the habits! How could anyone wear those clothes in the Australian climate?

Although in my senior year I was chosen as head of the school, I always thought it had come about by mistake or only because my fellow students didn't like the girl being groomed for it because she was too pious for their taste.

When we had finished our matriculation exams and were close to escaping the convent forever, it was a time to relax, to help the nuns tidy up before the summer break and make ourselves useful one last time. It was also the time when I received a beautifully written note asking me to attend Reverend Mother in the front parlour. Here goes, I said to myself. Be strong, don't waver.

The room was dimmed against the afternoon heat and, like all convent parlours, was sparsely furnished but had a gleaming floor polished to perfection by the labour of 'lay sisters'. These working-class women slaved their whole lives to do the housework and cooking to support us children in the boarding school and the teaching nuns, a class system we students often questioned but only among ourselves.

Reverend Mother McGuiness began by telling me that as head girl I had been a wonderful influence on the school.

'You know, Anne, you have remarkable leadership qualities,' she added. 'We would welcome you into the order of the Sacred Heart if you wish to offer those in the service of our Lord.'

She was a formidable person, Mother McGuiness, remote from us most of the time, so I felt the need to be ready and had rehearsed this conversation. 'Of course, Reverend Mother,' I said, 'I want to offer my life to God, and I have thought about it a lot. But I do believe my vocation is to be a good woman of the world and bring up children in God's service.'

There, I had said it, and pretty much this was the end of the conversation.

What I didn't say was this: 'Look, Reverend Mother, after all those years enduring the comments of my family about my height, my spindly arms and legs, my skinny frame, I've been looking in the mirror lately and what I see meets with my approval. A swelling bosom, small waist, long legs (now an asset), brown eyes and brown hair and a complexion the envy of many. Throwing it all away under a black habit would not show gratitude to God, who gave me these gifts.'

In fact, on leaving school, this ugly duckling grew into a swan. Confidently stepping out into the world then, I was 'ready to rock and roll'.

book two
a girl in the country

But the cloud never comes in that quarter of the horizon from which we watch for it.
— Elizabeth Gaskell, *North and South*

13

sydney university

At high school, my first choice of career was journalism. At fourteen, I had started preparing for it by writing a detective novel in serial form, to pass around my class at school, one chapter at a time. I had been inspired by a young writer called Catherine Gaskel, a published author who had written her first novel at fifteen and went on to become quite famous. I didn't see why that couldn't be my future.

But it all came to a shuddering end when the novel was confiscated by our class teacher, Mother Judith Hill, and I never saw it again. Although it must be said, she was inspired to give me the prize for English at the end of the year.

When I voiced my ambition to my mother to become the Lois Lane of Sydney, I ran slap bang into her opposition.

'I'll not have you sweeping up shavings on the printing room floor,' she said. 'You'll just be sent to report on balls and weddings of society people, and do you know what male journalists are like? Hard drinkers, and who knows what their morals are like. It's no place for a girl.'

Well, I hadn't imagined any of that. It didn't sound like the newsrooms I'd seen in films, where women were often heroes of the day. There was no way though I could stand up to Mother.

Then I had to decide what my career choice would be. I didn't think I was bright enough to do medicine, my maths wasn't good enough for architecture or engineering, and law seemed to be deadly dull. Joan had studied at Sydney University and remembered it, in the postwar years, as a mecca for riotous partying – balls going all night and finishing with a swim and breakfast on Bondi Beach. After two years, she'd given it up to pursue a career in modelling, then met Bob, a British naval officer from Scotland, and got married. But among her partying at university, Joan had done one year of social work. That seemed like a worthy thing to do, and if I became a hospital social worker I might catch the eye of a good-looking doctor.

My first day at Sydney University was terrifying. There I stood, at the top of the stone steps off Parramatta Road, waiting for my school friend Catherine Honner to arrive so we could help each other through the first few days. We 'freshers' were everywhere. *Boys, boys, boys, all let out of their cages*, I thought. I tried to look cool. Then Catherine arrived and we set off together with our maps and brochures into this brave new world of learning, steering each other through the crowds of other students. We stood out like sore thumbs, with our uncertainties on show for all to see.

The first stop was the Great Hall, where the Vice Chancellor gave us advice we didn't really need to hear.

'Don't think,' he said, 'that because you've made it to university that you are part of society's elite.'

It hadn't occurred to us previously, but now we began to think we might be. He then went on to warn us that half of us would fail our first-year exams. *Not me*, I said to myself. *Certainly not me.*

Outside we ran into a girl Catherine knew, Alice Collins. They had both been at the Sacred Heart day school at Elizabeth Bay, across the water from the boarding school. Like me, Alice had been head of her school, but she had already spent a year at Sydney University. Exotically, she had entered the convent at the end of her first year, only to swiftly learn it wasn't what she thought it might be. Now she had returned for a second university orientation. In my eyes, she was so worldly-wise, and Catherine and I were happy to be taken in hand by her for the next few weeks as she guided us through the intricacies of university life.

That day, she introduced us to her circle of friends. They were doing a variety of studies – science, architecture, economics and arts with various majors. Catherine, Alice and I were enrolled in arts with a view to combining it with social work in our third year. All of us were from private schools – Frensham, PLC, MLC, Ascham, Kambala, Abbotsleigh and Rose Bay – and all of us had done well at school to have been admitted to university in the first place. Most of the friendships started there have continued, even to this day.

Every morning, my journey to lectures took me past a group of students lounging in the sun at the northern end of the quadrangle. They were waiting for a lecture from Professor Anderson, head of the Philosophy Department. Philosophy was one of those subjects I wanted to study but the nuns at school had warned us about this prof. It was said he preached free love, encouraged his students to become socialists – or worse still, communists – and that his influence would be a threat to my faith and therefore might lead to the loss of my immortal soul.

As I passed this group on my way to lectures it struck me how different from me they all looked. There I was in in my twin-set with a little Peter Pan collar clipped on at the back for easy laundering, a pleated skirt, court shoes and stockings. Their look, by contrast, was bohemian, a little eccentric, a little scruffy. Ankle-length gypsy skirts for the women, with scarfs wrapped around their hair. Worn suede desert boots and open-neck shirts and beards for the men. In coming years, many of this group – such as Clive James, Germaine Greer, Robert Hughes and Lillian Roxon (the only one who became a friend of mine) – would become internationally known as leaders in their fields of art, culture, social change and music.

My friends, by contrast, were an uncomplicated lot. Sober, mostly celibate, enthusiastic, funny and full of anticipation for the life that lay ahead of us.

A smattering of Colombo Plan students – beneficiaries of scholarships to foster development in South-East Asia – also peopled the campus. The Colombo Plan had evolved partly as a bulwark against communism. The Cold War was still with us, with 'reds' definitely under the beds. This was a time when wool prices were high; the Labor Party was split in two and in turmoil; the Democratic Labor Party held the balance of power in federal government; the New South Wales government was corrupt, as were the police. Mother loved Mr Menzies, as she called him. She loved the way he spoke. Abortion was whispered about behind closed doors but you could get one if you knew who to go to in Macquarie Street, the epicentre of medical practice in Sydney. Immigration from Europe was in full swing as refugees provided two years of indentured labour for the Snowy Mountains Hydro-electric Scheme, amid self-congratulations by the politicians at having dreamed up a way to redistribute water from the mountains to the dry western plains. The returning soldiers, with whom Joan happily cavorted at university, were now feeding an economy hungry for their skills; and young mothers were doing their bit to keep the white goods industry growing and giving birth to the Baby Boomer generation.

We looked forward to a wonderful future as we sat around the tables in Manning House, discussing all this as well as the ideas coming out of our studies; the state of romances, current, broken and emerging; boys and what we thought of the current 'talent'; who was going with whom to the college and faculty balls (fortunately, I always had an invitation); the ins and outs of politics as outlined in *Honi Soit*, the campus newspaper; or the latest political matter student leader Myfanwy Gollan (later Myfanwy Horne, wife and editor of the prominent intellectual Donald Horne) had presented us with at the end of lectures in Wallace Theatre.

Although we were far from a radical bunch, most of us did once block the pedestrian crossing on Parramatta Road, standing there with placards protesting about I don't remember what. Then there was Commemoration Day, a tradition begun in 1887 to honour the university's benefactors. The Commemoration procession through the city began in 1903 and here I was in 1954, in my second year, honouring the benefactors. This was by way of being perilously perched on the back of a float adorned with witty comments on the events of the day and facing a barrage of rotten eggs and soft tomatoes while the police, who occasionally got 'accidently' pelted themselves, kept a not-so-benevolent eye on the event.

Unlike students in medicine or science, I was not radical enough to remove my clothes to cool off in the city's Archibald Fountain; the statues had been painted with dye the night before. This escapade drew loud tut-tutting in *The Sydney*

Morning Herald the next day, although everyone knew it would happen again the following year and that it was just part of good old dissolute Sydney.

None of us had much money; most of us were chronically broke. To augment my minuscule allowance, I worked semester breaks. Peter Cahill, a science student who lived across the road from me on Edgecliff Road, got me a job serving Cahill's fruit drinks at the Easter Show and I also did a stint each Christmas in the china and glassware department of David Jones; at other times I worked at Better Brakes as a receptionist.

As my friends and I progressed in our studies, many weekends and some evenings saw us gathered at the Mitchell Library, where we widened our circle of contacts. I met law and medical students and a goodly bunch of other young males. Often one or other of them took me to coffee afterwards and occasionally drove me home in a car borrowed from their father. If I was alone with one of them, it was always time for a serious talk or even a pashing session, but not sex. My friends and I weren't prepared to risk pregnancy with all its complications and, besides, sex outside marriage was a mortal sin.

My arts degree included subjects like psychology and economics, which counted towards social work studies. During the summer vacation at the beginning of my third year, I did my first practical assignment. Miss Norma Parker, the head of the Social Work Department at Sydney University, chose it for me; it was with the Catholic Welfare Agency on Elizabeth Street, opposite Hyde Park.

One early morning a couple of weeks in, my supervisor handed me a file and said, 'I'm so snowed under, Miss Austin. I'm sure you could handle a home visit at Blacktown. It's on the way to the Blue Mountains.' She added, 'Here are a few notes.

The parish priest at Parramatta has rung about a deserted wife with two children. Just take the bus to Central and hop on a train to Blacktown. It might take you most of the day. Write it all up in the morning and tomorrow we can see what has to be done.'

Feeling both terrified and exhilarated, I hurried down to Central Station, stepped onto the train to Blacktown and into my first solo assignment.

Fortunately, a taxi was waiting at Blacktown station when I arrived there.

'Where to, miss?' said the driver.

I showed him the address.

'I didn't think those people lived out there any more,' he said, looking at my shiny shoes and stockings.

'Yes, I need to go there to see Mrs Every urgently,' I said.

'Never heard of her. It's a bit of a hike but we'll find her. Let's go.'

On the way, I glimpsed horses and cows grazing in small paddocks with old farm houses and sheds. Then I saw Chinese men and women working in neat market gardens. Dogs were in evidence everywhere, as well as chickens and their coops. When we arrived at the house, a woman who turned out to be Mrs Every was standing in her doorway with a baby on her hip and a toddler clinging to her skirt. Disused tins and other rubbish littered an unkempt, overgrown yard, and next door, an old car body sat rusting away in the summer heat.

Mrs Every had heard the taxi pull up and greeted me enthusiastically. As I entered the house, I almost reeled with the pungent smell of unwashed dishes and dirty nappies and the buzz of hopeful flies. She offered me a glass of water in a grubby cup, which it took all my courage to sip from as I prayed for protection from unimaginable germs.

'Miss Austin, I have no money and I know it's illegal but I've just come back from taking water in a jerry can from a hydrant down the road. I had to take the pram because I couldn't carry it otherwise. I didn't like leaving the baby in the house but what could I do? I'll have to do the washing in the morning and wash the dishes tonight unless I get the electricity back on. I've only got a bit of an old barbecue outside to heat things on and you can't do much with candles.'

When I asked about her husband, she replied, 'Dane brought us out here to start a farm, but he gave up when I had the baby because I couldn't help him much any more.'

'Where is he now?' I asked.

'He took off in search of work about three weeks ago. I haven't seen him since and don't know where he could be. I'm desperate, Miss Austin. Can you find out where he's gone?'

'What about your family,' I said, hoping for a breakthrough there. 'Can they be of any help to you?'

Mrs Every's mother lived somewhere in Queensland; she was no longer sure where. Other family members were dispersed. They'd all spent time in orphanages and she'd lost touch with them and her mother after she married Dane.

'We'll do our best to locate them,' I said and hoped I sounded encouraging. 'In any case, what are your plans? It doesn't look as if you can stay out here much longer.'

'No, I hate this place. Without a car or transport it's hopeless, and look at the dirt floor. There is nothing to stop the snakes and spiders coming in. Snakes and spiders, Miss Austin. With two children, it's just not safe,' she said and I could see that for myself.

I felt desperate for this young mother's situation and after listening to her story for two hours I knew she needed urgent assistance. I would paint a grim picture when I got back to the office tomorrow.

'I'll make sure we get the water and light put back on and hope we can get you some better housing,' I said.

Just as we finished our conversation, the taxi driver turned up again. I thanked Mrs Every for telling me her story, assuring her someone would be back in touch the next day.

'Had to get you back to catch the 4.30 train, love,' the taxi driver said, 'otherwise you might not get home till midnight.'

I wrote my report that night and gave it to my supervisor the next morning. She was full of praise and from then on she referred to Mrs Every as 'your client, Miss Austin'. How grown-up that made me feel.

I managed to get Mrs Every's electricity and water put back on the following morning by agreeing that the agency would pay some of the backlog. After making their own enquiries, the small state welfare department, as it was then, agreed she was eligible for the pittance of a small cash payment. We also arranged for a food parcel to be delivered, finally found her some half-decent accommodation (with a linoleum floor) and linked her with the St Vincent de Paul Society, who managed to catch up with Dane and arranged for him to return to his family.

No doubt the reason the agency sent me, a young rookie, into a situation like that was to strip away my middle-class inexperience and expose me to the worst of what lay ahead for me in the profession I had chosen.

More cases like that one followed in different agencies. At the end of that year I graduated as a social worker and then commenced postgraduate studies in medical social work.

As part of my postgrad course, I spent three days a week at Sydney Hospital – on pay. On my first day, having managed to survive the hospital's antique bird-cage lift, I was introduced by the head social worker to the sister in charge of the urology ward filled with long rows of old men with bottles of urine by the side of their beds. Ever after, they would greet me warmly when I arrived in the morning, no doubt keen to have the monotony broken by this pretty young woman in a white uniform.

In the morning, the doctors would do their rounds to assess the medical progress of their patients, with an entourage of resident doctors trailing behind.

'Where's the almoner sister?' a doctor said on a typical morning, using the term for medical social workers at the time.

'Here, doctor,' I said, disappointed he hadn't noticed me.

'Well, Mr Sweeney tells me he hasn't got his pension card – is that what you're saying, Mr Sweeney? Please see if you can help him, Miss … err,' he said, his voice trailing away on my name, which he had forgotten. So much for finding a husband in this environment.

Then I would make my own rounds to follow up on the doctor's instructions.

'Good morning,' I would say, holding my chart and clipboard up to my face to accommodate each man's distinctive odour.

'Mr Sweeney,' I said that morning, 'I understand you are having trouble with your pension card.'

'Yes, miss,' he said. 'I left it in my room at the Cross.'

'Do you have a relative who could call in to get it for you? I can ring them for you if you like.'

'No!' was the answer. Most of the men in the ward had lost touch with family or never had one to begin with, and were loners. Some of these men had been or were alcoholics and abusive or had a history of venereal disease contracted during the war. As they grew old and dependent, their close-to-the-edge families had abandoned them in pursuit of their own survival. Mr Sweeney was no exception.

In his case, a hospital orderly accompanied me to seek out his pension card. We found it in his one-room residence in a boarding house around Darlinghurst, on the strip that is now better known for the high and low life of drugs and traded sex.

The smell of stale cooking was the first thing that assaulted us as we made our way up the narrow staircase and the equally narrow passageway. Then there was the urine-stained unmade iron bed and clothing scattered over the floor. What I remember most, however, was the dead bird in the cage hanging in one corner of the room. This, it seemed, had been on his mind more than the pension card.

'I buried your birdie [as he called it] in the hospital garden, Mr Sweeney,' I told him, at which his eyes filled up with tears. He leant over and squeezed my hand.

During this last year in medical social work, most of our time at university involved discussion seminars rather than lectures, there were no exams as such but each of us had to complete a thesis by the end of our training.

As well as Sydney Hospital, I also had placements at the Children's Hospital, Royal Prince Alfred Hospital and Crown Street Women's Hospital. On graduating, I was offered a full-time job at Crown Street and joined four other medical social workers whose job was to take care of numerous pregnant unwed mothers and the parents who were waiting to adopt.

The question I sometimes asked myself about the women who signed over their babies to the many childless couples who came to our clinic was, would I ever have been able to do the same? The cruel thing was that the immense stigma and judgement associated with unwed motherhood resulted in secrecy and isolation from family and friends during the months waiting till the baby's birth. Thanks to the lack of financial support for anyone wanting to keep their baby, almost all these girls opted for adoption. In rare instances, an unwed mother went home with her baby, her mother pretending it was hers. Most of the women were very young and naturally wanted to be married eventually, but to someone who would provide them with a stable home and family. That is one reason why secrecy was so important. Being tarred as a loose woman might destroy all prospects of that for the rest of their lives and had to be avoided at all costs.

It wasn't until I had a child of my own that I really understood how desperate the situation must have been for the women who gave their babies away to strangers and how heavily their secret decision must have weighed on them.

14
the apple pie man

My school friend Sally was the first of my peers to take the plunge into matrimony. She got married in Wagga Wagga – we always just called it Wagga – at Easter in 1955. Catherine Honner and I both received invitations. Since we'd spent most of our Christmas holidays putting together our respective final thesis for the academic year while our friends cavorted on the beach, the wedding represented a welcome opportunity to let our hair down. At the unholy hour of eight o'clock on Holy Thursday morning, we boarded the Daylight Express at Central Railway Station, arriving at Wagga by 3.30 in the afternoon.

'Ten minutes' stop,' yelled the station attendant. 'Boarding passengers for Albury and Melbourne. All aboard, please.' He could hardly be heard above the noise of people crowding the platform to greet or farewell friends and family in the dusty glow of the warm autumn afternoon.

The Wagga station was typical of most such buildings in country towns around New South Wales at that time. A corrugated iron overhang trimmed with iron lace provided shade, and matching adornments supported the wooden seats. Opening the door of the train – which was air-conditioned, an innovation for 1955 – we were greeted by the accumulated smells of diesel and the steam that had embedded themselves into every post, beam and fabric of the station over close to a hundred years. There was another aroma: the whiff of human excrement mixed with railway-issue disinfectant wafting from the restrooms. Then, from the room optimistically labelled 'Refreshments', came the ubiquitous smell of heated pies. It was all so familiar, both toxic and … well … reassuring.

Catherine and I were both twenty-one years old and amply provided for in all the important ways for girls of that era. I wore a favourite frock: a bright blue, full-skirted, polished-cotton dress scattered with white clouds and nipped in at the waist. As I stood there full of anticipation, in my high-heeled strappy sandals, which showed off my red-painted toenails to perfection, what seized my attention was a pair of the bluest of blue eyes shaded by a broad-brimmed Akubra hat. Before us stood the epitome of rural masculinity, dressed in white moleskin trousers, polished brown elastic-sided boots and a green knitted tie. Stepping confidently forward, the apparition said, 'You must be Anne and you must be Catherine? Welcome to the Riverina! I'm Bruce Gorman and I have been given the privilege of escorting you both and taking care of you during your stay.'

We piled into the front seat of his grey farm utility and sped off down the long main street of Wagga. Over the next four days, being 'taken care of' included bunking down with an elderly pious spinster, a barbecue, swimming in the Murrumbidgee River, a race meeting, a dance, the wedding at the Catholic cathedral and reception afterwards at the golf club, and in between

Catherine and I carried out the usual manoeuvrings to be in the company of the boys we fancied. No time to let the grass grow under our feet as we flirted our way around the available talent. Our escort, in spite of *his* manoeuvrings, received little encouragement from me and absolutely none from Catherine. Early in the weekend, a kind soul had warned me he was unofficially engaged to some absent friend and more or less to keep my hands off him. No trouble; he wasn't my type anyway.

On Tuesday afternoon, exhausted, we climbed back onto the train. As we rode the 350 miles north-east to Sydney, we decided we were unlikely ever to visit Wagga again. Our major goal was to graduate with distinction and, until then, neither of us was interested in a serious liaison.

All around us, however, tales of romance from our early university days seemed to be morphing into talk of marriage. Catherine and I were both to be bridesmaids in the coming September at the wedding of our close friend Alice, who was giving up her studies to marry a doctor and move to a Northern Rivers town in New South Wales. I was glad for Alice that she was to marry a wonderful man but not to finish her studies was a disappointment. Another friend, Judy, turned up at Manning House sporting a large red, white and blue engagement ring. As she put forward her hand for all of us to inspect it, there was an audible gasp and then silence as everyone took in the ring's audacity. Then I found my voice and said, 'Judy, what magnificent stones.' From then on, I would be dubbed Miss Diplomatic.

Like Alice, Judy's choice of a mate meant she was going to live in the country. Judy had completed an economics degree; at least that would come in handy in running a rural property.

Now that our time at university was coming to an end my close friends and I began to develop an account of the kind of person who might make a good husband. A few of us were Catholics so we knew that if we made a mistake, divorce would not be an option. Moreover, we all knew who the men and boys you couldn't trust were, and had labelled them 'gorillas'. Belinda had taken the risk of going on a date with a gorilla and had, in her words, 'just escaped with my life, certainly with my virginity'. Gorillas didn't make it onto our list as marriage material.

During my practical work, I had dealt with a number of marriage tension situations and decided this subject was as good as any to use as my social work thesis. From then on I was referred to as '*the* expert on the subject of matrimony'.

Finally we came up with the template. The ideal husband would be: reliable, steady, unlikely to go off and have an affair, well educated, a lover of children and a good conversationalist. It never occurred to us to add sexual prowess to the list. If any of us had had experience of sex – and I certainly hadn't – we wouldn't have been sharing it with the group. In our naivety, we took it for granted that if the other aspects of the relationship were okay, your new husband would know the proper techniques for the enjoyment of sex and *your* enjoyment would naturally follow.

We nicknamed this paragon of virtue 'the apple pie man'. Alice and Sally had clearly found theirs. Maybe even Judy with the big ring. It was up to the rest of us to snag the remaining talent, before it all ran out!

Mother had been married at twenty-two, as had a couple of my sisters. It seemed, then, that twenty-two was the gold standard, whether you were ready for it or not. This was reinforced by comments such as, 'Whatever happened to Mary? Such a nice girl. Why is she still on the shelf at twenty-eight?' Being left a spinster was unthinkable – tantamount to the worst humiliation of your life and, indeed, the very end of life itself in many ways.

Twelve months after my Wagga adventure, I opened the Rosemont letterbox and found an envelope addressed to me, postmarked Yerong Creek. It contained an invitation to the Bachelor and Spinsters' Ball at the Lake Albert Golf Club, outside Wagga, from the very same man who had met Cathie and me at the railway station. He of the blue eyes and Akubra hat.

By now, I had completed my studies, graduated well and was working full-time at Crown Street Women's Hospital. After a few days' reflection, I wrote back and accepted his invitation – one wouldn't have made a phone call for something like that. What the hell; I was a year older than when I had met him and had matured a lot. Maybe Bruce Gorman was worth another look. Maybe he was an apple pie man. I had nothing to lose by accepting this invitation. Clearly, he had not married the mystery woman to whom he was supposedly engaged on my last trip.

At Central Railway Station, I boarded the *Spirit of Progress* and at the end of the long journey, Bruce was waiting to meet me at the station. We went to the ball at the golf club, then made the thirty-mile drive to his homestead at Yerong Creek, where his mother acted as chaperone, a task she took very seriously, much to Bruce's chagrin.

On Saturday, we were invited to a barbecue and on a brilliant warm autumn Sunday, we took off for a swim in the Hume Dam, near Albury. We travelled back to Bruce's home via Mangoplah to visit Bruce's sister Barbara and her family. It was obvious that the family were casting an eye over me as a potential partner. Bruce was thirty-three and, in their view, no doubt it was time, particularly since he had failed to progress the last good prospect, even the one his family wanted him to marry.

Over the weekend, as I got to know Bruce, I was particularly interested to hear about his war-time experiences. When he signed up at age twenty-one, he was the only male working on the property. He had sisters away at school and brothers engaged in war-related activities elsewhere. Then his father started to employ Italian POWs and Bruce was free to go. 'No one knew how long the war would last,' he said.

His initial training was at the Benalla and Sommers air force bases in Victoria and then, having got his wings, he worked as an instructor at Uranquinty, near Wagga Wagga, in New South Wales. None of these recruits knew how to fly in northern hemisphere conditions so when Winston Churchill called for more pilots from Australia to fly over Germany, Bruce was one of a group chosen to go to Canada. There, they learned to fly bombers and bigger planes in snowy and icy terrains being prepared to go on to that fierce European theatre of war.

Hearing this, I shuddered. The wartime exploits of the British air force were common knowledge and I'd also read books like *The Dam Busters* and knew how few came out alive from those campaigns.

'How did you feel about that assignment?' I asked.

'It wasn't the thought of going into battle in Europe that really worried me,' replied Bruce. 'There were only two things that scared the hell out of me. The first was the nightmare trip to Canada by boat. The Japanese subs were crawling over every inch of the Pacific Ocean and one of their torpedoes would have meant the end of us. I slept on deck most nights, where we had to be as quiet as mice. That way, I could jump overboard and swim or drown quietly and not be trapped below. No one was allowed to light a match or cough for fear of being heard or spotted. Smokers slept below decks. I was never so glad to see the North American coastline as I was at the end of that journey.'

'What about the second thing that scared the hell out of you?' I asked, eager to hear more.

'It was when I was flying solo over the Canadian prairies. It was covered with snow – feet-deep. White, white, white was all I could see. Not a landmark in sight. I just couldn't get my bearings and pick up one recognisable thing.'

'What did you do?'

'The most important thing was I kept my head and prayed!'

We both laughed, and he continued, 'No laughing matter really, and it was like that for fifteen minutes as I kept flying east toward what I thought should be the Calgary Air Base, where we were stationed. I nearly missed it at first. Then suddenly, I picked it up, looming out of the white landscape. At that stage snow had begun to fall right as I heard the controller calling me in to land.

'"Gorman," he said, "we thought we'd lost you. Dropped into the pub, did you? Aussie bastard, where have you been?"

'"Thank you, Captain. Sorry I'm late for dinner. Thanks for staying up for me."'

'But it wasn't really a joke, was it?' I said.

'No, it wasn't and although I wasn't much of a drinker and he knew it, I had a few that night to celebrate my survival.'

During his two years in Canada, Bruce met many Canadian girls who came to the base for dances and opened their Calgary homes to him and his fellow pilots. He also took advantage of opportunities to travel to Niagara Falls, New York and the southern states. Before he left he was given an officer's commission.

When the war ended in 1945, he came home, never to use the skills he had acquired overseas. The death of one of his best buddies in Canada shook him so badly that after the war he never wanted to fly again.

I went probing into Bruce's favourite authors and found they included Evelyn Waugh, Oscar Wilde and Nevil Shute. As a bachelor, he'd had time to take holidays to exotic places and was always broadening his horizons by meeting new people.

He liked ballet, knew the names of many ballet dancers and actors in the Old Vic Company and had seen Vivien Leigh and Laurence Olivier playing in *The School for Scandal* and Olivier in *Hamlet* at the Theatre Royal. Best of all, Bruce's favourite music was Dvorak's 'New World' Symphony, which was a favourite of mine.

I also gathered he had become the family leader since his father's death, and had organised the split-up of his father's estate and the management of his mother's assets. It was obvious to me that he was the one who cared most deeply about his mother's wellbeing and holding the family together.

Quite a lot for me to take in on one weekend visit.

Although we had a few sessions of kissing and cuddling, which felt safe and pleasant enough, there was no special spark that made me think this relationship might go anywhere. I gave Bruce little encouragement and was beginning to think this visit had been merely a pleasant interlude.

Not long before he was to take me to catch the train on Monday morning, we called in to see his brother Kerry and his wife Judy and their three young children, Laurie, Susan and Christopher, still a baby in a pram. They lived in a little cottage near the main homestead so we didn't have far to go.

Their eldest child, Laurie, had a serious disability that left him partly blind and with a speech impairment. I watched Bruce lean in close to Laurie's face and listen to what he was telling him. The little boy was dribbling all over him, but it didn't worry Bruce. As I watched, my heart did an unexpected flip.

Now just be careful, Annie, went my internal monologue. My mind raced. This man was a bit different, kind and loving. In that one action, I was seeing him for the first time. Yes, he was eleven years older than me, but what did that matter in the scheme of things? He was intelligent, well travelled and no ordinary cocky. His time as a pilot during the war had given him a wider perspective on life than most of his country brethren – certainly much wider than that of the young men I had been going out with in Sydney. He was also financially able to keep a wife and family.

It was clear, too, that Bruce was ready for marriage and fitted most of the template my friends and I had set for a husband. Maybe this relationship might be worth pursuing after all. These reflections continued as we drove in silence for the three miles to the railway station at Yerong Creek. As he handed me onto the train, I stuck my head out the door at the end of the carriage and gave him an unmistakably warm smile.

'Without that smile,' he told me later, 'I would not have contacted you again.'

'It was an invitation to do just that,' I assured him. 'I had just made up my mind half an hour before that I wanted to get to know you better.'

So began a whirlwind relationship, with phone calls, letters and trips by Bruce to Sydney and a few by me to his home. When he was in Sydney, he mostly stayed at the Hampton Court Hotel at Kings Cross, where we spent many evenings cuddling and kissing and talking. It seems incredible now that we didn't have sex, but both of us were mindful of our 'Catholic obligations'.

On Bastille Day, Sunday 14 July 1956, at the end of one of Sydney's clear, sunny winter days, Bruce and I took the ferry across to Manly and walked around the pathway beside the ocean to the tiny harbour at Shelly Beach. The sun had just gone down and the fullest of full moons was shining in the cloudless sky, reflecting off the water and lighting the pathway along which we had come. I knew Bruce wanted to say something – that 'something' had been hanging in the air all day. I thought it might be a proposal but didn't care if it wasn't. 'Whatever will be will be', as the song goes. We sat watching the gentle waves coming in and out; the small boats rocked themselves to sleep in the little inlet. With the extraordinary beauty of this sight, I was lost for words and so, it seemed, was he. Nothing but stillness filled the space as our silence stretched out across the moonlit water.

There are only five words in 'Annie, will you marry me?' but it seemed they encompassed centuries of commitments made by people like us on the brink of making a lifetime promise. My head began to spin.

After a long pause, the word 'yes' came out of my mouth. Then we kissed – a long, lingering kiss that took my breath away. Suddenly, I found myself inhabiting a dreamlike place, an observer in a film sequence, moving in slow motion – both in and out of it at the same time. My future was being determined right here and now.

We walked slowly back in the bright moonlight, our arms around each other. I was trembling slightly – no, it was more like a vibration, still feeling as though I was travelling in another dimension. How, in a moment, had I committed myself so completely and what would be the consequences of that commitment?

Just go with the moment, I told myself, and as it began to sink in, I started to feel very happy and at peace. We continued along the pathway, past the big pine trees bordering the ocean beach, to the Manly Pacific Hotel. By the time I stepped into the bright lights of the hotel's dining room, a sense of reality had returned, especially when we celebrated the occasion with a bottle of pink champagne and an expensive dinner of chicken Maryland, followed by meringue with stewed peaches and ice-cream, the epitome of fifties Australian luxury and sophistication.

A life in the country! This was to be my destiny.

Right up to the day of the wedding, I had a few misgivings. The night before my wedding, I approached my sister Phil – who at that point was still single, though she did marry some years later – with doubts about the whole thing. Earlier, she had expressed reservations about me becoming a country wife and offered to support me if I decided to pull out, even though the wedding dress was hanging in my bedroom, the guests were soon to assemble and the food and wine was ordered at Caprice, a beautiful restaurant at Rose Bay, on the edge of the harbour.

Maybe these misgivings were because Bruce loved me more intensely than I loved him at that stage of our relationship. I slept through the night, and with a clearer head the next morning, the marriage went ahead at the little church at Edgecliff on Albert Street, where I had grown up.

I had realised that after a lifetime of longing for security since my father's death, there was no better place to land than with this man.

15
facing reality

The honeymoon was over. We were fresh off the boat from Europe, driving from Sydney to Bruce's home in Yerong Creek, the property Fairfield and its sprawling weatherboard homestead. As each mile passed, we got further away from *my* home. We had been driving all day in the heat and as we passed through each town – Mittagong, Goulburn, Yass, Gundagai, Jugiong, then finally Wagga – I sank further and further into depression. Crying was not usually on my agenda, yet here I was, on the last leg of the journey, weeping silent tears, terrified I might be found out. So I let them fall unchecked onto the skirt of the same blue cotton dress I wore the first time I met Bruce at the Wagga Wagga railway station. Bruce, for his part, was intent on his driving, unaware of the drama unfolding beside him. Or maybe he was but diplomatically chose to ignore it.

It was eighteen months since the still waters of Manly's Shelly Beach witnessed my utterance of the word 'yes'. One simple word that was to change my life, a 'yes' that set off a flurry of wedding planning, bridesmaid choosing, wedding dress design and fittings, venue booking and, finally, an extended honeymoon in Europe.

Every one of those wonderful, long carefree days was an adventure. Every day there was something new to see and learn: the Edinburgh Festival, *Swan Lake* at Covent Garden, Kew Gardens, the Tower of London, the Pope, the Eiffel Tower, cathedrals, art galleries, gondoliers and glass blowing on the island of Murano, war graves, sites of Napoleonic wars, interesting food, conversations in broken French, Spanish, Italian and English with farmers down country lanes as we camped out at night under a full moon. But best of all people, wonderful new people everywhere we went.

Here was freedom from responsibility. We were young and in good health, had no jobs or study assignments to complete by a certain time, no deadlines to keep and we loved every moment of sharing it with each other. Being in love propelled us forward; we had nothing to fear and much to celebrate.

On our first day in France we bumped our way off the ferry in our little van to arrive in Calais. An hour later, on the road towards Albert, a scene of World War I trench warfare that Bruce's pilot father had flown over in his flimsy little flying machine, I spotted a restaurant half hidden behind a thick hedge. 'Stop, stop,' I said. 'I'm famished, darling. Aren't you? Let's see if this is a place we can get something to eat.'

Bruce backed the van into a small clearing on the side of the road and out came a man with a white towel tossed over one shoulder and sporting a long black apron. He led us up the stairs to the restaurant, grabbed a carafe of red wine from behind the door, poured us a drink and left us to it, re-emerging minutes later with appetisers of sweet, freshly picked tomatoes, basil and garlic, the aroma of sunshine still clinging to them, and sprinkled with French dressing.

The sun was still high in the sky, it must have been about five in the afternoon, but we were hungry. The soft buzzing sounds of small insects slumbering lazily in the warmth of the late afternoon rose from the overgrown garden below the balcony, and a faint hint of jasmine perfumed the air around us. We were off the beaten track, all by ourselves in the midst of rural France. How absolutely marvellous.

The restaurant filled up with local people who knew each other well. Our chef introduced his prize exhibit for the night, two people from far-off Australia. That caused a lot of interest as everyone seemed to have met people from Australia during the war. Stories of that time came thick and fast until a small band of musicians started playing and a tinkling piano regaled us with war songs and any other tunes the piano player thought might please Australian visitors, including, I was surprised to hear, 'Waltzing Matilda'.

From there, it was off to the wheat-growing areas of the countryside, where harvest was in full swing, and then to the Loire valley, the Pyrenees and on to Spain. On the rare occasions that conflict arose between us, it was when Bruce was frustrated with my navigation, which once or twice got us hopelessly lost. But even those occasions often turned out to be adventures, though I was annoyed and hurt at his castigations.

Some of the most memorable parts of the journey were those moments when we found it hard to resist each other and would pull up and make love just off the road – once by a running stream in Switzerland and again in the depths of Germany's Black Forest on a bed of fallen leaves.

Most nights we slept out, feeling absolutely safe. We chatted to shepherd boys on the steppes of Spain, inspecting their flock and offering them our store of Coca-Cola in the searing heat. We joined a family on the Italian Riviera under a full moon and shared their picnic, red wine and operatic arias. When our tyres were let down outside a performance of *La Traviata* at the Caracalla, the open-air Roman baths, they were pumped up again by a group of laughing Italian men who wanted nothing for their trouble but to see us safely back to our *pensione*.

By the time we boarded the ship for home, I was pregnant. Morning sickness resulted in me heaving into four of the world's oceans on the six-week voyage home.

Now here we were on the Olympic Highway. As these honeymoon memories crowded in, I knew I should be looking forward to this new arrival and to having a home of my own. But right now, all I wanted was to go back to the love and acceptance of the people I knew in Sydney. My tears were a mixed brew, not only for the end of the exotic honeymoon but for the end of the comfortable life in the city and the support and certainty of my family. Would all my years of university education be lost here in the country?

As we reached the ten-mile stretch from The Rock to Yerong Creek, the last of the sun's rays had gone behind The Rock Hill, that huge, seated lion landmark rising out of a flat plain, flanking the western side of the road. Soon, the long summer twilight would drop decisively into darkness. First the air and later the earth would begin to cool down, making the heat of the drive a distant memory.

The sudden darkness now swallowed the day in an ocean of blackness. No sign of paddocks, sheep or gum trees, there just a moment ago but now determinedly blotted out by the darkness. Black as pitch, we were suddenly in another world, the only sign of habitation the pale twinkling lights of scattered homesteads. A ribbon of road ran precariously ahead of us, the oncoming lights of a vehicle threatening our very existence.

As we moved over to the gravel shoulder of the road to let the truck pass, a rain of tiny dust-laden stones were thrown onto our windscreen. Now grasshoppers and insects of every kind came out in force to do battle with the headlights, committing harakiri against the windscreen. There was no escaping the combination of dying insects and earthy odours pervading the small cabin.

We were nearly there, and turned off the main road heading towards the house. The light of the homestead appeared, then was obscured completely, then seemed close at hand, only to be hidden again by the peppercorn trees on the western side, planted there fifty years ago as protection against the fierce western sun.

At last I saw the lemon-scented gum silhouetted against the light on the verandah, its branches stretching upward to touch a starless sky awaiting the arrival of the planets and all the attendant galaxies that had not yet come out for the night. Bruce's mother, Frankie, planted that tree when the war ended to celebrate his homecoming from Canada, not terribly long after my sisters and I had been released from that boarding school in the mountains.

We came to a halt beside the peppercorn trees at the side of the house. Bruce leant over and kissed me on the cheek and said, 'It's so good to be home. Welcome home, darling!'

For a moment I thought, *It may be your home but it's not mine*, an unworthy sentiment and one I immediately put aside. *Hide those feelings, keep up a brave front.*

With Frankie emerging from the house to greet us, this was not the moment to speak of my tears and apprehensions. As Bruce made his way around to open my door, there was only one thing to do: wipe away my tears under the cover of darkness.

the country wife

After a meal of baked beans on toast eaten at the mottled-green laminex kitchen table, I took a wander through the rest of the house. What I found astounded me. The accumulation of sixty years of occupation by my husband's family was in evidence everywhere. Books and sundry items were piled high on beds, pictures from bygone days were propped up against walls, old shoes and clothes were strewn around the floor of the sleep-out and everything was covered in a thin film of dust.

Although I had been to the house once or twice before Bruce and I were married, for the first time I began to grasp the substantial clean-up now lying ahead of me. 'Despair' was too mild a word to describe the emotion gripping me at that moment. I guess I had assumed some of the family might have come to collect their belongings before we got back or at least attempted to brighten the décor. But it would not even have occurred to Bruce's brothers living in Berrigan, eighty miles away – Brian, with a thriving business; and Peter and his wife, Pat, having just lost their first girl baby after six boys. Bruce's sisters, some more than an hour's drive away, were all juggling growing families. Bruce's mother, Frankie, had recently spent twelve months in a Melbourne hospital recovering from her grief at losing Bruce's father, Ted.

Frankie had married Thomas Edward ('Ted') Gorman in 1918 and had come to live in the weatherboard homestead. It was built in 1880 from Murray pine timber cut and milled on the property. A ten-foot hallway ran down the middle with bedrooms on each side. The two bedrooms on the western side gave access to a wide verandah, on which the hazardous cracked wooden boards cried out for repair. Sometime in the past, the verandah had been enclosed on the eastern side to form a sleep-out. Three of the bedrooms sported fireplaces, relics from the past, their tall chimneys on the roof giving the house an illusion of grandeur.

In 1921, Ted had borrowed money from his wealthy uncle, with whom he had a very special relationship. This had allowed him to build a new brick section on the back containing a kitchen, living rooms and a bedroom, transforming the original weatherboard cottage into a more substantial dwelling. Consequently, the house was in two parts; the newer section was joined to the older one by a long breezeway that had originally been open at both ends but had since been filled in with louvred windows, an innovation at the time. Three small rooms off the breezeway were probably meant to house domestics; one was now a store room but the others were closed and dusty.

Ted's adoptive father had imported a new brass bed from England in the 1890s. Although he and his wife, Anne, had begotten no children in the years they occupied it, when the bed was handed down to Frankie and Ted, eight conceptions had followed. Now Frankie had given it to Bruce and me as a wedding present, after sending it off to Sydney to be re-brassed. On its return, it had been hastily reassembled by Paul, Bruce's bachelor brother, who still lived in the house.

To celebrate our homecoming on our first night, Bruce convinced me to make love in this double bed, which stood slightly skew-whiff in one of the bedrooms off the wide hall in the old weatherboard section of the house. As soon as we climbed aboard, I realised that there was a problem. Its rickety bolts and screws complained of their incompetent assembly and I immediately regretted my readiness for love-making. But Bruce, determined to mark our homecoming with something momentous, was undeterred. He had omitted to carry me over the threshold and this was his way of making up for it. There he was, going at it, with me trying to respond but mindful of the rocking and creaking sounds echoing through the thin walls, fit to wake the dead, and certainly Frankie and Paul!

The next morning, Bruce showed no signs of embarrassment. *It's all right for a man*, I thought. For my part, I was mortified and found it hard to look Frankie in the eye over the cornflakes, although she was kind enough to act as if she hadn't heard anything. Fortunately, a new inner-spring mattress, a present from Mother, arrived at the train station that day. In response to my continuing encouragement, Bruce moved the bed into the brick part of the house, reassembled it and tightened the nuts and bolts.

Before we left for our honeymoon, Bruce and I had planned some renovations to the kitchen, dining and living rooms, which the workmen had finished off while we were away. The kitchen, which now boasted a new electric stove, had been remodelled. A wall had been removed, allowing the pantry to be reincarnated as a dining area, and the living room fireplace had been rebuilt to modern standards. Those changes, at least, were a consolation. Nevertheless, from my point of view, other parts of the house were completely dysfunctional.

So it was that four days before the new year of 1958, this city-bred daughter, European traveller and pretend sophisticate with a BA and a postgraduate degree in medical social work rolled up her sleeves. Under the benign eye of my mother-in-law, I began to transform this amazing dwelling into a home fit for my vision of how a farmer's wife should live.

16
thomas edward and frankie

Bruce's sister Barbara once told me that their father, Thomas Edward Gorman, would have approved of me.

'Why?' I asked.

'Well, for one thing your stocking seams are always straight and your shoes are polished.'

Tom, as he was known since birth, had grown up in Queensland, one of ten children in a family severely strapped for cash. His father had 'got a maid in the household pregnant', and had subsequently married her. Together the couple moved as far away as possible to avoid the 'disgrace'. When Tom was ten, his wealthy, childless Uncle Edward visited the family and made an instant connection with young Tom because of their mutual love of horses.

'Would you like to live with me in the Riverina?' the wealthy uncle asked young Tom.

Without a second thought, Tom packed his meagre belongings and left that day with his uncle, never to return to his family of birth.

Edward John Gorman, Tom's uncle, was a leader in his community and championed the declaration of a new Riverina state at the time of Federation. He was a man of standing, having amassed considerable wealth out of land, sheep and wool, allowing him to build a substantial homestead on one of his properties, Nangunia, where he and his wife, Anne, lived the life of rural gentry. He was, moreover, a regular contributor to the *Argus*, Melbourne's premier newspaper.

Although Tom was never legally adopted, for all intents and purposes, his Uncle Edward was his father. One of the many adjustments Tom had to make in his new life was the changing of his first name. Aunt Anne, whom nobody disobeyed, decided he would now be called Ted because her nephew Tom lived at Nangunia and there was a houseboy with the same name as well. Ever afterwards, he was to be known as Ted, except on official documents such as his birth certificate.

One can only imagine the look on young Ted's face the day he arrived at his new home, an architecturally designed, purpose-built homestead. Twelve-foot-wide verandahs adorned with elaborate iron lace friezes and railings shielded the house from the summer sun. There was a ballroom, a dining room for thirty, many bedrooms and a billiard room, lit brilliantly by morning light that streamed through a glass dome. The kitchen was enormous, and there were rooms for staff accommodation and storage.

Ted quickly adjusted to life as the only son of an established rural landholder. He was educated as a gentleman at Dr McCrystal's school in Melbourne, where he received a classical anglicised education heavily influenced by Jesuit principles, and could look forward to a prosperous future. When war seemed imminent, he enlisted in the Royal Flying Corps with thirty other young Australian men, long before

Australia had an air force of its own. They set sail for England on the SS *Medina* in 1914. Many more Australians followed, including Kingsford Smith. Three months training to fly and he was sent off to a posting in France, flying over trenches and bombing enemy territory, always inches away from a violent death.

Returning from World War I, Ted cut a dashing figure in his pilot's uniform, which, he wrote in his diary, he had had made by a London tailor.

Frankie was a stunning beauty, one of two daughters of a local stock-and-station agent, who was a business partner of Ted's uncle. Frankie and Ted had been childhood friends from the time of his arrival at Nangunia and when Ted took off to the war, they were unofficially engaged to be married. Frankie often told her children she had 'prayed him home from the war' and it worked, because in spite of the huge Australian death toll, he returned in 1918; many of his mates had been killed and he had experienced numerous near misses himself.

The couple was married at the end of this same year at St Patrick's Cathedral, Melbourne, and had a reception at the fashionable Windsor Hotel. Frankie wore an ankle-length dress with a big hat, while Ted wore his flying officer's uniform from Bond Street, London.

Until she was fifteen, Frankie had been educated in the feminine arts of music, sewing, literature and compliance at the Convent of the Sacred Heart, Bourke Road, Melbourne. During her marriage, she raised eight children and ran a substantial household. She had help: sometimes a cook; a governess when the first three children were young; a washerwoman, who was fetched from the village on Mondays in the horse and sulky; and a maid to clean up and help with the chores. She was well read and a champion golfer and tennis player and, like most well-educated young women of the era, her accomplishments included the pianoforte.

Frankie and Ted spent forty years raising eight children and watching every penny. During the Great Depression, they resorted to selling valued possessions to make ends meet. When the wool boom years following World War II brought newfound prosperity for them, Ted bought a large, powerful Buick sedan. The same year, 1954, he became the President of the Wagga Picnic Race Club, reflecting his lifelong passion for the sport of kings. It was a coveted position, one he'd hoped for after the war when events like picnic race meetings were reinstated in the district.

Returning one night from a race meeting in Wagga, in January 1955, his beloved Buick was hit by an unsecured hay frame that swung off the back of a truck being driven by a drunk driver. He must have died instantly. The impact sent his car careering over a fence and up a small hill onto the railway line just beyond The Rock. It was not until the following morning that trains were able to get through.

The first thing Frankie knew of his crash was when she was roused from a deep sleep. Bruce was standing beside her bed whispering, 'Wake up, Mother. Wake up.' The local policeman was waiting down the hall to officially tell her the news.

Frankie was one of that generation of women who deferred to her husband in most matters. Ted was, Bruce told me, something of a martinet and made almost all family decisions, including what they would eat for dinner.

'In the morning, he would open the fridge door or come up from the meat house carrying whatever he thought Frankie should cook. And Frankie never argued,' he told me.

Bruce spoke about his dad often, sometimes with a good deal of amusement, sometimes not. He regarded him as a good father – feared, controlling and strict, impressing on his family a set of strong Catholic values; a man who belonged to a generation secure in the knowledge that they were born to lead and born for heaven after a blameless life. Ted loved his children and wanted the best for his family. He saw to it that each of his boys could make a decent living off the land. As was common in his day, he didn't look far beyond a private school education and a good marriage for his girls.

Although she was a compliant wife, Frankie had a big personality all of her own and managed to negotiate her own place in the hearts of everyone who knew her. She kept up a copious correspondence with friends and was not only well liked but well loved by most people. But now that her husband had died, who was she to become?

'One evening a few months after Dad's death,' Bruce told me, 'Paul and I came in from the paddock expecting her to have prepared the evening meal. She was just sitting there staring into nothingness. She couldn't function and didn't know where she was or for that matter, who we were. After that, we took her to Melbourne, where she spent twelve months having treatment.'

Just like my mother, I thought. *How many other women had languished as semi-invalids, their condition little understood?*

By the time Bruce and I were married in March 1957, Frankie had recovered and was functioning well but was still prone to melancholy. As I came to understand her better, I realised that losing her son 'Boodles', as she called Bruce sometimes, to a city girl like me, who was just about to kick her out of her home, must have been another big adjustment. I didn't want to make it worse for her.

Paul, Bruce's younger brother purchased a house shortly before we were married, had it moved onto his property and was planning to have renovations finished before we returned from our honeymoon. Both he and Frankie were supposed to move out when Bruce and I arrived home. But nothing much had been done and it would take four more months, with Bruce's encouragement, for that reorganisation to happen.

At first I was annoyed, but in those four months I got to know Paul and Frankie better and was glad that Frankie was there as an 'educator' to introduce me to village life and the people and histories of that small community.

Frankie was a vulnerable soul and Fairfield had been her home since before 1920. With her still living with us as I embarked on a clean-out, it did seem potentially insensitive to start disposing of her home's historical junk. Nevertheless, I ploughed on – as gently as I could – clearing out the Gorman memorabilia no one seemed to want.

As time went on though, I longed to have my husband all to myself and to make a nest for our eagerly awaited baby.

So in the days after returning from the honeymoon, here it was – country life, the village, the house, family history and a community of family and owners of nearby properties who opened their arms of friendship to me without hesitation. This warm reception wasn't anything to do with me personally. It was all about my husband.

Everyone liked and admired Bruce and wanted him to be happy. Farmers had to be married – it was the order of things. A collective sigh of relief went up when, at thirty-four, he managed to pull that off, later than most of his peers and with the help of a younger lady from far-off Sydney. And, even better, we were about to become a family.

17
settling in

The first time I went shopping in Wagga with my mother-in-law, the whole exercise took much longer than I expected. Walking down the long main street of Wagga, she would frequently stop and talk to her friends from all over the Riverina. This was also her opportunity to introduce me to each of them.

My head was spinning. I didn't know how I would remember all of these people. Mercifully, one of them was Marion Montague who, because of her closeness to the Gorman family, had been invited to our wedding.

A few days later, she rang and asked the two of us and Frankie to dinner. Marion's husband had died about ten years before and she'd brought up her two daughters and a son and run her property since then. She was a much-admired woman and could hold her own with the best of men on the subjects of sheep, wheat, weather and all other rural preoccupations. Osterley, her property, was about ten miles west of Fairfield and it would take us no more than twenty minutes to drive there through a rough short cut across the railway line, called the Gap.

When I was getting dressed that evening, I asked Bruce to do up the zipper on my blue dress with the white clouds. It had a full skirt that hid my pregnancy quite effectively, or so I had been kidding myself.

'It's getting a bit tight, Annie. Won't be long before you have to start buying maternity outfits.'

Although I tried to hide my annoyance, I bristled at the prospect of having to wear a maternity tent. 'There's a maternity shop in Wagga. What if next time we go up there, I take a look? Do you want to come with me?' I asked. That would fix him. There was no way he'd want to be seen dead in a shop like that. Not unexpectedly, he replied in the negative.

Even though he realised he would now have to spend some money, he laughed as he said, 'You have to bow to the inevitable, Annie!'

It was all very well for Bruce. He was coming to fatherhood later than most of his peers and was much more excited about the prospect of becoming a father than I was of becoming a mother. It followed that he might be keener than I was to see me in a maternity outfit. He put his hand on my tummy.

'I still marvel on how one human being could be made just by having that night of love in Glasgow!' he said, looking wistful and giving me a loving hug. We smiled at each other, mutual recognition lighting up our faces as we remembered.

It had been summer in Glasgow but no one had told the elements, because it was like the coldest day in Australia's winter. We had been shown to a room sporting a double bed covered with an enormous eiderdown. It was all cosy-looking but the room was cold as ice. We braved the elements to collect our mail at Glasgow's poste restante and arrived back to the room chilled and wet. There was no alternative but to don another sweater and keep warm in bed under the covers, while we opened the bundle of letters from home.

The incessant rain beat at the windows as we read our mail to each other. 'Listen to this,' I said. 'Carmel's engaged to Les Downs. Do you remember, darling? She met him at our wedding.' I opened the next letter from her, dated nearly three weeks later. By then Carmel had graduated as a physiotherapist and was working at Royal Prince Alfred hospital. 'You won't believe this,' I said. 'She's broken it off and is now engaged to Neil Gallagher, a doctor she met at the hospital.'

Hunger finally got the better of us and, as the rain continued to beat a love song against the window panes and darkness closed in on the city, we repaired downstairs to partake of the ubiquitous high tea of fried eggs, baked beans on toast, hard rock cakes and cups of tea. Tomorrow, we would be up early, on the road in our little van, catching the ferry across to Belfast, then on to Londonderry, the west coast and the Ring of Kerry, Donegal and Dublin. But in the meantime, we had the night ahead of us. A night to remember.

Being good Catholic celibates, we were inexperienced lovers when we began our journey together, so inexperienced that we had devoured a book on technique before the wedding. Authored by a Catholic doctor and a priest, its purpose was to prepare Catholic couples for marital lovemaking. Aghast, the Australian Catholic bishops had withdrawn it from circulation soon after its initial distribution. Luckily for us, a few copies remained here and there in the hands of more enlightened clerics, and one of these was Stanley Hosie, the priest who ran the spiritual retreats for senior girls at Kincoppal in my final year. I had been comfortable enough then to speak to him about my lack of sexual knowledge. What's more, he was the elder brother of one of my closest school friends, another Catherine. Shortly after I left school, I went to visit her at the Hosie beach house in Ballina, six hundred miles from Sydney. There I met Stan again and cemented a lifelong friendship with him.

Five years later, on the brink of marriage, I introduced Stanley to Bruce and during our discussions we raised the subject of sex. He took pity on us and lent us a copy of the banned sex manual. For Bruce and me, that made all the difference to our early life together. As we travelled through Europe, we had grown in sexual boldness and our instincts of how to please each other had become more finely tuned. 'Practice makes perfect' became Bruce's appreciative mantra and we put in much practice.

Now fortified with news from home and Scottish stodge, we snuggled together in our Glasgow bed. We made love in a slow languorous way almost all the night. It could have been the rain, the letters from home, being an island of intimacy in a strange city or the comfort and passion of our closeness in that big lumpy bed that made it so memorable. In a dreamlike state, we took each other to heights of ecstasy and back again into sleep. There was so much love to share it seemed we had the whole world in our grasp, and by the time dawn began to light the curtains, I knew that we had surely made a baby.

After three wonderful weeks in Ireland, we arrived back in London and within another week, I realised I had missed my period. Ten days went by before I started to look at food with less enthusiasm and thought it would be best to see a doctor before we left for Australia. Sure enough, he confirmed a pregnancy.

To celebrate, Bruce booked us into the sumptuous Savoy Hotel for the last two nights in England. The eminent Harley

Street specialist prescribed a drug for morning sickness called Thalidomide. I took one dose but something told me I shouldn't take another, so I left the package in the Savoy's wastepaper basket.

After we sailed through the Mediterranean and then the Suez Canal, I was sometimes sorry I'd left the medication behind since, by then, I was depositing most of the food I ate into the depths of the Indian Ocean. As a result, I lost a stone in weight on the way home. When my family met us at the overseas terminal, they were shocked at the sight of their skeleton-eyed daughter and sister.

Even though we didn't realise it then, we'd had more than a very lucky break. Within a couple of years, hundreds of babies had been born without properly formed limbs and the blame was laid at the door of the drug company who made and marketed Thalidomide.

Back on dry land, the morning sickness abated and the rest of the pregnancy developed normally.

When Bruce asked me to marry him I wondered if I should divulge the sexual abuse I had endured at the hands of my brother during my childhood years. I chose not to, and for good reason. When I entered secondary school, I had made a promise to myself. I would not allow those childhood experiences to ruin the rest of my life or my prospects of a happy marriage. I held firm to that promise; otherwise this early sexual abuse could have coloured Bruce's perception of me and might have affected our life together.

Looking back on it now and remembering the taboos that wrapped themselves around anything sexual, it will be obvious to anyone who remembers that era how wise I was to stay silent. Bruce was a good Catholic. How could I know that it wouldn't be constantly in the back of his mind when we were making love? *No, don't take the risk*, I thought. And why would I take the risk? The times were not on my side. I knew this only too well from things I'd witnessed as a social worker in a maternity hospital. Women were much more likely to be victimised in court if they reported rape. Men, more often than not, escaped the consequences of their actions. Who was to blame? The victims who were said to be the seducers?

My last encounter with Allan had left me shaken. It took place during my second year at university when I was babysitting Joan and Bob's three children at their house in Bondi. The children were having their afternoon sleeps when Allan, whom I hadn't seen in ages, knocked on the kitchen door.

With few preliminaries, he proudly announced, 'I just came over to tell Joan my exciting news. Jack and I are going into business together. We have bought a property at Walcha, up in the Northern Tablelands. You are looking at a cattle rancher.'

'Cattle rancher?' I said, shocked. 'What do you know about cattle ranching?'

Then I caught my breath. 'Allan, are you mad?' I added. 'What are you thinking going into business with Jack?'

Jack had gone bankrupt and Mother had rescued him and his family by taking over their mortgage so that their home wouldn't be ripped away from them. I pointed it out to Allan.

'Oh, everything is going to be okay,' said Allan. 'Jack's stopped drinking. He's had a bit of bad luck, that's all. But now he has great new plans. He's got vision and is a tremendous businessman. I'm lucky he's taking me on as his partner.'

During my last years of school, Jack had tried to take away from Mother the textile business our father had established. She had to go to court to stop it happening. Then Jack had set up a business in opposition. That is when he'd gone bankrupt and Mother had rescued his house for the sake of his wife and children. Trying to convince Allan of his folly, I reminded him of this sequence of events.

'That's all a bunch of lies. Jack told me the full story. He's the eldest son and he deserved to take over the family business after Daddy died. That is his birthright,' he argued.

'Oh, my God, Allan, have some sense. The business put you through school. That's your birthright. All of our birthright, in fact.'

By then, Allan had a wife and children to think of, too. I said, 'You can't take Beverley and the children up there.'

'Yes, she wants to come and the children are excited about the idea of living on a ranch,' he said.

Poor Beverley, I thought.

Then it dawned on me that this might be my last chance to talk to him about his abuse and to bring *my* issues to a close.

'Allan,' I said, 'we need to talk about what you did to me all those years ago.'

'What do you mean?' he replied.

'Don't you remember how you sexually abused me when I was a kid?'

'Oh, that was just a bit of fun,' he said, looking slightly shamefaced.

'You call that a bit of fun? Don't you know how much damage it did to me, and probably Carmel and Christine till I put a stop to it,' I said, my voice rising.

'Don't be stupid,' he said, 'it was okay. All the boys at school were doing it. Some of the Brothers, too.'

I gasped, too amazed to speak.

He stayed silent. Then I found my voice again. 'You mean to tell me you still think that was okay?' I said, and by now my voice was shaking. I wondered if I could control myself.

'Well, yes. Admit it; you enjoyed it, too.'

'Get out of here, Allan. You have no idea, do you? No idea at all what I suffered. I will forgive you. But I hope you can forgive yourself.'

And with that he took off, banging the kitchen door behind him.

There, I had done it! Told him how I felt! It had taken a long time but I'd got it out of my system.

I don't recall ever speaking to him again after that. He disappeared into the hills of Walcha, where Jack's great plans were short-lived and sent Allan broke. Allan lost his marriage and his children and became a stranger to our family. He remarried, but he never made contact with any one of us again before he died and, as far as I know, none of us made contact with him, either.

18
giving birth

A few weeks into my rural transformation, Frankie was on the telephone speaking to the Yerong Creek President of the Country Women's Association. 'Would Anne be prepared to speak at our next meeting about her honeymoon travels?' she asked Frankie. What could I do but say, 'Yes.'

The two of us staggered into the local hall, burdened with my memorabilia, photographs and the inevitable cake cooked by Frankie that morning. A largish crowd had gathered to hear about our honeymoon adventure.

The village hall had been built with the same clapboard Murray pine timber as the local store, the Catholic church and the front part of the Fairfield homestead. After World War I, a local artist had painted a number of large portraits of soldiers at Gallipoli, one of the most prominent being of Simpson and his donkey. A lean-to construction off the side of the hall had been added years before to provide extra space for flower shows, small meetings and a drinks facility for dances.

Few of the women in that big hall had ever been overseas or

much further afield than Sydney or Melbourne. Some, indeed, had not ventured beyond Wagga or Albury. A few ex-service husbands had been posted overseas and several women had served as nurses in the Pacific but that was about it.

The women gathered in the hall that afternoon were very welcoming and seemed genuinely interested in what I had to say. Having regaled them with tales of our travels between England, France, Spain and Ireland, I told funny stories of mishaps, getting lost, being surprised by French farmers as we woke still in our pyjamas and about how I murdered the French language. We laughed together at these simple tales and I began to like them. At the end, as I saw their eyes glazing over and a small group leaving to make the tea, I brought the talking to a close and received a polite ovation.

The CWA's membership was mostly limited to people on the land. The wives of the policeman, the stock-and-station agent, the schoolmaster and the stationmaster were there as well. But rarely the spouses of shearers or railway workers. This was my introduction to the unwritten class systems that operated here in the bush.

'Well done, Annie,' Frankie said as we drove away. 'They liked you. Did they sign you up as a member?'

'No,' I said, 'I'll see to it next time.'

'They meet on the first Tuesday of the month,' she said, so I wouldn't forget.

When I was eight and a half months pregnant, I took the train to Sydney to stay with Mother to await the baby's arrival. By the ninth month, I had begun to develop silly fantasies, thinking I might be pregnant and misshapen for the rest of my life. *Will the baby ever come out? How can it come out?* went my thoughts.

Early in the morning of 10 June 1958, I woke to pains in my front and lower back. Bruce was still at Fairfield and was duly summoned so he could start his journey to Sydney as I was starting mine to Crown Street Women's Hospital. Mother drove me there and helped me fill out the admission form as we sat on a hard bench in the corridor outside the labour ward. Every five minutes, I paused to deal with the pain.

After Mother left, I was kidnapped by masked bandits who shaved my private parts, prodded and poked at tender places and shoved an enema up my bum, the most humiliating experience of all. I felt apprehensive and alone. Efficiently prepared now, I was laid out on a very hard bed to concentrate on labouring.

When I had worked at Crown Street Women's Hospital as a medical social worker, I had rarely needed to come to the labour ward. The hospital attracted a large number of recent migrants from Greece and Italy, who had settled in nearby inner-city suburbs. They came from cultures where not so long ago families and whole villages had done everything together. Their conversations were audible and expressive and they were not used to suffering in silence. Just down the corridor I could hear an Italian woman calling, *'Mamma mia! Mamma mia!'* over and over again. Nurses took no notice, efficiently going about their business in the midst of all that audible pain. And there I lay, too embarrassed to make a sound.

Eventually, I remembered the breathing and relaxation exercises in Dr Grantly Dick-Read's book *Childbirth Without Fear*. I had been trying hard to do them since my return home from England, but more often than not I had fallen asleep in the middle of my exercises. Concentrate, Annie, I said to myself now, regretting my slackness. I breathed and relaxed, breathed and relaxed between the excruciating pains that swept over me every few minutes. There was no going back now. She or he was on the way, hell-bent on becoming a person, through wave after wave of muscular contortions.

Bruce was on the plane to Sydney by now, but there was no way he would be allowed to attend the birth. The medical model still had a firm grip on childbirth, no matter what the Grantly Dick-Reads of this world had to say about it. No husband or support person was allowed into this most sacred and personal of all human enterprises. Surrounded by strangers, I had to achieve it by myself.

By mid-afternoon, three and a half hours after my admission, I was moved off the bed and wheeled into an operating theatre, where the gowned figure of my obstetrician stood waiting. 'Won't be long now, baby is nearly ready to come,' he said, smiling encouragingly as a nurse fastened his mask with gloved hands.

In an instant, he had become my lover, my husband and my saviour. The hero of the hour. No wonder so many women fall secretly in love with their obstetrician.

Through the pain, I heard a nurse say, 'Push! Push a little harder!"

The doctor picked up a scalpel and, without warning, my body was overwhelmed with a different kind of pain, like a red hot poker searing the skin between my legs. An ear-piercing scream came out of my mouth. He had cut my perineum to assist the baby's passage into the world. Then, within seconds, the theatre was filled with the cry of a newborn baby taking her first breath. 'It's a girl!' I heard the doctor say.

The squirming bundle was laid on my chest and I shook with relief and ecstasy. In that moment, I was the only woman in the world who had ever given birth. The surgeon set about stitching up the wound he had made with his knife.

'Did that hurt?' asked the obstetrician. An episiotomy without pain killers was routine then. Hopefully not so today.

'Yes, it did,' I replied but the pain was secondary because at that point I was so very, very happy. I was overwhelmed with joy, gazing on the miracle bundle of Alexandra Margaret.

Bruce arrived as I was wheeled into my new room in the private wing of the hospital; our newborn daughter had been whisked off to the nursery, where all babies were kept in those days. Mother, Phil and Carmel rushed in to see me. Everyone was very excited but I was grateful that the mob soon left to prepare for Christine's twenty-first birthday party that night at the Pickwick Club in the city.

That evening, when they rang the bell at visiting hours, Bruce viewed his own child for the first time through the glass partition of the nursery.

Bruce stayed a few more days then returned to Fairfield and ten days later, Alex and I were on the train to Wagga, where he was waiting at the station.

'Having a baby is as close to a miracle as one could imagine,' Bruce said when he took his six pound six ounce baby in his arms.

The happiest of happy fathers. I no longer felt the ambivalence about starting a family. I might even be able to wear that old blue dress again! And Alex was a marvellous baby. One of those good girls who slept and ate, smiled early and gave us joy in abundance.

After Alex's arrival, I cried at everything that could possibly be thought of as sad and over events that weren't. Yet I was deliriously happy. I knew it was all hormonal but that didn't make a difference. For a time, I became much more vulnerable and more compassionate. It was the beginning, for me, of a deep sense of responsibility.

the country wife

One of the joys of returning to Fairfield from giving birth was finding the house beautifully prepared for my homecoming. I hadn't expected it but there it was – flowers in vases, cakes in cake tins and a casserole in the fridge ready to heat up. My sister-in-law Judy had done it all and left a short note to welcome me home. I was overwhelmed by her love and generosity – as I was many times thereafter.

Judy and Kerry's lovely new architect-designed house was about a mile away, up on a hill looking over the countryside. Before the advent of a school bus service, their vehicles had to pass close by our house every day as they took their eldest daughter Susan to and from school. It meant there was a considerable amount of dropping in, in the afternoon with fresh bread, newspapers and mail. A very welcome daily event for a first-time mother with a newborn baby.

From the beginning of my life at Fairfield, I understood that having Bruce's family nearby provided a kind of safety net for all of us. We relied on each other to help out in emergencies and frequently were guests at each other's homes for barbecues and special events like birthdays and Christmas.

Kerry was younger than Bruce. During the war he had been the head prefect at Xavier College, the Jesuit school in Melbourne. When Bruce was discharged from the air force following the war, both brothers had returned to Fairfield as its badly needed labour force. It was never an option for Bruce to take up the opportunity of a free university place, as enjoyed by some of his mates. But there was another bonus to being an ex-serviceman: when new tractors became available, he got preferential treatment. Working together to restore the income the family lost during the war years, Bruce and Kerry were as close as two brothers could be, always communicating with a secret humour that only they could understand. When I saw it in action, I used to smile and was always glad of it.

My Bruce's work didn't involve him heading off every morning; he wasn't swallowed up by some distant enterprise that involved people and things that had nothing to do with me or our life together. I spoke to my husband many times a day, except during the frantic periods of shearing and harvesting, which took his full attention.

One morning, not long after I came home with Alex, Bruce arrived in from the paddock for morning tea as I was bathing her. She was now six weeks old. It was midwinter in this very cold climate. The bathtub was on the kitchen table and the air was warmed by the kitchen fire, glowing in the slow-combustion stove nearby. Alex kicked her little feet and cooed from the pleasure of warm water playing over her body. She had begun to smile back at us now, too, and watching her enjoyment gave Bruce as much pleasure as it did her. Then I wrapped her in a warm towel and handed her to him to cuddle while I prepared our morning tea.

With this kind of love and support, I threw myself into this life without a backward glance and sometimes wondered why I had ever had any doubts about marriage the night before our wedding.

Frankie, too, arrived one morning at bath time and cooed over the new baby revelling in the warm water. It was she, this time, who sat and dried Alex and Bruce who made the tea. The three of us sat together while we chatted and discussed the baby's progress, with Frankie giving me her own advice about baby care. From the moment she set her eyes on baby Alex, Frankie loved her.

Although by now she had many grandchildren, she welcomed every one of them with an open heart and loved cuddling and kissing them. The front door to the house was in the old part of the house, a long way from the living areas at the back, so it wasn't obvious to strangers where to alert us to their arrival. There was no doorbell so visitors used to call out or walk around to the back to gain attention. Frankie generally came in the side door, mostly unannounced because it was the door used by the family. As our numbers grew, the first I would know she was in the house was when I heard the joyful cries of the children shouting, 'Granny! Granny!' as she threw her arms around them.

Although I was happy at Fairfield there were things I still missed here in the country. One of those was the ocean. As a coastal dweller, I'd always seen the ocean as a presence, part of my own physicality, one that invited me in – 'Ah, there you are, plunge in; become part of my rolling white foam.' I imagined the sea was just beyond the hills to the east. Or I pictured myself walking along the water's edge as the spent surf kissed the sand and then retreated in surprise like a bashful lover.

I knew, in fact, that the ocean was four hundred miles away. Here, there were no sounds of water lapping, no surf pounding against a headland, no little boats rocking their way through the night, no heavy humid days or southerly busters to cool things down in the afternoon. When I thought of those things, I felt a deep sense of deprivation.

Instead, I woke to the caw caw of the crows calling us out of sleep and then listened as a flock of smaller birds began their daylight ritual, swooping and chirping in a cacophony of delighted song as they flew over the house. In time, I came to love those sounds of the morning, especially in summer, when I woke in the early-morning cool, knowing the heat of the day would be unrelenting, scorching like no heat I have known before. I came to know, too, how well the birds managed this climate, celebrating the cool of the morning, lying low in the shade of their favourite tree during the day and at sunset beginning their swooping and cawing again as the night came in, with its feast of flying insects.

Now it was winter, many days were wet, so drying nappies became a problem. Bruce erected a clothes line for me at the end of the verandah. After I had fed and bathed Alex and put her down for her morning sleep, I would wash the nappies and hang them on that line.

That was also the time to marvel at the whole beautiful vista of hills to the east, shrouded in misty rain as it fell on the greenest of green pastures. At such moments, I experienced a deep sense of tranquillity and thankfulness for all I had been given. Eventually, I stopped pining for the coast. I knew that it would still be there when I went back, however fleeting those visits might be. And with that, I began to love exactly what I had here now. One day, as I stood at the sink in the kitchen peeling potatoes for dinner, I became aware of just how happy I was. And in that moment, I experienced a sense of contentment and security.

As our baby grew, Bruce and I both marvelled at her development. When she started babbling in her cot and then letting out singing sounds, we thought our hearts would burst right open and we stayed in bed listening to this symphony. Breastfed, she grew very chubby. One day when she was ten months old, she said her first word. It was car. This was not surprising since she had spent a good proportion of her little lifetime travelling in the Holden – the one Bruce had driven when he picked both of us up at the Wagga railway station.

At sixteen months, she still wasn't walking. My philosophy of child-rearing was to let her take her own time. She was talking fairly well and my theory was that babies shouldn't be pushed. They should master one thing then go on from there to master another. Then my brother Ken and his wife, Libby, came to stay on their way to Melbourne. He was a disciplinarian and would have none of it.

'Come on, Alex,' he would say to her firmly as he held her upright by the back of her overalls while guiding her forward. 'Stop pretending you can't do it. You'll have a little brother or sister soon and you'll need to help your mother.'

The amazing thing was, by the time he left, she was determinedly walking everywhere.

19
three times lucky

With the encouragement of my mother-in-law, I soon discovered that having a baby was no excuse for not supporting the CWA. Actually, it was one of the reasons *for* supporting it. The CWA had lobbied the government to have a baby health centre nurse visit the village once a month. All the CWA had to do was provide a clinic space. The mothers who used the clinic were rostered to prepare the space the day before the nurse was due. That meant dusting, mopping the floor, providing a vase of flowers and afternoon or morning tea. As a new mother, I was put on a roster to do my share.

Although I found the CWA meetings pretty boring, the CWA women were far from that. They all had sharp minds and most of them could have gone to university. Precision! It was the last thing I thought I'd encounter here in the depths of the Riverina but whooo, these CWA women had it. Once I thought about it, I realised it takes precision to bake a perfect sponge cake and control an unruly group of pastoral women.

At first, I didn't really consider myself as one of them, or take the whole thing seriously, so I didn't fare well in the early stages of my attendance at CWA meetings.

'Are you speaking for or against the motion, Mrs Gorman?'

'Is this an amendment to the motion, Mrs Gorman? Or an addendum to the amendment?'

I was a university graduate, for heaven's sake. Why didn't I know this stuff? It wouldn't do. It was time I learned how to play the game.

Bruce searched around in his office and brought out a book called *The Law and Procedure at Meetings: A Concise Guide*, by P. E. Joske. I would practise with Bruce over morning tea.

'Now, darling,' he said, 'think about a proposal you want to put up. Anything. Really doesn't matter.'

'Madam speaker, I wish to propose we bring a circus to Yerong Creek.'

'Do you want to speak to the motion, Mrs Gorman? For example, do you want the proposal to include elephants?'

'Yes, madam president. It's high time we had a circus to brighten our lives, and the only people qualified to bring it here is the CWA. I think they could manage the elephants.'

Through his laughter, Bruce went on. 'Mrs Gorman, this is the time when madam president calls for speakers for and against the motion, et cetera, et cetera. Can you do both?' He had a gleam in his eye.

And so on we went. Next Bruce directed me to an evening course at the Wagga TAFE. There I began to meet budding shire councillors and other people like me, who thought life depended on learning how to run things properly.

In November 1959, when Alex was eighteen months old, I took another visit to the maternity section of Crown Street Hospital, this time flying to Sydney by way of Ansett Airways.

It was an easy labour as I was more relaxed. Only twenty-five years old – I would turn twenty-six three months after the new baby's birth – I thought I knew everything because I'd been through it all before!

We called our son Austin, a choice Bruce made, I believe, as a tribute to my family. Bruce arrived promptly to see him, a plump little fellow of over eight pounds. The nurses at the hospital said to him, 'How clever of you to have a "pigeon pair", Mr Gorman. Now you can relax.'

At this we both smiled wryly, knowing Austin would not be the last.

But this time, managing my newborn wasn't going to be to be plain sailing. Right from the start, Austin's feeding was a problem. Mother persuaded me to delay my departure from Sydney. Austin did a great deal of crying during the day and she thought a trip to the Karitane home, just up the road, where excellent one-on-one mothercraft help was provided, might be useful. She also cautioned that inland Australia was going through one of the hottest periods on record. Caught without air-conditioning in country hospitals, babies and very old people were dying.

After a two-day stay at Karitane, the diagnosis came down to this: Austin was a vigorous guzzler and the milk was coming out of me in torrents. His newborn tummy couldn't handle it. The advice was to feed him lying down so he would have to defy gravity by sucking up. That did relieve the situation a little. But try as I might, it didn't make a significant difference to his colic or his crying. Consequently, Austin became a permanent fixture on my hip for a lot of the day. Any adult dropping in would be invited to hold him while I did the odd chore. Mercifully, he slept well at night.

When we were back in the country, it was every bit as hot

as Mother had anticipated. On the advice of both the Karitane nurses and heeding my mother's admonitions, I draped Austin's cot in wet towels and had a fan set to blow through them.

Alex had been used to being number one, so now things were different for her. She understandably regressed and gave up toilet training. When harvest finished, we took both children to the seaside, hired a mothercraft nurse to look after Austin (a tremendous extravagance) and paddled with Alex in the ponds around the beaches so she had her parents all to herself for a few hours every day.

Her faith in us must have been restored because she started progressing again. At four months old, Austin had put on so much weight he looked like a six-month-old baby. And then his colic was over and we could relax and enjoy our children.

And here we all were. I had married into a wonderful family. I had the apple pie man as a husband, and he brought with him much, much more than that.

I was the luckiest woman in the world.

When Austin was nearly twelve months old, I missed my period. This could mean only one thing. *It must have been when we went to that wedding in Canberra last month*, I thought. According to my ovulation chart, that was a safe time. So much for the family planning method recommended by the Catholic Church.

When the familiar nausea arrived, my hunch was confirmed. The Gorman family was about to expand again and the baby would be born around my twenty-seventh birthday, in the middle of January 1961.

One day, six weeks into the pregnancy, stands out vividly in my memory. We'd been busy on the farm. Lamb marking was in progress and we'd all been out in the cold helping with castrating the poor little lambs and cutting off their tails. Austin was in a stroller watching from a safe distance, the dogs keeping him company to his delight. Alex, now a very adventurous two-year-old, hung off the fence watching her parents and our hired hand do the necessary damage to the livestock.

My sister-in-law Judy had suggested we go to the movies in Wagga that night. The film was *Auntie Mame*, starring Rosalind Russell, the story of an eccentric aunt and her young nephew travelling the world among the rich and famous. Most of our friends and neighbours had read the book and heard the film was hilarious so we were looking forward to seeing it and Bruce was happy to mind the children while Judy and I went to see it.

All day, I'd been having slight period-type pains but had taken no notice; I assumed they'd be gone again the next day. Halfway through Ethel Merman's performance, I became aware that something wasn't right.

'We'd better go,' I said to Judy, 'Something really odd is happening. I've got blood running down my legs.'

We made it up to Judy's sister's house and phoned our GP. He came immediately and called an ambulance, even though the hospital was only a few streets away.

'I think you've lost the baby,' he said.

I told him I disagreed and that the baby was still with us.

Fortunately, I was right.

Almost immediately after coming home from the hospital, I received a call from a Canberra GP friend I'd known at university. One of her patients – an eighteen-year-old unmarried girl – was pregnant. She came from a well-off family, was a Catholic and was looking for a place to live for six months to await the birth of her child. She also needed some advice about adoption.

What to do? If we took her in, there would be two pregnant women in the same household. I asked for Bruce's opinion.

'Why don't you ask the girl and her mother to drive over to see us?' he suggested. 'Then you can make your own assessment.'

Of course, that was the end of it. She stayed. I liked Barbara very much. And she turned out to be a wonderful companion and a willing helper.

By that stage, I was the Sydney Catholic Adoption Agency's registered agent in the Riverina, and they got busy arranging for a matching couple to adopt Barbara's baby.

Close to her delivery date, Barbara had a burst of energy cleaning out all the kitchen cupboards, although I kept telling her not to overdo it. It came as no surprise when she called to me early the next morning, 'Anne! Anne! There's water all over the floor.'

I came running. 'Don't worry, sweetie,' I said. 'Your waters have broken. I'll clean that up. It's time to call your mother and go to hospital.'

I stayed with her at Calvary Hospital (the Catholic hospital where I had had my threatened miscarriage seven months before), until Barbara gave birth to a healthy baby boy. Then her mother arrived and I went home. When I visited a few days later, I found her sitting up in bed feeding her tiny son. I cuddled him, a pink and blond beautiful boy of 8½ pounds. In the presence of couple of witnesses supplied by the hospital, I took Barbara's consent for adoption.

A week later came the day for the handover. I met the adoptive parents in a small waiting room at the end of the maternity wing's main corridor, with the Virgin Mary watching over us from the wall. We chatted for a while, then I went back to get the baby and placed him gently into the adoptive mother's arms. Both parents were ecstatic, peering into his face with the kind of focus reserved for newborn babies the world over. When he opened his eyes to look straight at them, I thought they would die of ecstasy. A nurse came in to give them advice about feeding and a package of various baby things, including a tin of formula.

Her efficiency was a contrast to the emotions she could see before her. But it forced the couple to come back to earth. 'He's taken to the bottle okay,' said the nurse, and 'seems to be all right with cow's milk, but here's a package of formula just in case. I'd advise regular visits to the baby health centre if you have one near you. Here's a list of where they are …' And on and on she went with the oh so relevant advice and information. Eventually, she said, 'How far have you got to travel?'

'About two hours' drive,' said the new dad.

'That's okay then,' she said. 'You'll make it home in time for his next feed.'

I said goodbye, wished them well, then watched them walk out the door, place the baby in a basket on the back seat and drive away.

Barbara and her mother came out to Fairfield to collect her things, and Barbara's parting words made me happy: 'Anne, I'm glad they like him. Now it's all over, I can get on with my life. I'm going to enrol at the ANU [Australian National University in Canberra]. In a way, it's a new challenge. One I'd never thought I could take on until I'd stayed with you and Bruce.'

Two months later, I gave birth in Sydney, a more complicated delivery than the previous time as the baby showed signs of distress towards the end. The medical staff hurried the process and there she was, the one I nearly lost at *Auntie Mame*,

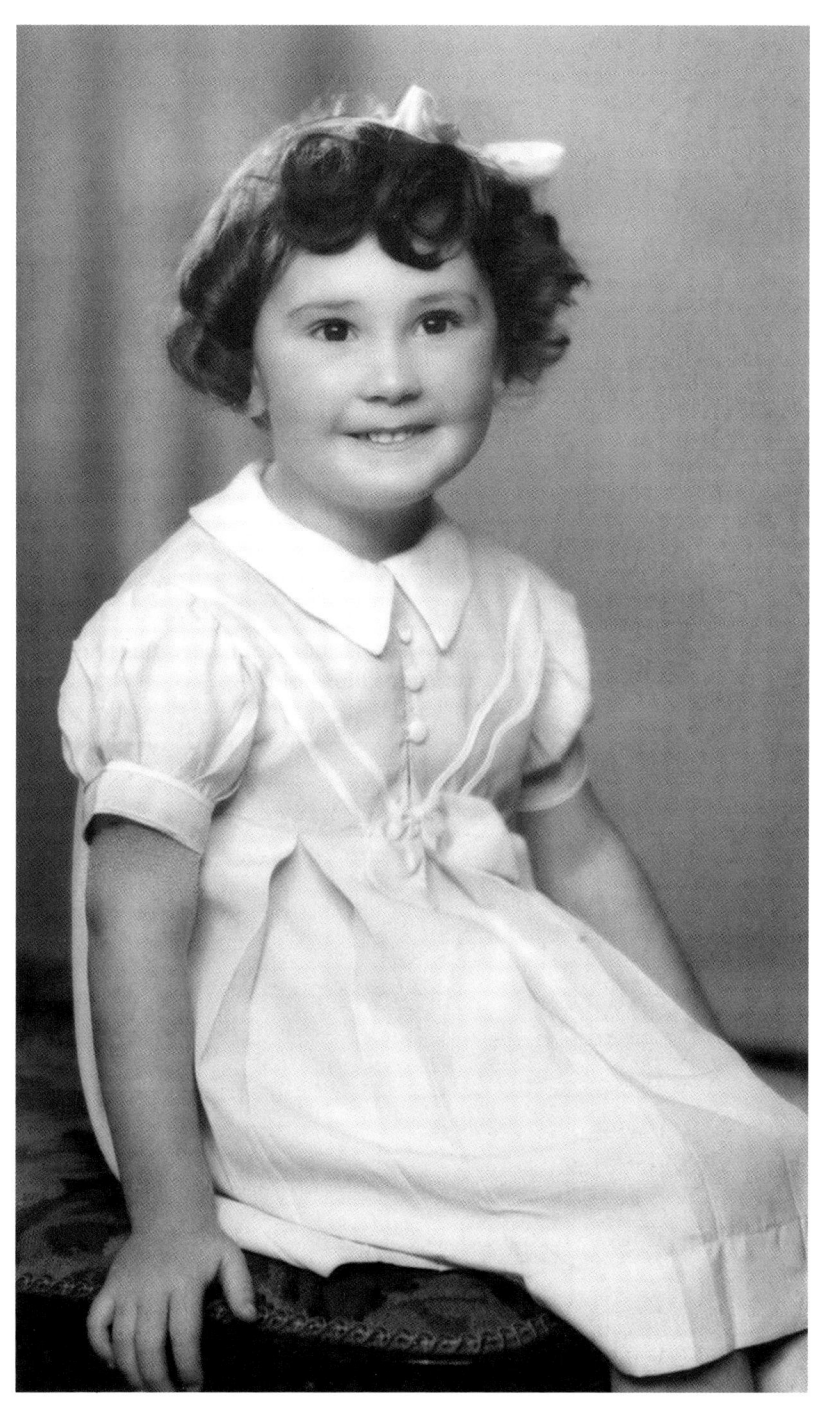

At the age of three, blissfully unaware that my world was soon to be turned upside down.

Such an innocent-looking and earnest fourteen-year-old bridesmaid at my sister Joan's wedding. Yet I felt I'd already lived a lifetime.

Beaming with pride and confidence. In my final year at Kincoppal-Rose Bay, to my surprise I was named as head girl.

The epitome of stylish young ladies, my Kincoppal teammates and I pose on the gantry of our plane before heading to Melbourne to play tennis.

Dressed to the nines for a ball at Sydney University in about 1953.

If only they still made such flattering swimsuits these days. Me on the beach at Cronulla, Sydney, around 1956.

So young, so happy and so full of plans to take on the world. Me and Catherine graduating from Sydney University in 1956, with close friend Elspeth cheering us on.

Newly minted medical social workers. Me (fourth from right), Elspeth (holding book) and Catherine (right).

The Gorman clan gathered to see Bruce off, looking dashing in his airforce officer's uniform and proudly displaying his wings.

Bruce in full kit about to take flight in his Wirraway.

Bruce and me on our wedding day. The deep red roses were unconventional for a bride but insipid white was not for me.

Honeymooning in Europe, Bruce and I pose with a hitch-hiker we met in front of Brussels' Manneken Pis statue.

Within months of our return from honeymoon, I had become both a country wife and a mother. Before long I would be president of our local CWA group.

Bruce adored being a father. Here he is with Alex on his beloved horse, Riverina Lad.

Every year Bruce and I would pack up and head for the beach with the children. From left: my sister Joan, her husband Bob, Lindsey Browne, me, Elspeth and Bruce at Avalon.

Bruce with Austin, aged eighteen months, at Farm Cove.

Bruce, always a keen horseman, encouraging the children to ride. Alex (foreground) and a friend wait their turn.

Our growing family – Bruce holding Austin, me holding Alex – visiting our friends the Palmers, who lived 50 miles away.

Lynelle came when we needed her most to help look after the children, and stayed for years. She was an absolute gem and we all loved her. Here she's keeping a watchful eye on Vanessa (left) and a friend.

Off to work in Wagga as a community social worker, with Bruce's encouragement and support. He told me it was unfair to inflict all my energy on the children!

Every year, Bruce bought a new hat for cricket. Twelve months later, it became his paddock hat.

Bruce and me at Lynelle's wedding. Thankfully he was well enough to join the celebrations but his weight loss was noticeable.

It shocked my conservative mother-in-law, Frankie, when I joined the Australian Labor Party and became swept up in the 1972 federal election campaign. Here I am wearing my It's Time badge with, from left, the mayor of Wagga, Tom Uren, local candidate Kevin Esler and an ALP staffer.

The Labor Party slogan for the campaign to elect Gough Whitlam was of course wildly successful. Here's a close-up of the badge I wore – almost a collector's item.

My other life – helping with a sheep at shearing time. By now I could discuss the finer points of wool as well as party policy with the best of them.

In my role as a lecturer at the Centre for Adult Education, I loved interacting with students and the counterculture was a new awakening for me.

Wielding the chalk during a CAE lecture. I loved teaching.

A publicity shot with the children for my preselection bid for the senate.

On official business as director of International Year of the Child, 1979.

Receiving the Prime Minister's Centenary Medal from the Hon. Michael Kirby in 2001.

With former prime minister Bob Hawke at the inaugural Bishop Kevin Manning Lecture, when I was Chair of the Catholic Commission for Employment Relations.

You've come a long way, baby. At my eightieth birthday party, from left, Rebecca, me, Vanessa, Henry, Alex and Austin.

another girl. And she was to be a delight – a beautiful, docile non-crying baby with blue eyes, more like the Gorman side of the family. We named her Vanessa.

This meant that by 1961, I had three children under three – one on the breast, another still in nappies, and the eldest, now two and a half, attempting to rule the roost.

Without Barbara to help me, there was not a minute of the day, and often the night, when I wasn't tending to someone: one being breastfed, another on the potty, another playing at my feet as he pulled all the saucepans out of the cupboard. My weight fell below eight stone; I was thin as a rake. My gums started to recede and I noticed my hair was falling out. The dentist advised me not to fall pregnant again and to stop breastfeeding because it could get worse.

Bruce did what he could to help. My mother came to stay and noticed that because Vanessa was a non-complainer, she wasn't getting enough attention.

'You can't leave that baby in her pram all morning just because she doesn't make a fuss,' said Mother.

That made me feel somewhat ashamed, and I remembered all the attention we had given Alex when she'd arrived, and the times I'd had to nurse Austin all day. Here was a baby who didn't cry much, was happy to feed and sleep, would gurgle away but not cry. To be honest, I was glad to have a docile infant so I could focus on taking care of a three-year-old and a toddler who was into everything, as well as attending to the household chores of the day. But I knew I'd accepted the easy path with Vanessa and I had to do better than that.

When I spotted my mother and husband sitting in the sun on the back verandah, I wondered what they were cooking up between them. Mother wasn't that good with small talk but she loved discussing matters of substance with men as she had spent so much time doing that as a managing director in her own business. She especially loved getting together with my husband on her own and I decided, early in our marriage, not to compete with that relationship. But this time, something told me they were cooking up a conspiracy.

Later, over dinner, I would discover what that was. Bruce announced, 'I think it's time we got some help in the house, Annie. It's either that or I give up working outside.'

That sounded like an ultimatum, and I said in response, 'How do you think we will find someone?' Apart from Barbara, I'd never employed anyone in my life before and I wasn't sure how to go about it.

'Oh, I'll let it be known around the district that we're looking,' he said. 'Let's see how that goes. Otherwise, we'll advertise in the *Wagga Daily Advertiser*.'

He also said that he would take Vanessa under his wing and give her a lot more attention. Mother looked pleased and went back to Sydney happy.

Presently, we had a candidate named Jocey, the daughter of a man who had been badly injured during the war and was so damaged he couldn't work the land any more. Jocey's mother, Dulcie, was one of those heroic wiry women who took over everything, undaunted – mustering sheep, putting in crops, taking crops off and everything in between. I didn't know how she did it all. Dulcie was a wonderful role model and although her daughter Jocey was only sixteen, I was prepared to at least give her an interview. It wasn't a classic job interview, just a kind of friendly conversation with Jocey and her mother in the living room while I nursed Vanessa and we all sipped tea.

'If you agree Jocey is suitable,' said Dulcie, 'I'd like her to work for you for a couple of years before she goes off to the Wagga hospital or the city to do nursing.'

Jocey started work with us a week later and turned out to be a companion for me, even though she was so much younger. To my surprise, I was a good teacher and I succeeded in introducing her to a wider perspective of opinions and ways of managing children than she had experienced before. Jocey loved the children and they loved her. I knew I could trust her with them and that because she'd worked on a farm, she understood the hazards for little people.

Thank goodness we made that decision to employ her, because Henry was born in July 1962, fifteen months later, with brown eyes and enough energy to fire a power station.

Even when he was in the womb, Henry was an extremely active baby. I used to lie in bed and put Bruce's hand on my tummy so he could feel him jumping about.

'Whoo,' Bruce exclaimed, 'what have we got here?'

In the delivery room, Dr Macbeth said the same thing as Henry jumped right into the world, all guns blazing: 'I can hardly hold him. Look at him go. Whoo, what have we got here?'

A new invention, called a bouncinette, had come on the market and I was visited in the hospital by one of its reps. The maternity patients there at that time were part of the trial group so we received one free. The label said 'Safe for babies up to eight months'. But when Henry was three months old, he managed to turn the new invention upside down and his face ended up looking straight at the tiles on the floor. No harm done to him as he was immediately rescued. We were given a new modified version for active babies.

My niece Angela, Joan's eldest daughter, came to stay during one of her school holidays and just couldn't believe her ears. When Henry woke in the morning, no one got any more sleep because he bellowed like a bull to get out of his cot. It wasn't long before he could climb out himself and toddle into our bed to get a cuddle. But he had to fight for his place in the sun because coming into our bed early in the morning was a common occurrence, with four of them snuggling up to us at once. A joyous time, one both Bruce and I agreed we loved and would always savour.

20
four little australians

When I think back to life with four children under four and a half, in my memory, everything merges into a time–space capsule of total focus on four small human beings, and learning to accommodate the differences between each of their needs and wants. Alex loved eggs, porridge and Weet-Bix, Austin liked peanut butter and banana sandwiches, while Vanessa and Henry would eat almost anything. They all loved ice-cream.

Always protective of their teeth with fluoride tablets, I was glad temptation in the form of a local shop wasn't just around the corner. The only time they drank lemonade or fizzy drinks or consumed sweets was when we went to a birthday party.

Of course, there were endless chores and I thought we all might as well enjoy them. The chook feeding was part of the children's education and it was always, 'Let me do it, let me' as each child begged to take charge of scattering the feed and kitchen scraps. Their greatest joy was collecting the eggs and, for a while, 'uh-oh' became commonplace as we lost many in the process.

Then the hens went broody and the inevitable chickens were born and had to be protected from small hands that loved to hold the balls of tiny fluff. It was always so cute to watch the children and their enthusiasm as the chickens grew up to become our egg providers of the future.

Eventually, I started a vegetable garden and that, too, had to became a joint project, with everyone having their own plot and plantings. I remember when Vanessa was little, she planted her seeds and the next day dug them up to see if they were growing.

Every morning, Bruce milked the house cow, Dawn, a gorgeous pure-bred Jersey who kept us in milk and cream for the first ten years of my marriage and, when I had the energy to make it, butter. At lambing time, orphaned lambs were brought to the back door and the children took charge of nursing and feeding them. One became a family pet.

'Look, Mummy. Lammie has learned to open the garden gate,' I heard Austin call one day.

With the children's tuition, Lammie learned to do other little tricks as well.

Bruce also taught him to lead the mob of sheep into yards and the shearing shed. He roamed the house paddock and the children delighted in playing with him. After that, I never called sheep stupid again.

Once a year, when winter was about to descend on us again, Bruce and one of his farm hands brought the chainsaw out of mothballs and towed it over to where a clump of old fallen box gums lay. I loved the distant repetitive sound of that saw. The wood was perfect for burning in fireplaces and slow-combustion heaters. The truck that would bring the wood home – to be deposited outside the garden, ready to make its final journey by wheelbarrow to the back door – was a most welcome addition to the landscape.

I became an expert at lighting fires. In my view, a cold house was not a happy home. In fact, so much lighting of fires went on that the 'Let me do it' cries of the children led to them becoming experts as well. Fairfield was unlike the house Judy and Kerry had built on the hill, with large north-facing windows and floods of sunlight in the winter. Our place was built by pioneers to guard against the onslaught of summer. Most rooms were sunless and protected by wide verandahs. There was a spot outside the kitchen where in the winter we sat to thaw out our frozen bones as we drank our tea in the morning sunshine. No matter what the weather did, the kitchen was always kept warm by the wood that had been piled up outside the garden gate. In time, when oil got to be very cheap, we installed a big oil heater in the middle verandah. It had its own flue and a line to an oil tank outside.

In the city, there were many practicalities of daily life I took for granted. One was that garbage would be collected by the local council once or twice a week. Here, there was no garbage man who called in a big truck. We had to be the original conservationists, composting some of the house scraps, feeding the chooks some and storing the rest of the garbage for burning once the danger of bushfires was over.

Then there was the business of running the farm operation on top of all of this domestic activity. There were shearers to feed and crops to sow. After rain, Bruce would be up all night in an effort to catch the best conditions for planting; six months later, out he would go in the heat to harvest those same crops. At other times, it was all about sheep-mustering, lambing and lamb marking. Agents would ring to report on our wool or livestock sale prices – more often than not, right as I was feeding the children their lunch.

At the beginning of Jocey's second harvest with us, which was a particularly heavy harvest, mice arrived in their thousands. It was a plague of biblical proportions and the little buggers invaded us through every crack or crevice, causing mayhem to every operation. Under the eaves, into the roof and from beneath the house they came, respecting nothing – our privacy, our food, our clothes, the grains in our barns, our farm machinery, trucks, tractors and harvesters. Judy and Kerry had installed a swimming pool and the first job they did in the morning was to fish out hundreds of dead mice, then bury them in a pit dug for the purpose. Crystal, our cat, had a field day but it was all too much of a good thing, even for her.

Then, mystery of mysteries, just as the weather began to cool off, as suddenly as they had arrived, they were gone – totally, absolutely gone to whatever heaven mice look forward to after they have done with ransacking everything. Now came the time for the big clean-up. Kitchen cupboards were emptied and washed out, floors scrubbed, linen taken out and washed, while over in the sheds, a similar process was going on. Bruce and a farm worker swept up the grain and either discarded it or rebagged it. There was much pulling out of dead mice that had inevitably got stuck; a few had become trapped in the farm machinery. And the smell of it all! Oh, I was glad Jocey and I were doing our bit in the house and felt for my husband and his farm worker.

Gradually, I came to accept that living in the country was unpredictable. We were only inches away from what nature wanted to throw at us – or was it what nature wanted us to understand?

During those years, I learned anticipation, flexibility, patience and vigilance, and at the same time how to live in the moment. I'm a fast mover, what is known as a 'doer'. I could let fly at times, especially if we were going somewhere: each child had to be dressed, shoes put on and the children were laughing or annoying each other and no one was taking the time limits seriously.

'Look here, you guys. You can see your mother is annoyed. Stop acting the fool. We have to get to Mass on time [or the plane on time, etc., etc.]. Now come on, be fair,' Bruce would say. They would begin to see that he was right and start to cooperate.

Reason always worked better than a threat of coercion.

I loved each of my children differently but with the same passion. My greatest fear was the possibility of losing one of them. Fatalities occurred often enough in our district for us to become alert to the ever-present hazards on a farm. There were desperate funerals and desperate neighbours – desperate with grief.

One day, we received a call that a neighbour had lost a child. The four-year-old had fallen off the back of a ute as his father crossed a swollen creek. Everyone was out looking for him. Would Bruce take part in the search?

He was out the door in a moment but when he arrived, the child had been found a mile down the creek, caught up by the branches of a big willow tree. He was dead, drowned and beaten up by the debris. Bruce was clearly shaken and didn't want to speak about it.

When very deep feelings overtook Bruce and he wasn't able or willing to express them openly, he sometimes went into a depressed state for a day or two. It didn't happen very often but I got to know the signs and accustomed myself to let him be until he came out of it. It was difficult for an extrovert like me, used to talking things through.

As I lay in bed that night silently cuddling up to Bruce, I grieved for the parents of the four-year-old boy. I knew it would be hard to recover from something like that. I couldn't picture how I could do so, and knew I had to be more vigilant. We were living in territory that could be lethal for children.

One day, when Vanessa was a baby crawling around my feet, I was under pressure, making the midday meal for the shearers. Austin was a toddler and I suddenly realised I hadn't seen him for a little while. I called and called and eventually saw him appear just off the back verandah. His face was purple and he was holding a bottle of Condy's crystals. I screamed and gathered him up, forgetting the shearers' lunch altogether, leaving it to Jocey. Dashing to the phone, I called the Wagga hospital and started to sponge the purple dye out of his mouth and off his face. I was eventually put through to a very sympathetic doctor who was consulting a textbook.

'No, you can relax,' said the doctor, 'Condy's crystals is not dangerous. He will not be poisoned.'

All these years later, I can't remember what else he said – only the terror and the guilt I felt. The thanks I offered to God that day must have loudly reverberated through the heavens.

When Alex was only twelve months old, she ran a high temperature and had a wheezy chest as well. We took her to the GP in Wagga and he admitted her to hospital. She was terribly upset and the next morning when I visited, she became hysterical when I left her there again. She was never one to suffer in silence.

After that, I learned how to manage these predictable illnesses myself and spent many nights in the farm kitchen when one or other of the children had croup. Mother, who knew she must have passed on her genetic disposition for upper respiratory tract infections, said, 'Keep the room warm and moist. You can have that kettle steaming on the slow combustion heater. That will do it.'

I would move a mattress into the kitchen, set the alarm clock to remind me to feed logs into the heater and refill the kettle so that the air stayed moist, while I lay on a mattress on the floor beside the baby's cot. It worked just as well as the hospital humidicrib, I realised, and was far less traumatic for the baby than being placed in a lonely clinical environment. Luck was on my side, and all of us survived and lived to tell the tale.

Getting mail from Sydney and keeping in touch with the wider world by way of *The Sydney Morning Herald* and the ABC news were big priorities for me. There was only one ABC radio station. Everything – from news, parliament, current affairs, book reviews, sport, the country hour to religious services – shared one frequency, as well as the never-to-be-missed lunchtime radio drama *Blue Hills* by Gwen Meredith. It's hard to believe just how involved we all became in that program. Bruce would come in for lunch on the dot of 1 pm on four days a week just to share it with me and and/or whoever else was in the house that day.

Alas, I had got used in Sydney to having an ABC station dedicated exclusively to classical music. We didn't have coverage on the farm. On occasion, its absence left me bereft and, on balance, it was probably my greatest disappointment.

There are certain things mandated by God and the weather is one of them. For us on the land, many activities had to be done at particular times of year, whatever was happening with the weather. Shearing was one of those activities. Unlike the old days, when shearers worked and slept on site, our shearers now drove the three miles from the village every day, starting at seven and finishing on the dot of five. It was a long day, so it was crucial to provide them with regular sustenance. Morning tea was at 9.30, lunch was at twelve, afternoon tea was at three. And all on time to the minute.

I don't fancy myself as a wonderful cook. Nevertheless, twice a year, when shearing and crutching time came around, I donned the mantle of shearers' cook, giving thanks for the *Country Women's Association Cookbook*. My menus consisted of traditional fare, such as roasts, corned beef and chops in gravy, all served with baked vegetables, followed by something like apple crumble, golden syrup dumplings or bread and butter pudding with custard or cream.

The men from the shearing shed stepped through the kitchen door, filing in, eyes downcast and grunting a mumbled greeting as they came. I was ready for them, because I learned the hard way that every moment of the midday break from shearing was precious and food must be on the old laminex table immediately. They ate without speaking, an awkward silence intermittently punctuated by the rattle of plates being readied for pudding. A washing down with tea would then follow, the whole meal being over within a half an hour from beginning to end.

Depending on the numbers of sheep to be shorn, this daily ritual continued for ten days or more. We knew the shearers compared notes in the pub as to who served the best food in the district. I never heard whose cooking came first, second or third and I was sure I didn't make the shortlist. Their clean plates were good enough for me.

There was an unwritten code I called 'The Shearer's Law'. Put simply, they didn't thank 'the missus' for the food and no thanks was expected. The shearers' wages and conditions had been hard fought, literally through blood, sweat and tears. Historic Urangeline Station, one of the sites of the famed shearers' strikes of the 1890s, was only forty miles west

the country wife

of Yerong Creek. Shots had been fired there at workers. This was very serious and bitter business. In Queensland there were deaths, workers were gaoled, demonstrations held in city streets and in retaliation, the pastoralists formed their own association, all of which contributed to the twin births of the Labor movement and the Australian Workers Union. Banjo Paterson's 'Waltzing Matilda' was also inspired by the events of that time. Since the Eureka Stockade and the time of Ned Kelly, residues of bitterness between classes had lingered in Australian bush culture and were still alive and well when it was my turn to play out the role of the boss's wife. Most shearers believed there was no one to thank but themselves for their back-breaking work, the industrial battles they had won over many years and the enormous benefits that flowed to the nation and its rural enterprises. Good meals were their natural right.

Yet every year, as they gulped down their last cup of tea on the last day of shearing, one of our farm hands, a fantastic Aboriginal worker called Bill, enacted a ritual that flouted The Shearer's Law. Rising to his feet on that occasion, and with some ceremony, Bill would say, 'On behalf of all of us, I would like to thank you, Mrs Gorman, for the wonderful dinners and morning and afternoon teas you have prepared for us.'

At that point, the other men looked down at their plates, grunted something unintelligible and hurried out the back door and through the garden gate to the security of the shearing shed. Once they were out of earshot, I clutched my sides and Bruce and I fell about laughing – not at them but at their discomfort.

Harvest time was just as busy as shearing time, but completely different. Round and round the paddocks the harvesters went, slicing off heads of wheat then thrashing them into the header's drum. When that filled up, the wheat was lifted into a waiting truck, using a machine called an auger. The truck dumped the wheat into a silo at the railhead three miles away, and from there it was sold to the Wheat Board, who would serially dispatch payments, sometimes over a two-year period.

During my first harvest, wheat was bagged and sealed with skewers or twine, the whole operation requiring four men and taking days or even weeks. The following year, after Austin was born, Bruce bought a header, which allowed the grain to be augered straight into trucks. Two men now did the work of four – one to drive the header and one the truck. I made three, sometimes four trips a day out to where the men were working, carrying ice, food and drink in styrofoam eskies. At night, after Bruce had a shower and dinner and the children were in bed, I might drive to Wagga to collect spare machinery parts from the farmers' co-op which, during harvesting, stayed open until late into the night.

At this time of the year, a steady vibration spread through the whole district as headers moved majestically clockwise around the paddocks like ships under sail, every farmer hell-bent on getting the crops off quickly in case it rained. The only days they stopped early were school break-up day, when they showered and changed for the concert in the village hall that night, and Christmas Day.

After harvest each year, when the children were young, we headed to the coast for our annual holiday. We packed up the Holden station wagon and set off at 4 am for a three-week holiday at the beach, children sleepily bundled up in rugs as we faced the treacherous Hume Highway. Seat belts were yet to be invented and car air-conditioning had not yet arrived for Holden. We made Yass by 8 am for breakfast at one of the newly built roadside petrol station eateries, then braved the last leg in anticipation of our first glimpse of the ocean as we descended past the Baha'i temple into seaside Mona Vale in time for lunch. Jocey came with us so we had a babysitter and could catch up with city friends, inviting them to barbecues at the beach or visiting their homes in the suburbs.

It was worth all the planning that went into the eight-hour drive, a just reward for Bruce to escape the hard work, heat, dust and flies of harvest and for me to get my toes back into the beloved ocean again.

21

the village

When it came to doing our bit in the local community, Bruce and I split our responsibilities. He covered the Hall Committee (a group who took care of the hall building and maintenance and payment when it was hired out for parties and dances), the RSL, the football club and the Bush Fire Brigade – all of which held evening meetings to accommodate the men. My job, according to Frankie, was to show up for the Red Cross, the CWA, the tennis team and church meetings. The die was cast and I was more or less committed to be an active citizen.

By 1961, it was time for me to become President of the Yerong Creek branch of the CWA – almost, it seemed, an inevitability, as everyone took their turn at office-bearing, especially if, like me, they'd been part of the association for four years. With all that tutoring from Bruce on how to run things, I was armed with the wherewithal to chair meetings.

Flower shows and sponge cakes were not, in my mind, a sufficient reason for continuing my involvement with the

CWA over the longer term. In the baking department, Mrs Yates, the local champion, had no rival, certainly not me. My interests lay in other areas and I began to look for wider opportunities where we could make a difference.

For a long time after the end of the Second World War, there was a growing fear that, like Okinawa or Nagasaki in Japan, the Australian population might be confronted with a nuclear attack, mostly from communist forces. As early as 1959, civil defence groups were set up in many communities to mobilise the population to protect themselves in the event of such an emergency. All over the country, meetings were held in halls, including in our village in 1961.

A retired military man showed us a film about how to survive should there be a nuclear attack. We were aware such an attack might lead to total destruction, especially in the city, and I used to lie in bed planning in my head what I would do if the dire event came to pass. I knew our home was big enough to squeeze lots of people in. People like my mother and some sisters and brothers. I thought we should buy extra mattresses and hold them in reserve in case there was a nuclear disaster.

'Do you think we could drain the water out of the cellar and develop a bomb shelter?' I asked Bruce in bed. 'How many people do you think it will hold?'

'Oh, about two,' he replied and I could picture him smiling in the dark. 'Go to sleep, Annie. It isn't going to happen. Too many people know that whatever side wins, everyone loses. Didn't you read *On the Beach*? Now go to sleep!'

I had indeed read Nevil Shute's book *On the Beach* before we married and had dreams about it for months afterwards. My mind kept working. *We need to stock up on water and blankets as well as tinned food.*

As I drifted off to sleep, I suddenly came up with an idea. The CWA could ask St John Ambulance Australia to run a first-aid course for everyone in the village.

And that's what we decided to do at our next meeting. The course was held in the hall and well attended. Everyone had a lot of fun and new friendships were forged. We were taught to treat various poisons, snake bites, broken arms and legs, concussion and spinal injuries. And that was our village's contribution to civil defence in the event of a nuclear attack from the communists!

Although I was accepted in the community now, I was still a relative newcomer and therefore liable to unwittingly step right into unspoken village traditions and informal understandings. With eyes wide shut, it was only a matter of time before it happened. And it did in 1962, when I organised the village Christmas party, which was held every year in Stanley Galvin Park, where the 'Last Post' sounded on Anzac Day. Mrs Russell, the policeman's wife, had always organised these Christmas celebrations but this once, she and her family took leave in early December. I offered to pick up the job in her absence. By then, I had been the CWA president for well over twelve months, after all.

It was always done like this. Santa waited in the park for the children to come.

'Could I do something different? I asked CWA members and no one said no.

That should have been warning enough, but undeterred, I ploughed right on, arranging to have Santa Claus travel in a horse and sulky from the school on the eastern side of the railway line to those waiting for him in the park. This would create a better sense of excitement as the children watched his progress, or so I believed.

Alas, when Mrs Russell returned a few days before Christmas, I was left in no doubt that I had made a big mistake. War had been declared. Telephones rang hot. People got into huddles.

'Oh, dear,' I said to Bruce. 'How was I to know?'

'Don't worry, darling. You are sure to make a few more blunders before you're finished. Just remember not to step on Mrs Yates's toes by winning first prize at the flower show with your sponge cake!'

So like a man to make a joke of it.

'Not bloody likely,' I said. 'But I'm not sure I can keep up with the politics of life in the slow lane.' We both laughed.

Mrs Yates, who was the Vice President of the CWA, called for an armistice, and hostilities ceased. We met in the hall under the eyes of Simpson and his donkey. Although I apologised profusely, everyone agreed it was too late to change the arrangement. A face-saver became necessary. Mrs Russell was invited to preside over all the park proceedings that Christmas, requiring our local shire councillor to temporarily relinquish his role. Next year, when Mrs Russell was back at the helm, strangely enough the CWA decided to continue with my innovation. Twenty years my senior, Mrs Russell was a good person, and we enjoyed a friendly relationship after the incident. But not before she took her revenge on the tennis court at the Mangoplah Easter tennis tournament.

Anzac Day was one day of the year when social barriers broke down unreservedly between everyone. At 11 am, ex-service personnel would assemble at the school, together with the pupils in their uniforms. A drummer led the procession, followed by the schoolchildren. Behind them, keeping perfect time, as they had in their fighting days, came the soldiers and ex-servicemen and -women, medals flapping away on their chests. Officers led the column, then sergeants, then the lower ranks. Bruce, an officer, was in the front row.

We civilians lined the footpath in front of the pub then followed the servicemen and -women past the stock-and-station agents and the baker's shop, then turned right at the end of the garden running down the centre of the main street. This garden had been built and lovingly tended by Stan Galvin, now one of the marchers in the sergeants' row. For that reason, he was universally known as the 'mayor' of Yerong Creek.

Once the parade was assembled in Stanley Galvin Park, which was flanked by the Bush Fire Brigade building on one side and the general store on the other, the 'Last Post' was trumpeted and the Ode was recited:

They shall not grow old, as we that are left grow old;
Age shall not weary them, nor the years condemn.
At the going down of the sun and in the morning
We will remember them.

As I listened, I felt that familiar tightening in my throat before tears and looking up at the bronze statue of a soldier, his hand gripping his rifle, I couldn't help thinking of all the village men on that plaque who had died in both world wars and what a waste it had been. Survivors' names were there, too, like those of Bruce and his father, and others who were standing beside me now.

A minute's silence came next, just in time for us to put aside terrible memories and compose ourselves.

The children, who had been ready to go for some time, took to the swings and monkey bars, and the servicemen and -women retired to the hall for a largely liquid lunch. I sat with Judy and Margie, one of our other neighbours, under the cottonwood trees just beginning to go yellow in response to the cooling weather and watched the children enjoy their antics on the crossbars, then swiftly rescued Henry from a swing about to hit him broadside as he ran over to join in the fun.

There was nowhere for me to go but home; women and children didn't go to the pub, and Bruce was standing here waiting to take himself off to the revelries in the hall. The revelries were different in every town in the district and ours had a unique flavour: Scotty, a railway fettler, would kick off his boots and squeeze into the high heels of Ronny McRory, a woman from the grazing community, as she donned his boots. Then they danced together to wartime tunes bashed out on the tinny hall piano. Others would be down the back of the hall playing Two Up while everyone else uninhibitedly sang and danced as though it was D-Day all over again, reliving the last glorious days at the end of the war. Few left the hall entirely unaffected by alcohol; some went on to the pub.

All this I heard from Bruce when he arrived home to find me cooking the evening meal and getting the children into their baths and pyjamas. But I was not one of those who needed to recapture D-Day's release of inhibitions. After all, I was ten when the war ended and was, even then, a budding peace activist.

Later, as the servicemen and -women's numbers began to dwindle, the event began to morph into something that even the children could attend, and liquor was relegated to a less important place in the scheme of things.

By 2014, long after I had left Yerong Creek, Henry – a frequent visitor to his old home town – told me that celebrations for Anzac Day have moved across the railway line to the bowling club, complete with a liquor licence and poker machines, and all are welcome. The pub has been sold, its historic liquor licence gone to a Sydney restaurant. The hall building has been pulled down; no one rescued Simpson and his donkey, so it probably languishes in a tip somewhere or has long since been consigned to the flames.

22
expansion

One Sunday morning after we came home from Mass, Bruce received a call from his brother Brian, who lived in the Tocumwal area, near the Murray River. He said his friend Danny O'Day was wanting to buy land in the Riverina, and asked if he could visit so Bruce could give him some pointers.

We agreed, and a few days later, Danny arrived – a nuggetty man about sixty, who disappeared into Bruce's father's old leather chair and, apart from sleeping and a short trip around our property, didn't emerge until it was time for him to leave two days later. He looked exactly like what he was: a rough diamond, weathered by work in the outback and the sun, someone who understood the land and all its 'droughts and flooding rains' and other vicissitudes. Danny had amassed huge wealth from buying rural properties in Queensland and now wanted to hedge his bets with more reliable country in New South Wales's southern regions. Over two nights and days, he and Bruce sat around the fire in the living room while Danny recounted how he came to build his empire and squeezed every bit of information about the Riverina from Bruce. Once he had imparted his colourful history, the two were firm friends. Danny's parting words to us were, 'Buy land and never sell.'

Soon after Danny left, we saw a 'for sale' advertisement in the *The Land* for Hills Park, a property of 1200 acres near Henty, three miles from Fairfield. It was a lovely property that could grow fine wool and yield a good harvest. The terms of sale were fifty per cent up front, with the balance to be repaid in equal yearly instalments over the next seven years.

When Bruce sought Danny's opinion, he said, 'Mad if you don't buy it.'

Bruce consulted maps from the land titles office and discovered that the land could be made more accessible to our farm machinery and sheep by opening up an old public road that had been informally incorporated into our neighbour Ben's property. Ben, who had grazed the disused road free of charge for some years, wouldn't be pleased if we reopened the old public road, but the alternative – transporting machinery and sheep on a much longer main road – would not be a feasible proposition.

The bank extended us a loan; we attended the auction and were the successful bidders.

After it was over, I wanted to celebrate but all Bruce wanted to do was go home to bed. In spite of all his talk with Danny O'Day of buying land and never selling, the purchase sent him into a state of shock, and he stayed under the blankets for two days, refusing to get up.

By the second day, I was so worried about him that I stood at the foot of our bed and said, 'Look, darling, if this is too much for you, let me ring the stock-and-station agent who sold us the property. I'll tell him we can't go through with it.

We will do our ten per cent deposit but it's better than you getting sick.'

Bruce said no and to leave things alone.

The next morning, he was up and running again, and said, 'I don't want you to tell anyone about this. I'm okay now. I just needed some time to adjust and think about how I will manage it all.'

For me, it had been a shock, too – but not about the debt. I had been given a glimpse of the vulnerability of the husband I thought I knew so well. He was the man who had laughed with Danny around the fireplace, who'd caught Danny's fire and had acted on it. But when it came to the crunch, he might buckle. Where would that leave me and the children?

Yet I also saw Bruce's courage. He recovered from the anxiety and got on with the work required to see the deal through. Our neighbour was upset about our plans to restore the old public road and had words with him.

'What have I ever done to you, Bruce?' he said. 'We've always been good neighbours.'

'It's nothing personal, Ben. You have had years to buy that road if you wanted to, but it could work well for you to have it opened up. It will give you a new access for moving your stock around your property, and the fire brigade has told us it will open up that back country to fire fighters if there is a fire up there.'

Personal slights can last for years among farmers. Even though Bruce doubted that Ben would ever speak to us again, we proceeded. In the long term, if relationships were strained over the matter, Bruce never mentioned it again.

On Christmas Day in 1962, we woke to a hot north wind. Bruce started the day with 'Happy Christmas, darling' and then just one word – 'Gosh.' The children came in to show us their new toys and after suitably appreciative oohs and aahs, he added, 'I don't like it, Annie. It wouldn't take much to start a fire. On a day like this a few years before you came here, a fire was started by a Railway Department's scheduled burn-off along the line.'

He told me the fire burned out crops and homesteads and killed thousands of sheep and cattle on a hundred-mile rampage between Mangoplah, thirteen miles east of us, and the Victorian border about eighty miles south of Fairfield. It became known as the Mangoplah Fires and cost the New South Wales government millions of dollars in compensation.

Closing up the house, we set off for Mass in the village, then hurried home. Bruce always insisted on a traditional Christmas lunch, regardless of the weather, so I had a turkey in the oven and a plum pudding bubbling away on the stove. The table had been set with flowers and Christmas crackers the night before and the children had 'helped' in decking the Christmas tree out with lights and shiny baubles.

We were about to sit down to a glass of champagne and open presents under the tree before lunch. My friend Elspeth had arrived with her husband-to-be, Lindsey, a widower, who had brought two of his children from his first marriage; older than ours, they were were playing with Alex, Austin and Vanessa. Henry, only a few months old, was having his morning sleep but the other three were jumping up and down with excitement at the prospect of opening more presents.

Then the telephone rang. A bushfire was heading towards a neighbour's crops and was proving difficult to contain. Lindsey and Bruce raced off to hitch up the Furphy, a water tank on wheels, always at the ready during the summer.

I turned the turkey down to low. If the wind changed, the fire could end up anywhere, even here. Next, I trained the sprinklers on the lawn in the direction from which the fire might come and sealed the house with wet towels as best I could against the likelihood of sparks flying under the doors. Alex, Austin and Vanessa were happily playing with their Santa Claus presents, and Lindsey's children helped with occupying them for the rest of the time. Then I said a well-directed prayer and opened one of the bottles of champagne for Elspeth and me to nourish our spirits and ... wait.

Two hours later, Bruce and Lindsey returned, red-eyed from smoke; Elspeth and I were a little bleary-eyed from champagne. The fire had been halted before it did too much damage; the danger was past. Roll on Christmas celebrations.

This was the first time I'd ever faced a fire risk like this but I knew what to do. It's one of the first things Bruce taught me when I came to live at Fairfield and often on days when the weather was hot and windy, we would go over it again. Bruce was my best teacher.

Our life on the land wasn't all work, of course. There were the predictable rounds of social events, including barbecues and tennis parties on people's properties, picnic races and winter balls. And we always seemed to have a full house. Visits from family and friends during school holidays might last for a week or two as the city-dwellers absorbed themselves in adventures such as pulling lambs out of ewes, pressing wool in the shearing shed, riding horses, learning to light fires in the house, feeding poddy lambs or helping Bruce milk the cow.

Ours was an idyllic, sometimes frantic, one might say innocent, but stable life. I relished and came to love it, often wondering what I would have done with myself if I'd lived a life in the suburbs after the variety and drama of this rural existence.

Eventually, we succumbed to black-and-white television, which widened our horizons. In 1963, we cried with the rest of the world as we watched President Kennedy's funeral procession make its way down Pennsylvania Avenue. Jackie and JFK had been the hope of the future, or so we thought. My best dress was an identical design to one Jackie wore when she visited the Queen at Buckingham Palace, a smartly tailored short-sleeved dress of creme wool, with a flat bow setting off the eased skirt just below the waist. Phil, my sister, had spotted it in a couturier's sale in Double Bay and sent it to me as a surprise.

With television in our living room, the world seemed to be encroaching not only on us here in the bush but also on our national psyche. We were now living in a much smaller world, one that was in our face as we watched a US president shot. Would our world ever be the same again?

When Jocey had turned eighteen, she left to pursue a career in nursing. I gave her a send-off and a well-deserved glowing reference, but I missed her and was sad when she left. One of my neighbours told me she said of us, 'I really love that family' and we took that as a great compliment.

It was hard to replace her. I turned to the Commonwealth Employment Service for help and was sent a series of young women who didn't exactly meet my specifications. The first one, Sharon, nearly expired when she saw the open country.

'Oh,' she said, 'look at those paddocks. I'm terrified. I can't look at them.'

I tried to console her at first and soothe her worries, but then I used a more practical approach, telling her, 'This is a farm, we live here in the house and the sheep live in the paddocks. That's their home. There's nothing terrifying about that.'

But her fears would not be quieted and she left the next day on the train back to Melbourne.

Another young woman, Susan, brought her baby daughter with her. She was not a happy child and cried a lot. I needed someone to help me but instead I spent my days giving Susan lessons in mothering, taking her to the clinic and to the doctor and trying to get her to give up smoking. In the end, I gave her the address of somewhere in Sydney she might receive help and put her on the train to Central.

Then there was Trixie, the blonde English girl from the East End of London – a relative of friends in Wagga, who suggested we might give her a try. She couldn't get used to the idea that we didn't have a fish and chip shop just around the corner.

Two days into her stay with us, I thought I could trust her enough to take care of the children one afternoon while I sorted their clothes for the coming winter. She was sitting on the back verandah and all four children were playing in front of her on the back lawn. About an hour later, I came out to see how she was getting on. She was still happily reading a magazine and the children were nowhere to be seen.

'Where are the children, Trixie?' I asked.

'Oh, I don't know', she said, 'they were here a minute ago.'

'Oh, my God, Trixie. You were meant to be minding them, not reading a magazine.'

Bruce was out in a back paddock on the tractor so I couldn't get hold of him. I ran down to the dam nearest the house and breathed a sigh of relief when I saw they weren't there. I sent Trixie over to the sheds to look and told her to keep calling. As she went, she called out behind her, 'I don't want to ruin these shoes.'

'It's children we are talking about, Trixie. Never mind your new shoes. You were supposed to be keeping an eye on them.'

Distraught, I rang Judy. 'Can you see them from up on your hill?' I asked.

She ran out into her garden and looked down the road. There the four of them were, walking up the gravel road to her house – Alex leading the pack, dragging a shovel behind her, Austin, Vanessa and little Henry bringing up the rear, each also dragging some sort of implement.

My heart pounding, I jumped into the car and sped after them. In half a mile, I caught up to my brood as they were about to reach Judy's front gate.

'Where are you off to? I asked, pulling up behind them.

'We are going to help Judy in her garden,' Alex announced.

A pretty extraordinary response. So great was my relief, I didn't say anything but simply hugged them, put them in the car and didn't let them out of my sight again.

Later, over dinner, when Bruce quizzed them about their excursion, Alex said, 'We wanted to go on an adventure. You know like the children in *The Faraway Tree*.'

Trixie went with me back to Wagga the next morning; we'd agreed to call it quits. Bruce stayed home to mind the children for the day, which was a rare treat for them.

'Let's do an adventure today,' he said over breakfast and Henry ran around the table and jumped on his knee, which was the signal for the others to leap all over him, too.

The 'adventure', as it turned out, was rounding up sheep and moving them from one paddock to another. Next Bruce took them to the dam, where they helped him build a little hut to accommodate a couple of geese. The object of that exercise was to use the geese to deter the children from visiting the dam, in case they fancied a watery 'adventure'. After that, they caught yabbies for dinner.

'Did you have an adventure?' I asked when I returned home.

'Yes, yes,' they all sang out at once.

Then Bruce reminded them, 'It's only an adventure if it's a secret.'

'Yes, yes,' said Austin. 'Who can keep the secret?'

'Me, me, me,' said Vanessa.

Henry wasn't so sure and whispered it later into my ear as I was tucking him into bed for a well-earned sleep.

Then a local girl called Margaret came to try out for the job. Margaret was a terrific worker and she knew how to cook farm food, and even though she sometimes had a short fuse with the children, they liked her.

At the end of a year, though, I knew something was wrong when she couldn't keep her breakfast down. 'Look, you should go to see the doctor. I'll take you there.'

'No, no,' she said. 'I'm pregnant.'

'Oh,' I said, realising how clueless I was because that possibility hadn't even crossed my mind. 'Who's the father?'

It was Barry, one of the local shearers. Bruce had spotted them one night when he was coming home from a meeting. They were canoodling in Barry's car down the back lane into the village. Finally, I found out Margaret had been climbing out the window of her bedroom at night for these assignations so that's why she was often so tired at breakfast. That did cause me to wonder how Barry's sheep felt about his shearing at seven o'clock in the morning.

Barry's father, also a shearer, said to Bruce one day after Margaret and Barry announced their engagement, 'Try before you buy, mate; that's the way we do it around here. My boy has got the goods and so has Margaret.' It was all very matter of fact.

A couple of months later, we attended their wedding in the Lutheran church and afterwards went to the reception in the Yerong Creek hall, catered for by the CWA.

After that, we placed an advertisement in the Wagga and Albury newspapers. The first person to answer was Lynell.

She was well spoken, had a lovely smile and I liked everything about her.

A week later, she started to work for us and straightaway the children took a shine to her. She laughed with them, played with them, read to them and gently castigated them when they were naughty. And she fitted in with us as though she was one of our family. We all loved her. Now I knew we'd struck oil.

23

branching out

By the beginning of 1963, pupil numbers at our local public school had dropped and it was about to lose one of its three teachers. At four and a half, Alex was young to be going to school, but to keep the third teacher, the school needed to find every child who might be old enough to attend, so we enrolled her. From the school's point of view, it was a wonderful reprieve. From Alex's point of view, it wasn't. She told me she fought back by scribbling outside the lines of her colouring book and threatened to do even worse things than that. She'd become a colouring-book terrorist in revenge.

One day, I called in to the school to drop off some papers to the headmaster. Alex saw the car through the window of her classroom and ran out into my arms, all the while screaming for me to take her home. I took her home that day but Bruce thought I'd made a mistake.

'Next time that happens,' he said, 'stand your ground.'

And next time I did. The lovely young kindergarten teacher, Miss Hamilton, intervened and put her arms around Alex. All

I could hear as I walked away was, 'Mummy, Mummy, P-L-E-A-S-E don't leave me here. Mummy, Mummy, take me home. I'm dying.'

My heart was breaking as I drove off into the village to do my shopping.

After a while, Alex bowed to the inevitable and began to make friends, so by the end of the year she was bringing stories home from school and taking back others, to report on us at story time.

We joined the Parents and Citizens Committee a number of times a year to mow lawns, clear debris, mend fences, clean and paint classrooms and catalogue library books. Inevitably, flasks of tea and baskets of scones emerged by magic at 11 am, a part of the morning working-bee ritual no one wanted to miss. This was a time to compare notes on farming conditions and gossip about the goings-on of people in the district.

One beautiful late autumn morning in 1963, as we ate our scones, Rob, the president of the P&C, convinced me to take on the role of delegate to the Parents and Citizens Regional Council. This role required me to travel four times a year with other delegates to different parts of the region and once a year to a state council meeting in Sydney. Most of these meetings were only a few hours' drive away and held on a Saturday. Bruce said he could manage the children by himself on four Saturdays of the year and we might all take a trip to Sydney for the one-day meeting. I always relished a trip to Sydney!

Meeting delegates from other towns around the district, I learned about what were known as central schools; these featured in medium-sized towns such as Henty, Culcairn and Holbrook. They provided an education for children only up to the age of fifteen. Presumably, they were based on the assumption that children in those medium-sized towns had limited expectations: a boy's goal in life was to work as a farm labourer and a girl's was to be a wife and mother. It was a self-fulfilling strategy if ever there was one, because it placed full secondary education beyond the reach of lower-income families. Bruce and I always hoped we could send our children to high schools in capital cities – both of us had completed our education in settings like that – but we knew that if our income dropped, we would want to have the option of sending them to a local high school.

Some of the farmers who could afford to send their children away to finish high school, I discovered, had ideas about education that shocked me.

'Listen, love,' said one local. 'Why do you go on so much about education? I'm pretty successful and didn't go past intermediate. I don't expect my kids to do any different.'

He went on to tell me that Peter, his son, would leave school and work on the farm with him, and his daughter, Carole, would probably marry a farmer; what use would education be? 'What use has it been to you, Anne?' he asked me.

I ignored his little jibe at me and said, 'Don't you want to introduce them to a wider world than that? Carole is a very bright girl. She could go on to be anything she liked, like a doctor or something else. We can't even imagine what the future holds. If our kids have an education, it's the only thing no one can take away from them. Your daughter deserves that chance.'

'What! And leave home just when she's old enough to give her mum a break. Over my dead body' was his fierce response.

Our little group of education delegates – Brian from Culcairn, Ian from Henty and Geraldine from The Rock – all met up outside the Paragon Café in The Rock at 7 am one Saturday morning and set off together to drive to an all-day meeting in

Griffith. The guest speaker was to be the flamboyant federal member of parliament for Griffith, Al Grassby.

Dressed in a patterned jacket of green and red woven silk, with a matching scarf around his neck, Al brought the house down with his opening jokes and anecdotes, and he left us with a challenge: 'What can you as delegates and individuals, each and every one of you, do to enhance the cause of quality education for all Australians?'

At the end of the day, we drove home tired but inspired, talking all the way about what we could do for education.

And that's the evening when we began to hatch a plot. We would make an appointment with the Area Director of Education to discuss amalgamating our three central schools into one high school offering education all the way up to senior year and university entrance.

A few weeks later, we went to Wagga to meet the Regional Director of Education, Mr Bingham. Outside, the sun was shining, the birds were singing and blossoms were dropping their petals in the park and on the pavements. It was as though they were blooming to welcome our little delegation before we went into the more austere and restricted headquarters of a government department.

Our three-person delegation consisted of Ian, Brian and me: two farmers in their best wool sports coats, elastic-sided boots and Fletcher Jones trousers, and me in a pleated tartan skirt from the same supplier and a red twin-set. We sat on one side of Mr Bingham's desk; he and Wal Fife, who was the state Minister for Education and also Wagga's local member, were squashed into the space on the 'power' side, determined, it seemed, to assert the authority of their respective offices.

In those days, community activism was greeted with deep suspicion. Very few people thought it safe or, indeed, their right to demand changes from government, let alone the type of innovation we had in mind. Not surprisingly, the 'power couple' behind the desk was obstructive to begin with. Our delegation was fearfully polite, fearfully formal, but we pressed on and weren't going to leave until we got what we had come for. Finally, we pulled out our trump card.

'We will do the work,' I said. 'We think it requires a feasibility study.' In other words, we – not they – would take the risks. That seemed to change things.

The period around Christmas 1962 was memorable for more than the near miss with the bushfire. Alex had turned four in June of that year, while Austin was three, Vanessa was two and Henry was a baby. The harvest was still in full swing, and Lynell had taken a few days off over Christmas.

'Are you sure you will be all right?' Lynell had asked before leaving.

Always the optimist, I said, 'Yes, yes, you go. Enjoy Christmas with your family.'

But as the Christmas break progressed, changing nappies became unbearable because I had developed a rash on my hands. Tending to four small children meant I had my hands in water constantly. There was only so much I could do for the children while wearing rubber gloves. With the hot weather, the rash became infected. Every job I did around the house brought me close to despair. Bruce was out taking the wheat crop off and the children and I were constantly on the move taking food and drink out to the workers. I hid the rash from him because I knew he shouldn't be distracted from harvesting.

On the day after Boxing Day, he came in unexpectedly from the paddock and caught me there crying in the bedroom, close to the end of my tether. He must have had a premonition and I never found out what brought him into the house that day.

'Oh, Annie I had no idea. Those hands look awful. We have to do something about this situation,' he said.

'What about the harvest, darling? I didn't want to tell you before,' I said through my tears. 'Lynell won't be back until tomorrow.'

Bruce immediately left the room and rang a skin specialist friend. As luck would have it, he and his wife had not gone away for Christmas.

'Tell Anne to pack her bag,' he told Bruce. 'She might have to go to hospital.'

Judy offered to mind Henry, and the other children piled into the car. On arriving in Wagga we went immediately to the specialist's rooms and then to Calvary Hospital, where I was given a private room looking out over the garden.

Harvest was halted till Lynell came back the next day.

Travelling with me to hospital came a book called *The Feminine Mystique*, by Betty Friedan, which a good friend called David had bought in America and given to me as a Christmas gift. He often stayed with us at Fairfield and believed it his duty to keep me in touch with what was happening outside my engrossing world of infant chaos.

So infected had my hands become that I was not allowed to cut up my own food in hospital; instead, I found myself bathing them in freezing water and then anointing them with cortisone cream. But I propped up David's gift on the bed tray in front of me. The nuns thought the title sounded devotional. Mystics they did understand and I was not about to enlighten them further

The more I read, the more I realised just how much of society's norms I had absorbed and how these very same norms had been responsible for keeping women in their place – largely, safely at the kitchen sink. I also became aware of how my own subscription to an American magazine called *The Ladies' Home Journal* had sucked me into attitudes frequently at odds with my wider feminist instincts and the instincts of my mother.

My condition stabilised, I was discharged after five days and life went on as before, except now I was changed and started to look at the world around me in new ways. One consequence was that I approached the issue of our high school feasibility study with more vigour. I realised that, more than ever, girls needed to complete their education.

Having received a cheque for $3000 from the Education Department, my fellow delegates and I divided the research project up between us, went out in our cars to interview people, then sent out a questionnaire to parents of children at the schools in the three areas under consideration. The research findings came to this: if a high school was built at Culcairn, ten miles equidistant from the other two towns, Holbrook and Henty, most children would need to travel for less than an hour a day all up.

Then the project lost a bit of momentum for a while because of developments closer to home.

Bruce and I had decided four children was enough. It was a number we hit on before we were married. Despite our best family planning endeavours, now came the familiar symptoms of early pregnancy – an odd taste in my mouth and a queasy feeling as I lay in bed in the morning. I knew somehow this might be the last time I would carry a baby.

Bruce had once been told by the obstetrician, Dr Macbeth, that a little food and drink before getting out of bed was a good way to fend off morning sickness. Now he insisted on bringing me 'get-up' food in the morning – a cup of tea and a piece of toast. For the time being, he and Lynell took care of the children and managed the breakfast chaos. Listening to it all from a distance was worse than lying in bed, and after a few weeks, I declared myself cured and continued with my parental early morning routine so Bruce could get out of the kitchen door and on with his rural duties.

Once I was feeling more energised, we delegates followed through on the research. We published the outcome of the research in all the local media, took to the road again to consult with community leaders in each district and then called a public meeting to see if we could get approval from the communities to clinch the deal.

The meeting was held in the RSL hall at Holbrook, a town on the Hume Highway. It was where we had struck the most resistance during the research phase; many individuals were opposed to having their central school closed in favour of a half-hour bus journey for the students. Consensus was by no means a done deal and in the depth of winter, as we walked into that hall, the capacity crowd made us very apprehensive.

Given the probability of resistance to a woman driving this agenda, and a pregnant one to boot, we decided Ian should chair the meeting while the rest of us sat in relative anonymity in the audience. It began politely, as these things often do. Then some of the perpetual naysayers started getting niggly.

'What's wrong with the central schools we have?' one farmer said.

Another asked, 'What do you guys from Henty and Yerong Creek think you are doing coming over here to foist this idea on us at Holbrook?'

Then it became personal. 'Who do you people think you are?'

The mayor stepped in and said, 'Now, ladies and gentlemen, we're not here to insult each other. Keep it nice.'

Gradually, the dissenters began to realise their jeers and jibes were not cutting much ice.

There were some who wanted to start again with a brand new proposal. Others wanted to amend and yet others thought they should formulate an addendum to an old motion. *Thank God for Joske*, I thought.

In the end, no doubt out of a desire to go home to their warm beds or to get it over before the pub closed at ten, someone moved that 'the motion be put' and another person seconded it.

By now it was 9.30 and as the local P&C volunteers rattled cups and saucers down the back of the hall, the issue was finally brought to a vote. Would they vote for the change? Drum roll! For a 'yes', three-quarters of the hands went up. For a 'no', a tiny group expressed their opposition. In spite of the heated debate, no blood had been spilt, and we had won the day. A miracle.

24
the dinner party

It was November 1964, and we had four guests coming to dinner for the last night of entertaining before the baby's birth in four weeks' time. Frankie was also staying because the roof on her house was being fixed. As soon as the weather warmed up in another few weeks, harvest would begin. Like a well-oiled domestic machine, I'd prepared the home for my departure. A student harvest worker from the Wagga agricultural college would be coming to live in the house during harvest and I'd prepared his room and made it look welcoming. I'd paid all household bills, labelled and filled the freezer with prepared food like meat and cakes and, importantly, I'd finished the Christmas shopping and the children's presents were all hidden away in the grain shed.

Jovially, I said to Bruce as we hid them there one night after the children were asleep, 'If I die in childbirth, darling, promise me you'll give them a Santa Claus Christmas.'

'Don't even joke about it, Annie,' he replied as we walked hand in hand back to the house.

For that night, I had prepared one of my signature dishes, beef stroganoff, to be followed by a chocolate mousse for dessert. Hardly what master chefs of the new century would recommend, but advanced for the Riverina in 1964.

It had been raining all day, a light misty spring rain, perfect for finishing off the crops swaying gently under a deepening sky. As I stood on the verandah, looking up to the hills beyond, I was overcome by a deep sense of contentment. As if to confer approval of this moment, the baby in my belly moved determinedly. The crop of plenty was one promise, a new human being's arrival into the world a more momentous one.

A few hours later, a log fire was burning in the living room. I had received full praise for my culinary efforts and we took our coffee cups and went to sit in easy chairs around the fire, now casting a brilliant glow over everyone. Outside it was cold, but inside nothing could detract from the warmth and contentment of a host and hostess basking in the bonhomie of the evening. Someone had told a joke and we were all laughing – a perfect Saturday night.

All of a sudden, Bruce rose from his father's leather chair beside the fire and staggered out of the room, shouting for me to follow. His cry was like that of a wounded animal and by the time I reached him, he was lying on our bed, writhing in pain.

I rushed back to our guests and said, 'Bruce is in terrible pain. We need to get him to the doctor; we should take him to Wagga to our GP, Farmie Joseph.'

The guests, now shaken, gathered up their belongings. The men helped me get Bruce into the station wagon and as I slid behind the wheel, I called to Frankie, who had been standing at the back of the men:

'Ring Farmie Joseph and tell him what has happened. Tell him we are leaving now and will be there in thirty-five minutes. Tell him it's urgent.'

'No, dear,' she answered. 'Take him to The Rock; it's only ten minutes away. I'll call the doctor there.'

If I had trusted my own instincts, I would have headed for Wagga, thirty miles away. But this was not the time to assert my idea over my mother-in-law's judgement.

The back way into The Rock had an unattended rail crossing and sometimes nothing but a four-wheel drive could make it over the old track on the other side, especially at night. *Don't chance it*, I thought. So I chose to go onto the main rail crossing near the station, only to find the railway gates firmly closed and padlocked. At that point, I might have chosen to go on to Wagga, but no, I got out of the station wagon and, in my pregnant state, my breath making little crystals on the cold night air, ran up the line to rouse the duty officer, who was dozing in front of a coal fire.

The startled attendant hastily put on his coat as we ran down the track together. He opened the gates, allowing us to cross over the line to the small hospital, where Dr Zeigler was waiting. The doctor confidently diagnosed kidney stones, gave Bruce a shot of morphine to ease the pain and put him to bed in the hospital. I returned home relieved and exhausted. Bless her heart! Frankie had cleared the table and stacked the dishwasher. *She was right*, I thought. The Rock was the best place to go.

On Sunday, I collected Bruce from the hospital. The next day he insisted on joining the manager of our other property Hills Park, three miles away, because it was crutching time, so I made a doctor's appointment for him in Wagga for Tuesday morning. Late Monday afternoon, I got a call from Beryl, the manager's wife at Hills Park: 'Come quickly. Bruce is in great pain,' she said.

Out I raced onto the road Bruce had restored to give us direct access to Hills Park. There I picked up Bruce, then it was back onto the Olympic Highway to go north to Wagga's Calvary Hospital, where Farmie our GP, was waiting to meet us. Farmie immediately diagnosed appendicitis. Within fifteen minutes, Bruce was in the operating theatre, undergoing an emergency appendectomy.

Farmie greeted me later, pleased with the result.

'A success,' he said. 'You were just in time. There were a few peculiar features about this. The appendix had wound itself around the intestines but it's okay. Don't worry, Bruce is a fit man and won't take long to recover.'

A week later, Bruce was still in hospital and I delayed taking the plane to Sydney for the birth because every time I went to leave, Henry, now nearly two and a half, seemed to run a temperature and get very distressed. The third time, though, it really was time to go and I left him clinging to Lynell's arms whimpering his little heart out. I rang from the airport. He had miraculously recovered and was happily playing.

Our fifth baby, Rebecca, arrived a few days later, on 5 December 1964. Mercifully, it was a quick labour. It was all over in an hour, including the ten minutes it took to get from Mother's home to the hospital.

Bruce came straight from the Wagga hospital by plane to arrive in Sydney to meet his new daughter face to face. By now, the rules about babies were more relaxed and mothers were allowed to keep the babies in their rooms except at night. We celebrated the safe arrival of a healthy baby, but in the back of my mind I wondered how I'd managed to get myself into this situation: five children under six and six weeks before my thirtieth birthday!

At times like this, I always remembered the words of that intrepid heroine Scarlett O'Hara: 'I'll think about that tomorrow.' Not any more for me! This baby was the turning point. It had to be thought about now.

25

a pope, a priest and a bishop

The Second Vatican Council, in the 1960s, gave me hope that the Catholic Church would wake up to discover itself in the current century. There were signs I might be right. Inclusiveness was one of Pope John XXIII's main platforms: parish councils were set up to give the laity a voice; the Mass could now be performed in the vernacular. Women were allowed to participate in the liturgy and be on the altar; nuns were shedding their veils and coming out from behind their cloisters, where St Augustine had put them seven centuries before. Questions that might have hitherto been considered irreligious could be asked and even answered in ways that were beginning to make sense.

    Along with like-minded Catholic friends, Bruce and I believed it was our duty to support Pope John's reforms and to keep them moving. Inertia, we knew, would be their death knell, because in many church halls and chapels lurked the naysayers, just waiting for it all to go back to how it had been before.

Towards the end of the Vatican Council, the new medical miracle, the contraceptive pill, sparked a vigorous debate among theologians about the legitimacy of the Church's position on contraception. A special commission was established to come up with a recommendation to the Vatican Council. Most people believed there would be a change in policy.

Stanley Hosie, who had given us the banned sex manual before we were married, had been sent to Rome by his Marist order as an Australian observer to the Vatican Council. If anyone had a handle on this one, I thought he would. So I wrote to him, pouring out my frustration about the method we had used up till now, namely, tracking ovulation cycles.

Around this same time, this technique had been rebadged with a new name called 'the Billings Method', after the husband and wife Catholic doctor team who together had carried out so-called research to give it some spurious medical legitimacy. Catholics in Wagga and Melbourne had been told it was the only form of contraception acceptable to the Church. Going unremarked was the fact that the Billings had eight children. All I knew was that the Billings Method had resulted in three unplanned pregnancies for Bruce and me.

Not surprisingly then, the letter I sent covered all this information, including the fact that both of us felt that five children in six and a half years was too much for one human being to manage in this time and place and citing my mother's nervous breakdown as an additional argument.

Three weeks after sending off my plea for advice, we picked up our mail from our box outside the Yerong Creek Post Office after Mass one Sunday. Among it was a letter postmarked Roma from Father Stanley Hosie SM. I was excited to have heard back from him so soon. As Bruce drove home, with Rebecca on my lap and the other children preoccupied in the back of the station wagon, I read the letter out loud to him. Father Hosie wrote that the pill had changed the way theologians were thinking about contraception. The discussions within the Commission about it were in the balance. 'Even if the Commission stayed with the existing rules,' Stanley wrote, 'nothing would ever be the same again, because once there was doubt on a theological question, and certainly within the Commission itself, there were different opinions on this longstanding issue, the Canon Law perspective was that Catholics were free to consider the question and in good conscience take whatever action they felt was right for them.'

Instantly, I felt as though I had been thrown a lifeline. No more anxiously waiting for my period month by month. I was so happy!

Bruce went along with my decision to take the pill as he could see the sense of Stanley's argument, set against the debate raging in Australian and overseas publications, and in the Vatican Council.

We didn't do anything immediately, because I was still breastfeeding. A painful lump in my breast turned into a breast abscess and I began to run a high temperature. Rebecca and I had to be hospitalised while the abscess was drained and dressed several times a day and the fever was tamed. The nuns at the hospital were delighted with a cooing, smiling baby and were happy to spoil her. Unbeknown to them, this let me get on with my research on the pill.

By May 1965, I gave up limping through the last stages of breastfeeding and weaned Rebecca. I knew I would soon be entering the danger zone: as my milk dried up, ovulation cycles returned to normal and another pregnancy became a possibility. Time to take action.

I went to Sydney for my long-overdue postnatal check-up and to discuss the pill with my obstetrician. I explained to him that the Wagga bishop had forbidden Catholic doctors in Wagga to prescribe it or for Catholic pharmacists to supply it. Knowing my fertility as he did, he was sympathetic and I walked out of his rooms with a supply of the pill from his bottom drawer and a long-term prescription to go with it. Once I started taking the pill, I could relax in the knowledge that I would not be having any more children.

Some months later, when Stan came back to Australia, he introduced me to Denis Kenny, a Marist priest like himself. Denis had grown up on the north coast, had taught in Marist schools and moved on to become an academic. Soon after I met him, he published a book called *Catholics and Freedom*, challenging the notion that Catholics should rigidly follow the Pope's directives about everything from contraception to the Vietnam war.

When the book came out, he was interviewed on TV and radio and caused something of a sensation. Soon after this, he invited me to Melbourne to a conference on the writings of Pierre Teilhard de Chardin, a Jesuit paleontologist who had developed a set of theories on the origin of man and an interpretation of the Catholic faith.

While I attended the conference, Bruce took the children sightseeing and showed them through his old school, pointing out his name on its honour board. When they returned later in the day to pick me up, Austin greeted me with 'Mummy, Mummy. Did you know Daddy was the boss of the cricket team at Xavier College?'

'And Uncle Kerry was the boss of the whole school,' said Alex.

A few months later, my friend Shirley and I decided to invite Denis to give a public lecture in Wagga. The audience would be mostly Catholic but there were others who were interested, too. We booked the Methodist hall and phoned around to let people know. The word spread. A good crowd seemed assured.

A few days before the lecture, Bruce and I were preparing to go to a dinner at a friend's property when the phone rang. Lynell answered and came running down the hall to tell me: 'Anne, it's Bishop Henschke on the phone. Come quickly.'

I took the call from the longtime Bishop of Wagga in the office off the middle verandah. It had been a warm day and the late afternoon sun was flooding the room, shining through the peppercorn trees flanking the western side of the house. Without any preliminaries, the bishop's voice came booming down the line: 'I hear you are organising a meeting in Wagga for that priest Denis Kenny,' he said.

'Yes, M'lord,' I answered.

'Well, I'm telling you to cancel it. I forbid you to have that meeting.'

'I can't cancel it, M'lord. We have a lot of people coming and we've booked the hall.' Big mistake, I realised, saying 'a lot of people' and 'we've booked the hall'.

'Cancel it,' he said, his anger mounting.

'M'Lord, for heaven's sake; he may have some views that might be different to yours but we are just following the spirit of the Vatican Council and opening the way for Catholics to have these kinds of discussions. Since Father Kenny's book came out, many people want to hear what he has to say. They are grown-ups. They can make up their own minds.'

I thought the telephone might explode. 'Don't talk to me about the Vatican Council,' shouted the senior clergyman. 'I was there!'

Bruce had taken me to meet the bishop in his parlour when we were first engaged and I had a nodding acquaintance with him at public functions after that. I could not say I really knew him or that he knew me. What I did know was that our bishop wouldn't like being challenged by anyone, least of all a farmer's wife thirty miles from Wagga or a Marist priest outside his jurisdiction.

The bishop was a very conservative priest. He was old and his world order was being shaken by a worldwide revolution in thinking, now insinuating itself into his very own domain. This must have seemed intolerable for someone who for years had ruled the Catholic faithful in the Wagga Diocese with a firm hand. He was vehemently opposed to communism and a close associate of B. A. Santamaria. From time to time, the bishop invited Santamaria to speak in the Civic Theatre, complete with terrifying graphics on how the 'red menace' was spreading like a virus, would soon reach Malaysia, then Singapore and the Philippines and would close in on Australia as it took over the world.

The heat of the sun matched the heat of the conversation and I was beginning to sweat. I took a deep breath.

'M'Lord, I don't believe you have the right to ask me to do this. I will speak to Father Kenny and it will be his decision, of course, but if it was left to me, we should go ahead with the meeting.'

His reply astounded me. 'I will do everything I can to stop you.'

Undaunted, I continued, 'What do you mean?

'Never mind. You can be sure your Father Kenny will know about this through his superiors. There is a bishops' meeting in Melbourne next week and I will raise it there.'

'This sounds like a threat,' I answered with some feeling.

At that, he hung up; the click reverberated in my ear.

For a minute, I sat in the chair reflecting on my audacity. It was scarcely believable that I had taken on a bishop. I did not feel good about it but I felt justified. In another time and place, I might have been interrogated by the Inquisition and decisively burned at the stake but now I wondered if I had the right to offer Denis up for 'execution'.

My turmoil contrasted strongly with the tranquillity around me. A flock of birds swooped in unison over the house as they went through their last joyous ritual of the day before bedding down for the night. At that still moment, from a place deep within me, came these words from the Gospel of Matthew: 'Consider the birds of the air, for they neither sow nor reap nor gather into barns; yet your heavenly Father feeds them. Are you not of far more value than they?'

Well, that was the truth of the matter. The birds of the air were free and the bishop had no control over them. Wasn't that the way we should be, too?

There was no time to ring Denis now; I knew he was giving a lecture in Melbourne that night. I would call him in the morning.

We climbed into the car and sped the seventeen miles to our friends' property west of Henty, Bruce listening patiently as I recounted the phone call, letting off steam.

'Don't let it ruin your night, darling,' he said. 'These are people we like and they like you a lot, I know. They will have gone to some trouble to entertain us. They aren't Catholics and can't give a fig about the Bishop of Wagga. Just put it aside for now and in the morning it will all come clear.'

'Okay,' I said. 'That's good advice.'

I did as Bruce suggested but probably drank too much wine. When we got home, I fell into a dreamless sleep.

The next morning, I rang Denis early, catching him as he was finishing breakfast with his fellow priests. After recounting my conversation with the bishop, I said, 'Look, Denis, this might be your vocation at stake. I will understand if you pull out and we have to cancel. It's perfectly okay with me. Honestly it is.'

'Anne, the Marist order will survive. It won't be the first time they have had a problem with a bishop! Orders don't come under a bishop's jurisdiction anyway. As for me, if *Catholics and Freedom* means anything, then of course I must come.'

Soon afterwards, I received a call from the Moderator of the Methodist Church in Wagga. He told me the hall had been double-booked by mistake and we would have to find another place for our meeting. Somehow, I had half-expected that. But even so, I was surprised the bishop crossed the sectarian divide to put pressure on a man who had been supporting the peace movement and quietly spreading its message among his parishioners. *What*, I wondered, *does it take to have the courage of your convictions?*

We held two meetings at our home. In all, over two nights, seventy people drove the thirty miles there and back to hear Denis reiterate the contents of the arguments in *Catholics and Freedom* about contraception. He argued that the Church's ban on contraception could not be sustained and that as Catholics had become better educated, they were now able and willing to make their own decisions about the size of their families.

the country wife

Some of the audience wanted to test Denis's knowledge about the Vietnam war. His position was that the US government, obsessed by fear of the spread of communism, had engineered the whole thing and then had to invent a cover-up to justify the death and destruction of the Vietnamese people and its own troops. His knowledge was deep and backed by solid research but his views were a revelation to many people. To most of the audience, all this was new and controversial material.

Denis had brought some of the books about Vietnam that he'd studied. He was happy to lend them as long as they all came back to me. He had also brought copies of his book and gave them out to the keenest participants.

Later, I heard from a partner in the largest Catholic legal firm in Wagga that the bishop was far from pleased. Not only was he furious at the meeting's content but he was angry that he had been disobeyed. Of course, he also now understood that he couldn't control people if they wanted to hold meetings in the privacy of their homes.

At the next Sunday Mass, our parish priest, Father John McGrath, said nothing and was as friendly as he always was, accepting an invitation to lunch at Fairfield the same day. Not a word was uttered about our defiance of the bishop.

A few months later came Denis's punishment, in the form of a suggestion from his superior: 'You've upset the bishops and been offered a position at Stanford University in California. Take a sabbatical there until this all blows over.'

Denis rang to tell me he was leaving and to keep his library of books on Vietnam. I felt guilty to be the cause of his banishment from Australia.

'Don't worry about it, Annie,' Bruce said. 'Bureaucracies are the same everywhere, whether it's inside the Church or otherwise. Pope John knew it was. Unfortunately, he didn't have a long enough life to complete the job while here on Earth. But in the long run, someone else will have to.'

'In the long run, we will both be long gone,' I said and with that, we both laughed.

26

the labor party

Living as we did in the country, we were among people whose major concerns were the weather, farming subsidies, taxes, cattle and sheep, spare machinery parts and the next picnic race meeting. Wagga was essentially a traditionalist town, happily slumbering under the umbrella of a fading past.

Outside, in a wider world, the Age of Aquarius had dawned and a new generation of people was singing songs of liberation. Peter, Paul and Mary, Bob Dylan and Joan Baez reflected the feelings of many of us under forty that the 'times they are a-changin'. How could I, living in the country, participate in the movement towards liberation of the body and the spirit?

Bruce and I began subscribing to the *Catholic Worker*, a Melbourne liberal-minded Catholic monthly with a sound reputation for independence. Through that, we heard of another publication, the *National Catholic Reporter*, an American weekly newspaper whose editorial policy was to spread the good news of Pope John's Vatican Council changes and to oppose the drafting of young people to fight in the

Vietnam war. It was from this newspaper that I got to know the story of the Berrigan brothers, Jesuit peace activists.

The Berrigans were prepared to give their lives, if necessary, to the cause of peace, and this was because they were men of God. Every anti-war activity the Berrigans and their followers embarked upon was deliberately designed to bring their message to the public in the most audacious way possible. For them, if the 'government of the people' was in essence ungodly, it was their God-given right to shout it from the rooftops.

Watching their defiance and seeing them thrown into gaol by an uncompromising US government added fuel to my growing fire. I became involved in Christian Women for Peace, where I met a number of prominent women activists, such as Dorothy McRae-McMahon, a member of the Uniting Church clergy; Anne Schlebaum, a well-known children's psychiatrist; Bridget Gilling, a public commentator with ABC television; and Noreen McDonald, a housewife-activist and the convenor of Catholics for Peace Movement. Bruce encouraged me to go to Sydney every few months to participate in the group's meetings, and the phone ran hot, even though it seemed that the monopoly telephone company, Telecom, could charge whatever they liked for phone calls, especially from the country. I was now in the thick of an extraordinary burgeoning movement; we felt as though we were all riding a huge wave to the shore of a peaceful future.

'War is not healthy for children and other living things' became our motto. My daughters and I often wore bronze pendants inscribed with this motto, to remind everyone of its significance.

At one of the Christian Women for Peace meetings, a member of the Australian Labor Party took me aside and suggested I join the party.

'We have a very active Labor Women's Forum and it's growing in influence. We need women like you from the country,' she said.

And so it was that I joined the ALP one Sunday morning after Mass in the late spring of 1965. I was standing in the sun outside the Yerong Creek weatherboard Catholic church. It was warm, the paddocks were green with lucerne and the tall wheat and oat crops promised a bumper harvest. The talk around the churchyard was not, as bush poet John O'Brien's Hanrahan might have said, 'We'll all be rooned' but, more optimistically, 'Looks like a good season, Bruce.' And then, as if not to tempt the weather gods, 'We'll need a drop or two soon to finish things off.'

Bruce knew what I was about to do and smiled as he squeezed my hand.

At that point, Mick, one of the parishioners, walked me across the culvert, bridged by two old railway sleepers, to where the cars were parked at right angles to the little church. Until very recently, the only thing I knew about Mick was that he was a member of the Catholic congregation and I had seen him on Sundays in the Driscoll pew, a bowed and wizened figure, burnt by the sun and by the hard life of a widower forced to raise six children alone. Over time, though, I realised there was something else driving him – a kind of pent-up rage.

One of my letters opposing the Vietnam war had been published in *The Sydney Morning Herald* and Mick and I began to have regular conversations after Mass on Sundays about the issues I had raised. That's how I came to know Mick better and realised he was more interested in world affairs than in farming and would have done better as a union organiser or university firebrand than as a tiller of soil and a tender of sheep. Consequently, he was not regarded – including by Frankie – as one of the most efficient farmers in the district. People's opinions of Mick's farming prowess didn't interest me; courtesy of our mutual interest in the anti-war movement, I had found a kindred spirit.

As the custodian of the local Australian Labor Party membership book, Mick reached into his coat pocket and placed it on the bonnet of his car. I fished for a pen in my handbag, then filled in the form and we both signed on the dotted line. It was now official; I was a member of the Yerong Creek branch of the ALP.

'Welcome to Australia's first lady Prime Minister,' Mick said.

'That's impossible, Mick!' I said, laughing. 'But thanks for your encouragement.'

I was mildly flattered at his faith in me.

'You have it in you, you know, Anne,' he added.

I laughed and shook my head again and then said goodbye as Vanessa came running up to me with, 'Mummy, can I go home to Debbie's place for the day?'

'If Daddy says yes,' I said.

'He does, he does,' she said, jumping up and down with excitement.

Bruce drove the three miles home and we discussed my decision while Alex, Austin and Henry in the back were absorbed with their ice-creams – a rare treat on some Sunday mornings after Mass. Rebecca was too young for ice-cream.

'Frankie won't be happy, you know, darling,' he said.

'Yes, she's already mentioned something like that to me,' I said, hoping to avoid this discussion.

For Frankie and her ilk, it was largely a class issue. I was stepping out of my class by joining this party. She worried, I suppose, that my actions might reflect on the family and maybe even damage our social standing in the district. What

I realised, though, was that I had grown beyond the girl who came teary-eyed to Fairfield's farmhouse and that complying with other people's expectations would never make me happy. I had done as much as I was prepared to in order to please her – or anyone else, for that matter – and now it was time to follow my own direction.

Frankie was not a snob in the worst sense of that word. She was universally liked and respected by everyone who knew her. She would never dream of arguing over current issues and had once told me, 'Anne, I always trust that "they"' – by which she meant people in power – 'will do the right thing.' So she was truly bewildered as to why I would want to challenge anything.

When she heard I'd joined the Labor Party, Frankie said, 'Labor is the party of unions and they go on strike all time and don't have much in common with farmers.'

But being non-combative in personality, she seemed to accept what I had done and I never heard another word from her about it.

book three

a woman of the world

Can I see another's woe
And not be in sorrow too?
Can I see another's grief
And not seek for kind relief?
　　　　　– William Blake, 'On Another's Sorrow'

27

the horse without a rider, 1965

When Rebecca was still tiny, Bruce came in from the paddock shortly before lunch and found me in the middle verandah, the long enclosed breezeway space where we did most of our living in the summer. I was going through a dressmaking phase, busy at my sewing machine, and stopped mid-seam as he lay down heavily on a divan with a sigh of distress.

'What's the matter, darling?' I asked, getting up and coming over to sit beside him.

'Annie, I feel very strange. Every time I ride Riverina Lad, my gut is in turmoil. I don't think I will be able to ride him any more. It's too uncomfortable. I have the strangest sensation here,' he said, and pointed to his abdomen.

He loved that horse Riverina Lad and rode him almost every day. Back in the wet year of 1956, Bruce and his brother Kerry had entered him in the Wagga Picnic Cup then quietly trained him on the property. 'The Lad', as they called him, was more than hot to trot on the day. But the bookies didn't know that and gave him only an outside chance, with very long odds. To the consternation of all the punters, all except the Gorman punters of course, the horse romped in easily at a hundred to one. It was a family bonanza and the horse's one moment of glory, which established him in the halls of family legend.

Although this was now ten years ago and the horse was getting old, for Bruce to not ride his champion was tantamount to deserting his best friend. Deserting your best friend is serious. We had to take action.

My response was to immediately book an appointment with our GP, Farmie Joseph, who had removed Bruce's appendix two years earlier. Maybe this was connected. At the consultation, Farmie's advice was, 'No, it has nothing to do with the appendix operation, just wait and see. It could just be a passing thing.'

But the discomfort intensified. The horse grazed riderless in the paddock and Farmie could shed no more light than we could on the problem. Finally, we decided to go to Sydney for more extensive investigations. Exhaustive medical and personal histories were taken.

Bruce had grown up among sheep, handled dead wool, mixed chemicals for sheep dip and for spraying crops and lived close to the earth. No matter that the utmost care was always taken with chemicals on the Gorman properties, all manner of disease over that time could have invaded his body.

'Could it be hydatids?' I asked one physician at Royal Prince Alfred Hospital's clinic. Hydatids are intestinal tapeworms that can, in rare cases, be transmitted from sheep to humans, so it was a possibility.

'No! If it is, I'll drop my strides in Missenden Road,' he answered heroically.

Backwards and forwards to specialist doctors we went, but Bruce's condition steadily worsened. When nearly two years had passed, we embarked on yet another round of investigations. This time, it was suggested he could be suffering from stress, caused by the debt we had incurred by buying Hills Park.

'Perhaps the strain of that is causing a problem in the gut,' said one specialist.

Although I knew this was a long shot, we had to do something. I waved Bruce and his mother goodbye as they set off to Melbourne by car to see a psychiatrist, Dr Eric Seal, who was one of Bruce's schoolfriends. He referred Bruce to a surgeon, a friend of his. The surgeon's opinion was that Bruce had 'cystic growths in the abdomen'. He could only be sure if he carried out an investigation under anaesthetic. He would call us when a hospital bed became available. Bruce and Frankie drove home the next day.

On Thursday the following week, Bruce was in the shearing shed baling up wool when the surgeon's nurse rang.

'Bruce needs to come at once. The operation will be done on Saturday morning and your husband should book into the hospital no later than Friday morning at 9.30,' she said.

The train came into Henty just on 5 am and I waved Bruce goodbye as a glimmer of light began to emerge over the hills to the east. *Cysts. That doesn't sound so bad*, I thought. *Thank goodness this illness is being nailed at last.*

The drive from Henty to Yerong Creek takes about twenty minutes. There was hope in my heart as I watched the purple and pink sunrise light up a bank of clouds made translucent by the play of the sun behind them. A flock of birds followed me along the highway, weaving from one side to the other in their mischievous play by the morning light. *All this beauty and joyfulness must be a good sign for the future. It must be!* And by the time I arrived home to see a sleepy-eyed group of children coming out to greet me in their pyjamas, I was smiling.

It was just me and the kids at home that weekend. Lynell had left us some time before, to help out at home after her father had fallen from a roof and sustained brain damage. We had been sorry to see her go but had a new helper called Debbie, a robust young woman, pleasant and willing. Debbie had gone home to Holbrook on Friday afternoon after the children came home from school.

When I hadn't heard from the surgeon by lunchtime on Saturday, I phoned the hospital.

'Mr Gorman is resting comfortably. He has come out of the anaesthetic well,' the charge sister said, but would tell me nothing more except, 'The surgeon has left for Geelong to operate there; I am sure he will ring you soon.'

I went off to play tennis with the Yerong Creek team; the children played with their friends within eyesight of the court. Frankie had moved into a little cottage near the showground at Yerong Creek just before Paul got married but was away visiting one of her children. Twice, during set breaks, I ran over to her house to use her phone, tracking the surgeon from place to place but without reaching him. Finally, that night, after the children were tucked up in bed, I rang the surgeon at his home, only to receive his curt, brutal assessment: 'I don't want to discuss this now with you, but it's not good news.'

All my in-laws were away except for Paul's wife, Wendy. She was pregnant and about a month away from giving birth for the first time. I had to speak to someone, so I rang her and she was wonderfully consoling. She was a nurse and had trained at St Vincent's Hospital in Melbourne, so I assumed she might shed some more light on what the surgeon had said to me.

'Maybe it's not as bad as you think,' she said, and in the next breath she offered to sleep at our homestead that night and generously insisted on coming to Melbourne with me on Monday morning.

I spent a sleepless night tossing and turning, hearing the 'not good news' words over and over, slicing and dicing them for a more hopeful interpretation. In the morning, I woke the children for Mass. The only one who still needed help with dressing was Rebecca, so we managed a quick getaway. *Ah! The little blessings as each child grows up a bit more*, I thought as we drove toward the small Yerong Creek church The priest gave a sermon but all I could hear were the words 'not good news' playing like a tormenting soundtrack in my head.

After Mass, we toured the property, looking for sheep that might be on their backs needing assistance to right themselves. The sheep and cattle were okay, the wheat crops and the pastures thirsty and the water troughs full, their ball cocks working. Best of all, there were no sheep stuck in the expanding mud around the edge of the dams. How long would the feed last if the rain stayed away? Another couple of weeks? Well, we'd wait and see. I had bigger things to worry about now.

28

the surgeon without a soul, 1967

After I'd had another long night without sleep, Paul pulled up with Wendy at 4.30 am to catch the train to Melbourne. At last, I was moving towards the destination – the destination that would free me from forebodings, the best news or the worst, whatever it might be.

Travelling south, the same purple and pink streaks of sunrise I saw a few mornings ago were breaking over the Bonegilla Hills outside Albury. What a contrast my feelings were now to the hope I held in my heart just three mornings ago, when I farewelled Bruce as he left for Melbourne. As early morning sunlight flooded the interior of the train, we visited the dining car, as much to pass the time as anything else. Wendy ate breakfast; I had a cup of tea. At 9.30 we arrived at Spencer Street Station and took a tram up Collins Street to a small hotel opposite the surgeon's rooms.

By 10.30, we were walking across the road, confident we would be seen straightaway. The receptionist pointed us to a waiting room on her left. Pictures of Cambridge and

Melbourne universities hung on the dark panelled walls; a small leadlight window offered a glimmer of natural light; old dog-eared magazines sat untidily on side tables, the dim light hardly conducive to reading anyway. The uncomfortable, straight-backed chairs reminded me of a convent parlour. I greeted the two people waiting to see the doctor.

'Waiting long?' I asked them.

'No, not very long,' came their reassuring reply.

I had a vision of Bruce in his hospital bed, waiting for me. He knew the train would have arrived by now and we would be in Melbourne.

An hour went by. Then another.

A steady stream of people came in and out, each being seen almost immediately. Sometimes the waiting room was empty except for us. A middle-aged man came hurrying in and spoke to the receptionist.

'Yes, Mr Smith. Your GP rang from upstairs and said he'd send you down,' she said. 'Doctor will see you right away.'

Dear God, I thought, *surely not before he sees us*. But he didn't see us.

'How long do you think it might be?' I asked the relieving receptionist when the first one went to lunch.

'Doctor will see you soon.'

'Does he know we are here?'

'Yes,' came the curt response.

Lunchtime now over, the room emptied and filled again. Here was Wendy, visibly very pregnant, sitting all day on a hard chair. I tried to persuade her to go back to the hotel and have some food and a rest, but she wouldn't go.

Two o'clock came, then three. Finally, at 3.30, I was called into the doctor's room. I should have taken Wendy with me; she would have been able to keep a cooler head, ask better questions and help contain my anger.

A tall, good-looking man in his forties sat behind his desk and nodded. 'Take a seat,' he said, motioning me to a chair opposite him on the other side of the desk.

I opened the conversation with, 'We have been waiting outside since 10.30 this morning. I'm worried because Bruce will be wondering where I am.'

My tone was meant to send a reproachful message. He appeared oblivious. He went right on, without any preliminaries.

'I'm afraid your husband has only a short time left. His abdomen is riddled with cancer. We went looking for the primary but couldn't find it. But it would have metastasised, no doubt about it.'

Here it was finally, the fearfulness of it. No more doubting the callous truth.

Clutching at straws, though, and hoping against hope, I asked, 'Is there any possibility of doubt?'

'None at all,' came the matter-of-fact response.

'How long do you think he has?'

'Oh, about three months, maybe four or five but no more. I sent the pathology tests off for analysis. They should be back by Thursday.'

He rose from his chair and went to open the door.

I didn't wait out there for five hours to be fobbed off so quickly.

'Look,' I said, staying resolutely glued to my chair, 'we have five young children. Is there no chance at all that the diagnosis might be wrong?'

He came back then and stood beside me, a tall, well-built man towering over me. I wanted to punch him in the stomach, if not the balls.

'None whatsoever,' he said, and with that he turned to the door again and opened it.

'What about chemotherapy or radiation treatment?' I asked, rising reluctantly.

'No! No!' he said, impatient with me now. 'That won't make any difference. It would make things worse. If I were you, I'd go home and help Bruce get his affairs in order.'

'Have you told Bruce this news?' I asked.

By now he had one foot in the corridor. 'No, not yet.'

'I don't think this is something I should tell him. I'd prefer for you to do it.'

'Yes,' he said. 'I'll wait for the pathology tests to come back and explain everything to him then.'

I walked by him without saying another word.

Like a sleepwalker, I made my way up Collins Street, towards the hospital. Wendy, her face anxious, was beside me. The light was fading fast and as I stepped off the footpath to cross Victoria Parade, I heard a shriek of brakes. Inches away from my knees was a silver fender. A driver's ashen face stared up at me, wide-eyed with shock. I had been moments away from death – that driver knew it and I knew it. I came quickly back to earth. The black sedan crept slowly past, the driver's eyes focusing resolutely ahead.

I hear an inner voice say loud and clear, *You are to become the only parent of five children. You must do everything you can to stay alive. Pay attention, pay attention to that!*

Wendy, who saw the car coming and was still standing on the footpath, was as shocked as I was. In that state of shaken awareness, we both walked through the hospital door and up to the airy surgical ward on the first floor.

The nurse nodded and gave us a weak smile as I pointed to Bruce's bed. He was propped up against a bank of pillows with his eyes closed, a drip attached to his arm while another tube fed him through his nose. I fought back tears and turned my head away in case he woke to see me in this state. Then we waited beside his bed until he opened his eyes.

'Hello, darling,' I said, leaning in to kiss his cheek. 'How are you feeling? We had to wait a long time for the doctor; he was very busy today. Did you see him early this morning?'

'No,' he replied. 'I don't think he's been in today.'

Then he asked the question I was dreading. 'Well? What's the verdict?'

Standing right behind me, Wendy placed her supportive hand on my back. What to do? What to say?

'Look,' I said, 'it's just a bit more complicated than we first thought. Dr Ryan is the best one to explain it all. When he comes tomorrow, perhaps he will.'

'Oh ... Oh ... Okay. I'm sure he'll be in tomorrow. I'll quiz him then,' Bruce said.

'He did tell me he would know more when the pathology tests come back on Thursday,' I said. 'The main thing for you now, darling, is to just get better and on your feet again.'

Was I convincing enough? Too evasive? *Coward!* my mind shouted. *Coward!*

A few days later, I saw the surgeon striding down the hospital corridor like God himself. I called out to him. 'Dr Ryan! Dr Ryan!'

When I got close enough to avoid making a spectacle of myself, I said, 'I'm sorry to bother you, but you said Bruce's pathology results would be back by yesterday. Do you have the results?'

He paused, dazed, as if trying to recall who this person invading his territory and personal space could possibly be. 'Ah ... ah ... ,' he muttered, collecting himself. 'Yes, yes, they confirm what I thought and what I told you to expect.'

Then quickly he turned on his heel, strode down the

polished corridor and took the steps to the next floor two at a time.

I wanted to ask him if he had explained the diagnosis to my husband. I wanted to ask him if I could see the pathology report. I wanted to know if he even knew who I was talking about. I wanted to scream with frustration at his retreating back, but I knew it would make no difference. He had ticked us off as a hopeless case and didn't want to deal with us any more.

Now he was gone and that was the last I ever saw of him. Case closed.

29

melbourne

While Bruce recovered from his operation, I stayed with his friend Bob Cuthbert, who was in the air force with Bruce, and Bob's wife, Gwen; my lovely sister-in-law and guardian angel Wendy had returned to Yerong Creek. The Cuthberts' home was in North Balwyn, a leafy suburb with late spring blossoms in evidence everywhere. Fortunately, off Bob's study, they had a small self-contained flat for guests and I stayed there, sheltered from the busyness of their domestic life. Back at Fairfield, Debbie was happy looking after the children during the week, and my sisters-in-law Barbara and Judy took them at the weekend.

 The morning trip to the hospital on the Balwyn tram took about forty-five minutes and provided me with an opportunity to compose myself after weeping half the night. My task was to cultivate a cheerful face for Bruce during the day, sometimes reading him the newspaper or the avalanche of cards and letters he began receiving once the news of his illness became known. Flowers came, too – lots of them – and Bruce insisted I take them home to the Cuthberts. We chatted about current affairs, about people, about events in our own or our extended families' lives. Yet a deep silence had developed between us. I knew that he knew, and he knew that I knew that he knew. And still, there I was, talking as if there was nothing but chitchat on my mind. At night, I rang home so that I had news of the children to tell him the next day.

'Alex is one of the angels in the school concert ... Austin scored a goal in the school finals for the season.'

'Up there, Cazaly; it looks like we have a champion on our hands.'

'No rain yet, darling. We'll be home in time for the concert. I'll do some Christmas shopping here at Myer. Any suggestions? What should we buy Frankie for Christmas?'

One of the most vivid memories I have of that time is of the day I walked down to the city to Myer, the only store I really knew, to get a few things Bruce needed. The city was decked out for Santa's arrival. Shop windows sported mountains of tinsel, their windows stuck fast with fake snow, while coloured lights blinked on and off in every window all over the city. As the displays became ever more garish, my mood became ever more anchored in despair and by the time I walked into Myer in the middle of a hot November day and heard the store's invitation to go 'dashing through the snow on a one-horse open sleigh' I wanted to scream to the heavens: 'Don't you people know what life is all about? It's about death and loss. Turn off the Christmas lights. Turn off the music. Stop the cash registers. Look at what's important.'

I bought a pair of pantyhose, still a newish invention at the time, and soap and shaving gear for Bruce. As I passed over the money and the smiling sales girl handed me the change, I wanted to ask her, 'What is your life like? Do you know sadness?

Do you know about death? Are you just thinking about your boyfriend or chasing utterly useless entertainments? Don't you know? Don't you know?' But instead, I weakly smiled back at her and walked on.

Totally absorbed in my own despair, I left the store and walked across a small laneway into the entirely different atmosphere of the city church of St Francis. Here, among the peace of the flickering candles, wooden pews, statues of saints, muted light, soft organ music, Latin prayers and priestly vestments, I was at liberty to give vent to my misery, weeping my way through Mass. I went up to communion with tears still on my cheeks; the priest stopped and looked at me before moving on. Perhaps he was giving me a blessing. I hoped so.

Having visited that place at the conjunction between life and death, there was no going back to where I was before. I was touching something deep within me, a place only those who have experienced it can really understand. I was thirty-three but, for me, something young, fresh and optimistic had died here in this city. Would it ever be reborn?

Bruce and I had spent the last almost ten years getting up in the night to one or other of the children, watching over them, reading to them, loving them together, laughing with them, snuggling up with them when they climbed into our bed for a cuddle, sharing all the fresh and funny ways they looked at the world. The future would be different. What would doing it all alone be like?

When Bruce finally left hospital and we were sitting together in the Cuthberts' little flat, I knew I couldn't put off any longer the discussion we had to have. As I opened my mouth to begin, he grabbed my arm, then my hand, and held them firmly. Turning to face me full on, he said, 'Annie, darling, I don't want to talk about this with you. All I want to say –' and he lifted his hand to my lips, thinking I was about to speak. 'Please don't say anything after I finish. You are a wonderful woman and you deserve the best. I would like to think that when I go, you will marry again and, when you do, you will choose a husband who's your intellectual equal.'

He didn't want to talk about it. No doubt, he was coming to terms with what lay ahead for him. Talking about it would only make it more real. It was clear that, from now on, the subject would be taboo.

Yet Bruce would find himself able to discuss his feelings with some of my closest friends. After a conversation that my friend Dottie Pope had with him, she told me that the thing troubling him most was the probability that he would not live to see our children grow up. He allowed himself a few tears as he said to her, 'You know, Dottie, parenthood is not always easy but many of the rewards come with watching the children grow to maturity.'

When Dottie told me that, I too wept at the thought that the long-term satisfaction and joy, worth all the effort of those early years, would be mine but not his.

It puzzled me why Bruce felt he could have these conversations with other people he trusted but not with me. Was he shielding me or himself? Was it all too close to home?

For the first time, I felt alone in my marriage. Bruce and I had always openly shared our thoughts and feelings. Arguments between us were rare. Now we were facing different futures and different challenges. One of us needed to deal with the reality of letting go of everything, and the other needed to hold on ever more tightly, so that nothing fell apart for the children while the other inevitably moved on.

I entered a time of complete focus on my husband and children, when all other considerations but their welfare were secondary. I was torn between the grief of impending loss on the one hand and needing to find the courage to endure what lay ahead on the other. Making Bruce's life bearable was the first and immediate priority. *Pray hard, Annie, pray hard,* I told myself, *just as you used to do as a child.*

30

hope

After we returned home, it took a few weeks for Bruce to feel well enough to cope with a body close to his. But we eventually resumed sleeping in the double bed together. For me, the physical closeness was a relief and helped me deal with the emotional separation that had begun in Melbourne.

There was so much to be done. So much to think about, so little time to do it – and in that mindset, I was not aware of how driven and tense I had become.

One day, after Debbie had swept the hallway linking the bedrooms at the front of the house, I noticed she'd missed cleaning a section of the floor. It was quite dirty and needed a good scrub.

'Look, Debbie. Didn't you notice these tiles? Someone must have spilled something on them,' I said, my voice a little bit too shrill, and it wasn't the first time I'd spoken to her like that.

She turned on me with some ferocity and said, 'I was coming back with a special brush to clean that section. I know you are anxious, Anne, but you don't have to take it all out on me!'

I was stunned at the courage of that young woman and, after I recovered, said, 'I'm sorry, Debbie, you are right. I have been cross and it's unfair. You held things together while we were away and I am very grateful to you.'

At that point I had to ask myself, if I was tense and cross with Debbie, who else might have been the recipient of my anxieties? From then on, when the going got tough, I would pull back and try to imagine what it must be like for Bruce, facing a death sentence. When I felt tired of holding things together, this is what would give me strength to go on supporting everyone. I constantly reminded myself to stay calm – sometimes successfully, sometimes not. My best resort was the abiding thought, *It's not about you, Annie, it's about them.*

Putting one's own needs on hold is a noble sentiment, no doubt about it. But it has its consequences. I didn't want to risk a nervous breakdown like my mother had endured and thought that by being stoic I would avoid that disaster.

At that stage, my friend Shirley was going through problems with her own husband, and one day I unburdened myself to her. She was someone who would listen to my worries and not make judgements.

'I didn't choose this, it chose me, Shirley. I never expected to be cast in the role of a Joan of Arc,' I said. 'I don't know what I expected of the future but it wasn't this. You know, I find it hard even to cry any more. It's as if I left all that grieving behind in Melbourne.'

Shirley listened to more of the same and her reassuring comments helped me put a lot of things into perspective. Talking to her made me less sorry for myself and I began to count my blessings.

Even so, somewhere deep inside me was a worm of anger that said, 'Why me?', fuelled by another idea wriggling its way to the surface: maybe the diagnosis was wrong. Maybe there was another way of dealing with all this.

I was born with a 'fix it' mentality. There was always a solution to every problem, or so I thought.

Soon after this conversation, I took a trip to Sydney to spend time with my sister Philomena and Mother. While in Sydney, I also had to see a specialist tax adviser who was developing a tax plan for us which would come into effect in the event of Bruce's death. Mother picked me up at the train station and as we drove towards Rosemont she told me her news.

'The doctors have discovered a cancerous growth in my right leg,' she said. 'Next week, after you go home, I will have to have the leg removed.'

'*The* leg', I noticed she had said. She had spoken as if she had already disposed of it. Mother was very calm, presumably because she'd known for some weeks and had come to terms with it. It was a terrible shock for me though and, in that moment, I felt my stomach turn over and I couldn't speak. This is what I always feared. Her loss. At seventy-three, she didn't deserve the agony and discomfort she was about to go through.

When Mother's leg was gone, she battled on with a prosthesis, continuing with her work in the business, although she gave up driving.

When she next came to visit us at Fairfield, the children began to learn how to help her on with her leg in the morning, although it was far from their favourite task, or mine either. But I explained to them that there were things that happened to people when they get old and things we need to do for each other, like changing dirty nappies or cleaning up after people are sick. 'It's part of life,' I said. 'It's part of supporting each other.'

As time passed, Bruce seemed to get stronger and more or less resumed his life working between both farms. The two of us made love, we all went to Sydney for beach holidays, he took the crops off and supervised shearing. He did lose weight and there were certain things he wouldn't eat any more. The food we ate at home became simple and bland. But if we went to dinner at a restaurant, I always ordered something exotic, while Bruce could continue to eat 'proper Australian fare'. He had literally become the apple pie man of my earlier imaginings.

At the same time as he lost flesh on his arms, legs and around his neck, his abdomen became more and more extended and he began to resemble a thin pregnant woman. The following summer of 1969 when we took a house at the beach, small children playing on the sand laughed and pointed at him while their parents looked the other way or tried to silence them. It was something we all became accustomed to and Bruce found ways to make jokes about it. But it wasn't only children.

With some amusement, after Mass in Henty one Sunday morning, Bruce was chuckling to himself as we climbed into the car.

'What's so funny?' I said.

'It's Frank Connors,' he answered wryly. 'He never misses an opportunity to use his "death" voice on me.'

'What did he say?'

'He came in close and peered sadly into my face and said, "How are you feeling today, Bruce?", as if I was about to drop dead on the spot. He always has some tragic story to tell me about someone dying or being diagnosed with a deadly disease. He told me about a friend who developed the same body shape as me and died recently. I think he must think he's being kind, that's what's so funny.'

'Oh, God; what can I do?' I said.

'Nothing,' Bruce replied. 'Just keep him away from me, if you can.'

'Maybe we shouldn't go to Mass at Henty,' I suggested.

'No, no. It's nothing. I just can't help laughing at him. He hasn't got a clue.'

But most people did have a clue and took it all in their stride, treating Bruce no differently than they had before.

Thank God for that because in a strange way it helped to buoy him up for the coming years, where hope lay in waiting.

Later in 1969, Bruce began visiting a cancer specialist at the Wagga Base Hospital, who came each month from Prince of Wales hospital in Sydney. I decided to go with Bruce on one of his monthly visits. That day we learned that, unbeknown to either of us, the specialist had booked Bruce in for a series of radiation sessions in Sydney, to commence the following week.

'Why is this treatment being recommended? It is so radically different to the advice we received in Melbourne,' I said to this new doctor.

The reply I received was vague and unsatisfactory.

For the first time, I demanded to see Bruce's medical notes. The specialist slid the notes across the table and pointed to Bruce's diagnosis with his index finger: Myxoma Peritonei. No one had ever mentioned that before.

'Can you tell me more about it?' I asked.

'It doesn't change anything. It's still a form of cancer we can't do much about', was his response.

My next move was to see our GP, Farmie Joseph. He cautioned me against seeking another opinion from a different specialist.

'Look, Anne, Bruce doesn't have much time to live and why would you want to prolong his agony?'

That made me angry – so incensed that I was lost for words.

When I returned home, I phoned my sister Carmel's husband, Neil, by now a professor of gastroenterology at Royal Prince Alfred Hospital. I told him about the diagnosis and the planned radiation therapy. The following day, Neil called and told me he had discussed Bruce's case with a surgeon friend of mine from university days, Miles Little.

Miles rang the next day. 'You know, Anne, I think we might have a case of misdiagnosis here,' he said. 'Bruce may not have Myxoma Peritonei but Pseudomyxoma Peritonei, a rare condition, slow to develop and it's often misdiagnosed. This disease is invariably preceded by an appendectomy in men and an ovarian cyst in women.' Then he went on to give me more details and offered to send me an article from a medical journal which might provide more information.

'Oh, my God, Miles. Bruce had an appendectomy five years ago.'

'Yes – Neil told me. I think that's it,' he said. 'Almost certainly.'

If Miles's suggestion was correct, then it appeared that radiation therapy was contra-indicated. 'It's not like an ordinary cancer,' he explained. 'Pseudomyxoma Peritonei doesn't act like most cancers, nor does it spread beyond its source or through the bloodstream or the lymphatic system. It just keeps spreading inside the abdomen as the mucus collects there, and the only way to remove it is through surgery.'

'Is that how Bruce should have been treated right from the start?'

Miles didn't reply directly to that question, choosing to focus on his suspected diagnosis: 'We will only know if Bruce comes to Sydney, we do some tests and perhaps undertake exploratory surgery. I'll cancel the radiation treatment.'

He went on to tell me, 'When treated early, people with this condition have been able to live for years.'

'Have we lost too much time in between the first diagnosis in Melbourne in 1967 and now?' I asked.

'Let's wait and see,' Miles said.

Bruce was admitted to Royal Prince Alfred Hospital for diagnostic surgery and Miles's suspected diagnosis turned out to be correct.

When he returned home, he continued working on the property as usual. We never quite knew when the build-up of mucus would determine that he would need another operation. We lived in hope but in a kind of limbo.

Some time into Bruce's new treatment, Miles informed us that a team of French researchers was working on a new drug to quell the mucus growths inside the abdomen. The optimist in me jumped for joy.

31
the deep end

Not long after our hopes had been raised by the new diagnosis and the possibilities of a new drug, we were sitting in the sunshine on the back verandah sipping tea when Bruce said, out of the blue, 'You know, Annie, you really need to develop your professional skills again. You have too much energy to inflict it all on the children. It would not be fair to them.'

Bruce was as hopeful of a cure as I was. Our priorities had shifted from preparing for death to looking toward the future.

Looking back on this conversation, as much as they contained humour, Bruce's words might also have been an attempt to make me reflect on the demands I sometimes placed on the children. In those days, I did ask a lot of them, anticipating, I think, what might lie ahead. My focus was on creating a stable life, doing everything I could to keep Bruce in good health. There was no place for chaos.

One day, Bruce, Alex and I were in Wagga sitting in a coffee shop together when I realised that I'd forgotten to pick up

Bruce's supplies from the chemist. Alex offered to go, and I gave her a large note to pay for it.

When she came back with the package and handed me the change, I realised she had been massively short-changed and scolded her for not being more careful. I went on and on about it, not noticing she was now close to tears.

Then Bruce spoke up: 'It's all right, darling. You did your best. We'll get it back from the chemist before we go home. Don't worry. Mummy is just a bit tired today.'

That little episode stayed in my mind for a long time and I was shamefaced for the part I played in it and grateful for Bruce's intervention.

There was always much to do on the farm and Bruce not only directed the work but took an active part in it – crutching, wool-classing, mustering sheep, sowing and stripping crops – in spite of his intermittent bouts of surgery, one of which came at the beginning of the next year, 1970.

The large kitchen in our house was really the centre of things. In the morning, that room resonated with anticipation for what the day would bring. The first one up in winter would light the fire in the kitchen and in summer would close every door to seal in the cool night air. As breakfast got under way, everyone crowded in to eat fruit, porridge, cereal, chops or eggs as I packed school lunch boxes.

Bruce was first out the back door while the children left by the side door to walk the one hundred yards to the school bus. This was a dangerous journey for the brief part of each year when the magpies would be out in force to protect their young. We soon solved that problem with hats and sticks. They looked like an advancing army as they made their way together to join the bus, leaving a small pile of weapons beside the mailbox for the return advance against the 'maggies' in the afternoon.

The kitchen again was usually the place the children would find me then, and we would swap stories of how the school day had been and the homework set for the night. As in any good rural household, a new invention called Tupperware would emerge from the cupboard; the biscuits and cakes stashed inside would satisfy the children's hunger until dinner. Then they'd be out the door saying, 'Where's Dad?', running to the shed to find him.

Bruce delighted in having the children around him and they took an active part in the farming operation after school, at weekends and during school holidays: rounding up sheep, pulling lambs out of their mothers, and handing up those same lambs to him at lamb-marking time, or steering the ute while he fed fodder out the back to the waiting sheep. From the time they were six or seven, they all learned to steer a car or ute around the property. Bruce also took endless trouble to teach his sons and daughters about the reasons he did things the way he did and the changing circumstances of life on the land.

It was a busy life, especially when children were sick or there was some other emergency, like a cow having trouble calving. There would be a visit from the vet, car headlights shining on the distressed and noisy cow, and maybe a dead calf at the end of it – those were days that never ended.

All of us managed to survive. How I sometimes wondered. The answer might lie in the fact that both Bruce and I were good sleepers. When things looked grim, I, for one, adhered to this rule: never make a decision at night; often the decision at night to do something was different to what it would be in the morning after a good night's sleep.

I would fall into bed – some nights utterly exhausted – and curl into Bruce's warm body as he put his arms around me. Occasionally, I would allow myself to wonder what it would be like to lie there alone in that bed after he was gone but quickly put the terror of it back into its box, slamming the lid tightly shut.

The emotions I had briefly experienced so intensely at Bruce's first diagnosis settled into a low-level extension of that pain as I learned to live with uncertainty. While the ebullient me was on sabbatical leave, I learned to live with a kind of numbness. I remember one night wishing I could simply crawl under a stone until this was all over. But what would 'over' mean? Bruce's death, a cure or some long slow debilitation?

Only much later would I realise that I was parking my feelings out of sight, in dark corners, so the pain of it all would not stop me from functioning. After all, I had to get up in the morning, make the porridge, fill five lunch boxes and get the children onto the school bus on time.

Living with fear of the future is never easy, least of all for a natural optimist. Regardless of evidence to the contrary, I never expect misfortune to come my way. The worm that had prompted me to act and obtain a revised diagnosis was still there, of course. But now there was a Mack truck in the way blocking my progress. Moving on, my favourite way of coping, was not remotely possible. That would be to deny the reality staring me in the face every day of the week. I was stuck, and resigned to being stuck for a long time.

And then something remarkable happened. Bruce cornered me one day as I reorganised the bookshelves in the living room and told me to sit down because he wanted to talk about something serious. Then he fetched a cup of tea for each of us.

'Now, Annie,' he began. 'Remember what I said to you about needing to take up your profession again? Well, I've been thinking. You are a woman who has much to give to the world.'

At that, I must have looked surprised.

'Don't tell me you don't want to,' he said.

I had been volunteering with a group of about twenty women in Wagga who had decided to establish what they called a 'Good Samaritan' service but didn't want to go much further without some professional help.

'Some of those people in Wagga you've been meeting with want you to do some work in Wagga. Paid work, I mean,' Bruce continued. 'One of them asked me if you would agree to it. You need to take up that offer if it arrives – and I need you to.'

Wow, this was something new. Something worth thinking about. It was also a bit terrifying.

From the moment of that conversation in the living room, I realised Bruce knew something that I didn't. He understood that the key to my survival as a resilient wife and mother lay, paradoxically, outside the family. And it wasn't long before the opportunity he mentioned arrived on my doorstep.

It was clear for anyone who had eyes to see that regional areas had more people living in poverty than the city. To make matters worse, they didn't have services to alleviate the effects of poverty. The Good Samaritan women thought they could go some way to closing this gap. The group had encountered families in dire need of assistance. There was family violence and a degree of poverty as bad as any I had come across in Sydney. And the Good Samaritans had discovered, to their shock, that child abuse was lurking just beneath the surface of all levels of society in Wagga. Over the years, as the extent of child sexual abuse has become better understood, as a society we have developed a deeper understanding of its corrosive effects. It is now out in the open and receiving greater attention and there is no longer any excuse for turning a blind eye or for failing to protect children from abuse. Our Wagga group was in the vanguard of that development.

The main obstacle we faced in tackling the issues of being 'Good Sams' was the attitude of the local council. Basically, they were only concerned with showcasing Wagga as a perfect place to live and they didn't want to know about the dark side.

It followed that if everything was wonderful, there was no need to establish services for those who didn't fit the required citizen mould. Outcasts would always remain outcasts and would be shipped out of town as quickly as possible. I once asked one of the city fathers why we never saw Aboriginals in the town.

'We have done well with that,' he said. 'I'm pretty friendly with the head of the police force here. They appreciate our way of thinking about this problem. The minute they show their faces around here, we move them on. That way, we tackle the problem before it develops.'

'Where do they go?' I asked.

'We don't care really, but Cowra can keep them, or Leeton and Griffith.'

Since becoming a wife and mother, I had been out of the workforce for ten or more years. Yet I had kept up my membership of the Social Workers Association and remained in touch with new developments and people working in the field. In this respect, I knew I was more equipped than the volunteers, reminding myself of the old saying, 'In the valley of the blind, the one-eyed man is king.'

Although I was not averse to jumping in at the deep end, I knew I would need back-up. My friend Elspeth, who by now had a job as a lecturer in the Social Work Department at the University of New South Wales, became a kind of mentor.

While other councils in New South Wales were building community centres, I began work as a community social worker in a back room of an old hut set aside by the council for its senior citizens. The location spoke volumes about what the council thought of their Wagga elders. The army surplus-to-requirements building sat well away from the centre of town beside the Murrumbidgee River. How people were supposed to get there without a car or survive the heat in that metal building seemed to be nobody's business. I had to compete with senior citizens' activities such as bingo and community singing, so after a few months, the Good Samaritan women found me an alternative office in the centre of town.

I spent my small wage on a car of my own – a small red Renault, a symbol of my newfound independence. Although the council had provided a stipend to pay me for three days a week, tucked away in the Nissan hut with the uncomplaining 'olds', they believed they would never hear from the Good Samaritans again. But as we all began to discover the true extent of unmet need in the community, we started to pressure the council to take more responsibility. Other councils in suburban areas had begun to employ community development officers and set up community centres. We wondered why Wagga hadn't heard about what was happening elsewhere.

Not surprisingly, we met resistance, especially from the town clerk and the chief engineer, whose bonuses were tied to capital works. The higher the expenditure, the bigger their bonuses. Their mantra became, 'There were no problems in this town until we had a social worker telling us what to do.' And the mayor and other aldermen and -women backed them to the hilt.

Our genteel and polite approaches got nowhere. A head-on campaign seemed to be the only way forward. Over our first twelve months in operation, we built community support. We approached Peter Matthews from a group called Australian Frontier, who agreed to run a community program called 'Visioning for the Future'. Over an eight-month period, a thousand people participated in neighbourhood group discussions focusing their minds on the question of what they might like the future to look like for their city.

When the groups had finished their work and their deliberations were collated into a report, the results were presented to a large public meeting and were published in the paper. It was found that a significant proportion of the population wanted to be more closely involved in planning. They also wanted the city to provide better facilities, especially for families with children. A new hospital that had long been planned and promised by politicians was high on the list as well as psychiatric and psychology services, which were sadly lacking. It was suggested that a facility be set up for people from the rural countryside – a place to rest or take care of their babies during their visit. It was also thought that Wagga needed to become more welcoming to newcomers: to shift the focus of planning from building big monuments to meeting people's needs. Most supported the appointment of a community social worker or some special person to implement the changes. None of these proposals seem earth-shattering now, but they were a shock to council in that era.

Peter and I went to see with the mayor and town clerk and presented them with a copy of the report.

'Look,' said the town clerk, 'we're not interested in this kind of thing. "The community", whatever that is, can come up with all sorts of newfangled ideas but who is going to pay for them?' The mayor nodded in agreement.

'This isn't a wish list,' said Peter. 'It's just a set of ideas, many of which don't cost money at all but require a different way of looking at possible futures for the city. The futures that are fast approaching for a forward-looking city like Wagga.'

'We were voted into our positions because the people of Wagga thought we were doing a good job. We continue to operate on that basis,' said the mayor.

'Maybe this report might help some of your councillors with new ideas,' Peter continued very evenly. 'When you read this report, you might see something you want to know more about. This is just what the community thinks. It's nothing more or less than that.'

The conversation was interrupted by the mayor's secretary with a cup of tea. Then there was silence and we felt frozen out. There was nothing for it but to drink our tea, eat our Arnott's biscuit and leave as quickly as possible.

As time went on, many residents began to show their faces in the visitors' seats at council meetings. There was no doubt they were coming as activist–observers. I was there, too, for some of these meetings.

The council was at a loss to know how to handle this unexpected change in community interest. Nothing like this had ever happened before. Good Samaritan women, inspired largely by their need to follow the Gospels' admonitions of kindness, were one thing, a community uprising entirely another.

The local newspaper and radio station had come out in support of the report's recommendations. This was less than positive publicity for council, who saw me as the chief protagonist, although by now I was more a shadowy figure in the background because Bruce's health was declining and most of my concerns were focused on him and the children.

the country wife

One day, a letter of dismissal from the council arrived in our letter box at the Yerong Creek Post Office. Since council had been subsidising the Good Samaritan organisation, they thought they had a right to dismiss me. I appealed to the Australian Association of Social Workers for support. A compliant organisation, with little stomach for conflict, they did nothing until my friend Elspeth 'inspired' them to send a well-worded letter to council – no doubt penned by Elspeth herself. She sent me a copy of the letter, which carried an implied threat of action against the council and gave a spirited defence of my professional integrity.

The mayor called me, apologised for the dismissal letter and invited me and Mrs Bingham, the president of the Good Samaritan group, to the next council meeting so they could apologise personally.

The meeting was filled with supporters as well as a journalist from the newspaper. When item two came up on the agenda, the mayor stood to attention and invited me and Mrs Bingham to approach him. He looked down upon us from the safety of his raised dais.

'Mrs Gorman and Mrs Bingham,' he said, 'the council herewith withdraws the letter dated the second of June, sent to the Good Samaritans and to Mrs Gorman, revoking the employment of the community social worker. We wish to apologise to both of you for the contents of that letter. We are reinstating the funds to continue with Mrs Gorman's employment and wish to thank you for the good work that you have both done.'

With that, he held out his hand. I thought he might topple over in front of us. Both Mrs Bingham and I stood on tiptoe, shook his hand and then the gallery erupted into applause.

Why, in that moment, did I feel as though I had lost, even though I had won? This was a strange feeling. Although I had been vindicated, I still felt I my reputation had been tarnished. The other strange thing was I began to doubt myself. Had I been wrong to stir up so much trouble? Was it the right thing to do? Even if I'd wanted to – which I didn't – it was too late to turn the clock back.

The community had woken from its slumber and a powerful group who supported the Australian Frontier project – but were more numerous and feistier than the Good Samaritans – had been formed to carry on the work begun in the Senior Citizens Centre two years before.

Bruce would soon need another surgical intervention, so I retired, leaving it to my successors, the people who were inspired to carry these issues forward.

Four months later, at the next council elections, the existing council was thrown out, a new mayor, who had participated in the Australian Frontier project, was voted in, and the council recruited a full-time social worker from Sydney.

32

academia

One Saturday morning, we travelled about fifteen miles to another property for a barbecue. There we sat in a beautiful outdoor setting, the men in their moleskin trousers and V-neck pullovers, and the wives looking our best in pleated skirts and matching twin-sets. Here was Bruce among his own. As usual, he sipped a glass of wine and was happy talking about the current season and local politics. The children had a great day; I helped with the salads in the kitchen while catching up on local gossip. On our return home, though, Bruce suddenly went straight to the bedroom and lay down, while I began the children's bath routine.

Then I heard him calling, 'Annie, come quickly.' Straightaway, I sprinted up the hall into the bedroom. 'Look,' he said, lifting up his shirt and pointing to the sticky goo oozing from a hole in his abdomen resulting from the pressure of the accumulating mucus.

'Don't move,' I said and ran to get a dressing to cover the wound.

I could hear squealing and splashing going on in the bathroom as Henry, aged nine, tormented his seven-year-old sister, Rebecca, while Alex, now twelve, tried to arbitrate. Henry's antics stopped when I poked my head in the door. I was in no mood to let him get away with it, so out he came wrapped in a towel and was sent to his bedroom.

'Put on you pyjamas immediately, Henry. I don't want to hear from you again tonight,' I said sternly. I knew, of course, it would make no difference but one had to take a stand.

I rang a local Wagga surgeon. He and his wife were the 'bright young things' of Wagga's social life and my call had interrupted their entertaining.

'Don't worry, it can wait. Come to see me on Monday,' said the surgeon.

I knew immediately this was bad advice so I called Miles at his home in Sydney.

'I don't want to take a risk with an open wound like that. It could trigger an infection. Have you covered the wound with a sterile dressing?' he said.

'Yes, as best I can,' I replied.

'Okay then, I'll ring the air ambulance. You get Bruce to Wagga airport. Let me know when it takes off and I'll have an ambulance at Sydney airport and be at the hospital to meet him. We might have to operate tonight.'

Frankie came out to sit with the children. I read the children the riot act, served them boiled eggs and toast and packed Bruce's suitcase. Then I drove him to the waiting air ambulance outside Wagga. Around ten o'clock, I received a call from Miles. Bruce had arrived safely.

'It's as I thought,' he said. 'We will operate tonight. We can't take a risk with an open wound like this. There's always the risk of an infection.'

On Monday, I drove to Sydney to join Bruce. He had come through the operation well and surgery had relieved the pressure on his abdomen.

Miles told me that the French researchers were making progress on the development of a drug to kill off the rogue cells. Some of Bruce's cells had been sent to France and we hoped they would arrive in a good enough condition to help the researchers make the hoped-for progress; his was a rare disease.

When I arrived home a week later and looked in the message book we kept beside the phone, I saw that Dr Cliff Blake, the head of the newly created Riverina College of Advanced Education, wanted to see me. Up I drove to Wagga the next day and knocked on his office door at the college.

'Would you consider coming on staff to develop a new course for welfare workers?' he asked, and then continued, in a highly persuasive tone, 'Mrs Gorman, I believe you are just the person to do this for us.'

His offer didn't altogether surprise me, since while I'd been the community social worker, Cliff had asked for my help in assessing the merits of providing campus or off-campus accommodation for his college students.

Excited, I rang Bruce, who was out of hospital recuperating with Phil at Rosemont.

'Well, Annie,' he said, 'of course you must take it. It sounds better to me than that last job you took with the Good Sams.'

So I said yes to Cliff and began work the next week, beginning my new career teaching students in the Faculty of Education while designing a new course for degree accreditation by the Higher Education Board.

In 1967, the creation, more or less at the same time, of a number of new regional colleges by state governments to provide many country areas with regional opportunities for vocational education had resulted in an acute shortage of academics in Australia. Cliff was proactive in filling his places and was even successful in getting accreditation for two degree courses in the time I was there. He was not only adept at finding local talent but also at recruiting academics from America, where he had completed his own doctoral studies.

Coming with them in their suitcases was the peace and flower-power revolution that inhabited campus life all over America. The mixing and mingling of so many strangers was accelerated by the provision by the college of an abundant supply of fresh scones in the staff common room every morning. No one missed these occasions and it achieved the desired effect.

Because I was new to teaching and didn't carry the burden of too much old theory, I embraced the company of those American newcomers. Consequently, my intellectual horizons quickly expanded beyond my boundaries on the farm and fed my own set of values. All of a sudden, here I was working with people prepared to share their knowledge of the latest thinking in education and the humanities, academics with diverse views and a largely liberal approach to life. It was so different working in this atmosphere after my time with the council. I felt appreciated, valued and I was making fabulous new friends.

There were liberal term breaks coinciding with school holidays. When I wasn't teaching or interviewing students, I worked at home, close to Bruce and the children. An ideal solution for a working mother with an ailing husband. Lynell had returned to be our helper as Debbie had married and moved away and Lynell's father had gone into permanent care. She had become more a daughter than a helper; I knew I could trust her implicitly and the children adored her.

Our students hailed from all points north, south, east and west of Wagga's hinterland – from towns such as Albury, Lockhart, Tumbarumba, Tumut, Temora, Junee and Griffith. These young men and woman were, for the first time, being offered a chance at an education close to home in affordable accommodation. For most of them, their education was free because they signed up to a two-year bond to work in the school system, wherever they were sent.

It was my job to open their minds to new ways of viewing the world beyond the narrow confines of their rural environments. Many of them had never read a newspaper and if anything, the *Women's Weekly* had been the most stimulating reading in their homes.

As I began my first day, teaching a course called First Principles in Education, I looked across the lecture room at the seventy assembled fresh-faced school leavers and a smattering of mature-aged men and women, some around the same age as me, thirty-seven.

'What are the current major issues facing Australian education at the moment?' I asked.

A few mature-aged students were prepared to have a go at this. 'Insularity, the tyranny of distance,' one of them offered.

'Poverty and the third world,' said another.

'Illiteracy.'

'Communism and the red menace,' suggested another. I knew there would be a Santamaria supporter as part of this class.

'All right,' I said. 'Let's talk about a couple of these today then. Are any of these issues likely to pose a challenge for you as teachers in the classrooms of the future?'

From that day forwards, I continued asking the class

to discuss the relevance such issues might have for them as teachers of young children. If we were discussing literacy, for example, we might first look for the statistics on literacy in Australia. At that time, twenty per cent of the adult population of Australia was illiterate.

'Why might this be so?' I asked. What were the life chances for a child leaving school if they couldn't read or write? As teachers, what could they do about it?

Many of them had opinions and gradually became eager to express them. Now I knew I had engagement and they would learn within the atmosphere of a free flow of ideas.

As new friendships grew with the other staff, our social gatherings began to morph into quite different affairs than the barbecues and dinner parties Bruce and I attended with our rural friends. Bruce enjoyed meeting these new people as much as I did. Here was Sandy from California in colourful kaftans and his partner, Barbara, sporting different native American headgear every day.

There was Denis, the charming education lecturer playing endless tracts of Bob Dylan's music.

Tony became my dearest friend. His wife, Linda, opened a shop in the main street of Wagga selling Indian cheese-cloth dresses and the wonders of all things Balinese. She did very well indeed as the population took to the never before seen exotic fare. What a pair they made: Linda, whose retail background meant she never stopped talking, and Tony entertaining us on our back verandah with Indian philosophy or jokes, generating enormous hilarity around the barbecue table.

One evening, when Bruce was in Sydney recovering from another operation, I attended a dinner party along with Tony and Linda. The night was warm and the food abundant with delicious dishes new to my palate: corn fritters, barbecued pork with honeyed sauce, mixed bean salad and berry upside-down cake. That night, I was introduced to the wonders of pot smoking and I was a willing participant in this initiation. I had no qualms at broadening my education.

It was the best stuff, smoked out of a water pipe, and in no time I was lounging in a beanbag off my face and laughing hysterically at Tony's jokes, even when they weren't that funny. We talked long into the night, and I fell asleep in the beanbag. As the sun came up, I cautiously made my way onto the Olympic highway. And there it was, a more brilliant sunrise than I had ever seen before, lighting the face of The Rock Hill with pink, purple and orange iridescence. I had a delicious feeling of oneness with a new universe.

It took a few days before the full effect of the drug wore off. I didn't smoke any more after that but now I understood the attraction.

33
an out-of-body experience

At the beginning of 1970, Alex, who would turn twelve in June, had gone to Sydney to board at my old school, Kincoppal-Rose Bay, where the flying boats still took off every day. She was pretty miserable to start with. Her letters home conveyed, in no uncertain terms, precisely how dreadful she felt.

When she came home for Easter and the May school holidays, she said she didn't want to go back. But I drove to Sydney with her, spoke to her dormitory mistress and was reassured that most of the time she seemed quite happy.

Alex's teary letters home continued. 'See the tears on this page,' she wrote. 'I walk up to the school for breakfast in the morning, no one walks with me and I'm all by myself.'

'I think we should bring her home,' I said to Bruce. 'She could go to Wagga on the bus.'

'Give it more time,' he replied. 'I was like that when I first went to boarding school. But I was never game to mention it in my letters home. At least we know she isn't bottling it up.'

He was right to delay a rescue plan because the next letter we received was totally different.

'I have made a friend called Belinda and we walk to breakfast together every morning,' read the letter, and she happily recounted all the other good things that seemed to be happening.

The cancer that had claimed Mother's leg eventually went to her lungs. Her condition deteriorated, and when Phil called to tell me she had only a few more days to live, I immediately booked a seat on the first plane out of Wagga the next morning. My suitcase was on the bed. I was ironing a dress to pack when the phone went at ten o'clock that same night.

'Mother has died peacefully behind her oxygen mask,' said Phil. 'Her lungs have finally given out. I thought she might live a bit longer. So sorry, Anne.'

Now there would be a funeral, which meant we would all take off for Sydney by car the next morning. As we drove along the all-too familiar highway, I had time to allow the tears to flow. That is when I was struck by how much Mother really meant to me, with all her strengths and weaknesses.

The family gathered to send her off. Phil invited us to stay and for Bruce and me to sleep in Mother's bed, where she had died the night before. It seemed like a sacrilege but in another way it brought me close to her. Her spirit was still there and I couldn't forget the times I had slept with her as a child and she had protected me from my dreams.

In that moment, I knew that I loved her more now than I did then. My love was tinged with regret about how much I sometimes resented her as a child – resented her for leaving us as children and being older than my friends' parents, who were young and did fun things with them; resented the fact she cooped us up in a flat and didn't buy a city house for us. But still, there was no way in the world I could have thanked her enough for providing my two sisters and me with such a splendid education and for passing on the values of love, kindness and generosity, plus everything else in between.

The church was full to overflowing and there were flowers in abundance. Among the mourners were all her children except Jack and Allan, twenty-five of her grandchildren, our teachers from Rose Bay, priest and nuns, the friends and neighbours Mother had generously helped over the years and all her spiritual buddies from the parish.

Much was said in her praise, songs were sung and then we made our way to the cemetery at North Head on this beautiful calm sunny winter's day while the navy blue ocean gently rolled in to provide a fitting salute to this woman. All these years after his death, she would be reunited in one grave with her husband; now the two of them would bask beside one of the most magnificent ocean views in the world.

Each of us filed past the coffin placing a rose on its shiny wooden top as it was slowly lowered into the hole prepared for it. Vale Christina Ellen Donovan, July 1970.

The following school year began with Austin's start as a boarder at Riverview College Lane Cove. We had our usual beach holiday at Avalon on the Palm Beach peninsula and at the end we all went straight from there to install Austin in his new school. Judy and Kerry's son Andrew, who was the same age as Austin, was starting school there, too. They had grown up together, went to school at Yerong Creek on the school bus together, and had been friends since birth. They were placed in the same class and slept in the same dormitory. All of us were relieved and happy for both of them.

After we had all made a tour of the school and said goodbye to Austin, we drove to the other side of the harbour and deposited Alex at Rose Bay, where the squeals and hugs from her friends put my mind at rest. She was now a veteran.

Around ten months later, Bruce once again went to hospital for a surgical attempt to control the rapid growth of mucus in his abdomen. It was his fourth operation since the initial one in Melbourne, four years previously.

Walking through big double doors at the hospital's professorial unit, I found Bruce across the corridor from two men sitting up enjoying their morning-tea biscuits. Bruce lay with his eyes closed, his post-operative drips once again pumping new life into him.

It was now 1972, and a year had passed since I had accepted the position at the CAE. I was enjoying the life of an academic and the new friends we were both making among the staff. Another lecturer had offered to take my classes while I took off for Sydney to be at Bruce's side.

I stood for a moment beside my beloved husband's bed, looking down at his tranquil face. Within minutes, he opened his eyes, sat up with some effort and began to speak to me in an animated whisper. His eyes were wild, like I had never seen them before, as if he'd had some kind of a vision. And indeed he had.

'I was lying here last night after I'd come back from the operating theatre,' he said, 'and suddenly I was out of my body, floating above the bed, looking down on myself lying here with all these tubes attached.'

Then he described how, in this weightless, painless and unattached state, he had moved around the ward and had read the charts of patients on the other side of the corridor.

'It was so liberating,' said Bruce. 'I felt powerful, as if it was the beginning of some new life. How could it be, Annie, that I was able to be free like that? It was like those dreams of flying I used to have. Only this time it wasn't a dream, it was really happening. Then I heard the sister coming and knew I couldn't shock her with my flying apparition so I returned to my sleeping body, where I had left it. What do you think it means, Annie? A cure perhaps?'

'Anything's possible. Maybe … yes,' I said, hedging my bets.

He was still in the experience and wanted to talk about it. Although taken aback, I was absolutely in no doubt about its reality for Bruce. There's so much we don't understand about death, dying and out-of-body experiences. Episodes like this occurred in novels, mostly about people in crisis, like soldiers, floating above their wounded bodies as they were being carried off the battlefield. So what Bruce told me that day, although a bit 'way out', was at least familiar.

When I mentioned the episode to Miles during the afternoon, he looked thoughtful. Unbeknown to me, this 'out-of-body experience' was a turning point. Some remarkable changes had begun. Changes I could never have anticipated.

Miles wanted Bruce to stay in Sydney for a while longer. He was getting weaker and Miles had referred him to both a physician and a psychiatrist to see what else could be done for him. If Bruce went home, he would not be well enough to work.

My eldest sister, Phil, had inherited the apartment at Rosemont from Mother at her death. Our family home since I was seven was now to become a refuge for my husband. Phil was happy to have him and she was the right person to give him the care he needed. It was ironic, really. She had been witness and supporter of my doubts about marrying Bruce the night before our wedding. We never referred to my pre-marriage doubts ever again, and over the years as she got to know him better, it was clear her doubts had been as short-lived as mine. She really loved him for the person he was.

The year's work at the college was nearly complete. The welfare course I'd designed and run had been awarded degree status and I had been promoted to a new position and elevated to a higher salary level. All I had to do now was deal with a pile of end-of-year assignments.

Excitingly, the federal election campaign had begun and I became involved in Labor's 'It's Time' campaign. We were anticipating a Labor victory after twenty-three years in Opposition. With Bruce away, I did voice-overs for radio ads, involved the children in handing out leaflets around Henty and The Rock and supported the ALP candidate, Kevin Esler, who because he lived at Tumbarumba on the fringes of the electorate, needed a more central spot to work from. He set up headquarters at Fairfield and took me and sometimes the children, doorknocking with him on his forays around the electorate.

Meanwhile, back in Sydney, Bruce had embarked on his own personal reinvention. He began to make plans for the future. His immediate dream was to stage a nativity play in Fairfield's front garden. I could hear the excitement in his voice when he rang me one night to announce that our niece Caroline would be cast in the role of the Virgin Mary. She would come into the garden on Penny, the children's small Welsh pony. 'Better still,' he said, 'I'll see if we can get a donkey.'

'Oh, no,' I reassured him, 'I'm sure Penny will do fine; we don't need a donkey.'

'The other thing, Annie, is Austin. He will play the role of Joseph and lead Penny into the garden. We can have invitations printed for the neighbours to join us and, Annie, you need to organise a small choir to sing throughout the pageant. They will be assembled on the verandah and I suggest devotional Christmas hymns, not your Seekers or Abba songs.'

He was joking of course, about The Seekers and Abba, but there was a manic edge to his voice.

Caroline was bemused. She was in Sydney at boarding school and, at sixteen, was two years older than Alex. She had come out of school for the weekend with Alex and was staying with my sister Joan when we talked on the phone about her discussion with Bruce.

I tried to reassure her. 'It's okay, darling. I don't think this is going to happen. But it will be lovely if it does. I think Uncle Bruce won't be well enough for it to go ahead. Let's wait and see how things unfold.'

Not content with organising a pageant, Bruce had other plans, most of which involved buying sprees. He had several expensive suits and shirts made at one of the best tailors in Sydney. For a man who showed so little interest in fashion, this was a big reversal in character.

I didn't say anything to discourage him. It was his money and he'd never spent much of it on himself. As he described to me his visits to the tailor, I had visions of the measurements they would be taking. An extended stomach, pencil thin arms, shrunken shoulders with no meat on his bones – what a challenge it must have been for them.

On his daily walks around Woollahra, he approached an architect supervising the demolition of a heritage home; a group of new townhouses was to be built on the site.

'What have you got planned for those iron gates?' asked Bruce.

'We haven't thought about it at this stage,' replied the architect.

'Well, I would be a buyer if they were ever for sale.'

'Okay,' said the architect, 'I'll take your details and get back in touch with you in a couple of months. As far as I know, no one else is laying claim to them.'

'Annie,' he said to me on the phone, 'those gates will be part of Fairfield's rejuvenation. I know just where we can put them.'

'How much do you think we will have to pay for them?' I asked, picturing the twenty-feet-tall and twenty-feet-wide antique gates standing in the middle of the paddock.

'Don't worry about that. I will do a deal when we know they're available.'

But I did worry. How far would all this go? Where would it end up? Grand suburban iron gates fronting a bush homestead. So different to the iron gate into the old cow paddock I had constructed so many years before. Ridiculous. But I said nothing.

Most disturbing of all were the conversations he was having with our eldest son, Austin, who was a sensitive twelve-year-old in his first year at Riverview. Bruce made an arrangement for Austin to ring him every night and Phil overheard some of these conversations.

'Austin, you are, after me, the head male of the family. It is your duty to carry on the family traditions when I'm gone', was the tenor of the conversations. Bruce instructed him about how to run the property and burdened him with a host of other expectations.

Now I know that all this was the last throw of the dice for a man who knew his life was coming to a close. Medically, we knew that was indeed the reality. The French research team still had a long way to go; Bruce was not going to be the beneficiary of their research.

After Bruce's out-of-body experience that night following his last surgery, an extraordinary thing seemed to have happened. He had gained a sense of omnipotence, yet behind the omnipotence there lurked another need. A need to imagine a different future to the one he was now facing.

Six weeks before Christmas, Bruce returned home and then it was time for him to pay the price for his exhilaration. One of the common attributes of manic behaviour is that when the mania dies, it leaves behind a deep hole of depression. That is what happened to Bruce. Descending from the highs he had been on in Sydney, he crashed. There were days when he found it impossible to get out of bed. Fortunately, the arrival of Austin and Alex – home from boarding school for the holidays – provided him with a reason to rally and he moved into an enthusiastic phase again.

One morning, I watched Bruce walk slowly across from the house to the machinery shed in the blistering heat, his old battered white cricket hat sitting firmly on his head. I knew the effort must be costing him. Yet I did not try to stop him. The last thing he needed was to be treated like an invalid.

Before Bruce came home, I'd placed an advertisement in the local paper for a farmhand, so our next priority was to interview the applicants. On one of Bruce's up days, we both interviewed them together, and in the end Bruce made the decision: 'I believe Phillip is our man. What do you think, darling?'

I liked Phillip. All of twenty-eight years old, he came from a family of six boys, all brought up by his father on a property near Griffith, eighty miles west of Yerong Creek, in the irrigation area. To me, he seemed like a copy of the quintessential bush Aussie worker. He was tall, lean and strong-looking, with a ready smile and a gift of the gab. He talked himself into our job – there was nothing, seemingly, he could not do – and gave both Bruce and me confidence that he could handle the job on offer.

'Yes,' I agreed. 'He's young, strong, keen and with a nice wife and two young children. And he likes the house in the village we're offering.'

We had signed a long-term lease on a place so we would have accommodation for a farmhand. Providing housing was certainly a big advantage in attracting suitable workers.

I began to prepare for what I feared might be our last Christmas together. The girls and I drove to Wagga to do our Christmas shopping while Austin and Henry stayed with their father to help him on the property. The yo-yo of Bruce's highs and lows continued. At the same time, I could see his physical health was failing.

When I had picked up Bruce to bring him home, because Miles suggested it would be a good idea to speak to the psychiatrist myself about Bruce's current condition, I took the opportunity then to visit him at the hospital. During the interview, he began to focus on some of the issues that I might be facing.

'You experienced,' the psychiatrist told me, 'what is known as premature grieving when you wept yourself to sleep in Melbourne after Bruce's first operation. You had let him go, to ease the pain of his final death.

'But Bruce did not die,' he went on, 'and because you had already grieved for his passing, you began to build a new life for yourself. In any case, that was what he wanted you to do. As time went on, though, I believe he wanted to reverse the situation. Yet the realist inside him knew that wasn't possible.

'Obviously, too,' he continued, 'Bruce is now suffering from the knowledge that his own time might be fast approaching and he doesn't want to let go. His highs and lows are linked somehow with these two conflicting pulls and pushes.'

Just like my mother all those years before, Bruce and I had developed seemingly sane reactions to an insane situation.

34
the rhythm interrupted

'Annie, get me out of here. I feel terrible' was the first thing Bruce said to me as we sat on the side of the bed together holding hands. He had been in the Caritas psychiatric hospital in Sydney, just up from St Vincent's Hospital, for two nights and now looked utterly miserable. Outside, it was stiflingly hot and humid and even more so in the ward he shared with four other patients.

I had to use some assertive language to get the sister in charge to ring the psychiatrist. After I spoke to him on the phone, he was there within fifteen minutes. It took a few seconds for him to realise Bruce was dangerously dehydrated. An ambulance was called and he was admitted to the casualty department of St Vincent's, well past the need for psychiatric treatment, if indeed he ever really needed it.

After Christmas, which had been a lovely occasion for Bruce and the children, his optimism had returned. We had engaged two students to help us through the harvest – Michael, a mature-aged agricultural student, and Julie, one of my students, who was to be our helper for a few months. Phillip and Michael had taken the crops off, and Bruce had orchestrated everything from the sidelines, 'just like my father, the gentlemen farmer, used to do,' he laughingly said.

He decided we should all go off to the beach for a holiday and booked the house we had taken the year before. Thinking ahead, I cleaned out the fridge, making sure everything had been put away ready for our return and planning what to take for seven people, including Julie. Bruce was busy leaving instructions for Phillip, our farmhand, and Michael.

Two nights before we were due to leave, Bruce's breathing became quite laboured and he started coughing violently. Then the realisation hit me: he was in no fit state to make the 350-mile journey by car to Sydney, let alone stay at a beach house outside Sydney for three weeks.

Waving him goodbye at the Wagga airport as he boarded an air ambulance, I had a sense of foreboding that this might be Bruce's last plane trip to Sydney.

The medical team, including the psychiatrist, convinced that his current health problems were associated with his mental highs and lows, immediately admitted him to Caritas.

I cancelled the holiday house and, with Julie's help, packed up the station wagon and took to the road with Julie and the children on board. Many times we had done this trip in summer, leaving at 4 am to avoid the worst heat of the day, though our new Holden now had air-conditioning.

We booked into a serviced apartment not far from the hospital. The children stayed with Julie and spent time in the apartment's pool and watched television, while I went to the hospital.

Once Bruce had been transferred to the casualty department of St Vincent's, I sat with him until Miles arrived to assess the situation.

the country wife

'Bruce, you should stay here tonight until you're stabilised, and in the morning we'll transfer you back to Royal Prince Alfred Hospital, where I'll see you again tomorrow.'

'Hear that, darling?' I said after Miles had gone. He nodded and then suggested I go back to the children.

'They need you, Annie, more than I do.'

It was getting late. There was only so much swimming and television to fill their time in that cooped-up space. *I'd better do what he says*, I thought.

'Let's go out to see what there is to eat around the Cross,' I said when I arrived back to see them meekly watching TV. At least that would get us all outside and walking.

'Fish and chips for me,' said Henry and Austin almost in unison, while Rebecca wanted a hamburger with 'the lot', something she had only recently discovered. This was one moment to indulge each of their fancies, so I didn't quibble.

When I saw Miles the next day, he shook his head. 'He isn't well enough to operate again. Anne, I think you should prepare yourself. I don't believe he has much time left.'

Next, I phoned my friend Alice Collins (now O'Connor), who had seen me through those first days at Sydney University. Over all those years, we had been close friends and kept in touch. She and her husband, John, had six children of their own. They lived on acreage with a pool and our children got on well together. Without my asking, she offered to have the children for a week or two.

The following afternoon, Miles looked fairly gloomy. But he said that if the chest condition Bruce had at Caritas cleared up, perhaps he might make it home again for a while.

Out of the blue, he asked me how I was coping.

Cracking hardy, I said I was fine. But Miles went on, 'Often what happens in cases like yours, Anne, is that all the attention is focused on the patient while the rest of us forget to look at what is happening to the other party.'

Apart from the issues raised in my interview with the psychiatrist, it was the first time any medical person had mentioned my needs in all those years. No doubt I looked self-reliant, keeping my end up with a cheerful face. But now, I realised I had suppressed my feelings for so long, I was not sure I properly understood the full depth of what was happening for me. I knew I was lucky: I had wonderful friends, fantastic family and support and was financially secure. Yet the past eight or so years of living with a sick, then dying, then not dying person were taking their toll.

But could I have had other choices? Perhaps I could have fallen into depression or worn the face of the long-suffering martyr, prayed a lot or gone into therapy. But I did none of these things. Instead, I chose the path of distraction, the path of doer-ship, the path of hope and the path of life. I was also realistic and knew that I had to prepare myself for a future without Bruce. A future that meant I had the full responsibility for the lives of five young people, all of whom deserved the best I could offer them.

We were by now about ten days away from the beginning of the 1973 school year. Vanessa was about to join her sister Alex at Rose Bay Convent as a boarder. Alex had moved into the senior school and Austin was about to begin his second year with the Jesuits at Riverview. The three of them had to be got ready and Vanessa's preparation was particularly important.

There were uniforms to alter, name tags to sew onto new clothes, books and sports outfits and tennis racquets to buy, forms to fill in and all the myriad of other large and small things children need to make the experience of boarding school happy and productive. As one-time boarders ourselves, Bruce and I both knew how important these preparations were, especially when the children would be so far away from home. I well remembered not having all the right equipment when I first went to Rose Bay Convent in 1946. I was determined to see my children didn't suffer from the feelings of embarrassment or lack that I had experienced.

Much to Alice's relief, I am sure, I picked up the children from the O'Connors and down the six of us went on the winding Hume Highway towards Fairfield in that white Holden station wagon. It had been sixteen years since that first journey as a bride in the old ute, a vehicle still sitting in the machinery shed as it rusted away in its well-earned retirement.

No crying for me now, only a grim determination to deal with what lay ahead. Farm wages had to be paid, the farm program planned, delivered via explicit instructions from Bruce, and the children pulled into service to help with crutching and the movement of sheep around the farm. I knew Bruce would want a detailed report when I got back to Sydney. In any case, since Phillip was new to us and to the property, it was important that he understood clearly we were on top of things, as much as that was possible under the circumstances.

After the Australia Day long weekend, Henry, ten, and Rebecca, eight, began their school year again at the Yerong Creek school. Julie stayed on to take care of them when, a week later, with all our tasks completed, Alex, Austin, Vanessa, Julie and I packed up the car with a full roof rack and the children and I began the eight-hour drive back to Sydney.

The three eldest children came with me to see Bruce before I took them to their schools. I reported back to Bruce at the hospital. He wanted to know everything in detail. How had moving the children into their schools gone, especially for

Vanessa? Were any sheep fly-blown back home, any troughs running dry? Had Phillip organised crutching? Eventually, he asked me, 'How did you manage it all, darling? How did you get the roof rack up on top of the station wagon? How did you get the suitcases up there?'

'It wasn't that difficult. I used the small ladder. Julie helped me lift up the suitcases and I remembered the way you covered them with the tarp in case we went through rain, and how you tied that on. I'm your best pupil, after all,' I said.

He looked at me solemnly and said, 'What a magnificent woman you are. I know why I married you!'

We both laughed but I knew he wasn't joking. Maybe I was a magnificent woman but I didn't feel like one at that moment. I was simply holding myself together so everything would get done and everyone would be taken care of – except, I now realise, me.

About three weeks later, when I thought he might be able to come home again, Bruce developed another bout of breathlessness and by the following Sunday afternoon began to lapse in and out of consciousness. Sometimes we might have a lucid conversation and then he would go off to another place, pulling at the medical paraphernalia attached to his body.

'Hold that pin in place, Bill. Where's that bolt?' he'd say, as if he was fixing a tractor or adjusting a bolt on the harvest equipment.

Once I heard him rounding up sheep and calling to the dogs. 'Come back here, Dusty! Go back, boy!' Familiar cries could be heard from the paddock of every farm around Australia.

Miles came in on Monday. 'How long has he been like that?' he asked.

'It started yesterday. He doesn't seem to be with us some of the time.'

'It's pneumonia again,' Miles told me. 'We can provide bigger doses of antibiotics, but this will only delay his suffering by a few days, maybe weeks. What do you think? It's really up to you.'

I went into Bruce's room and looked at his wizened body. He was on high doses of morphine, drips were hanging out of him, and an oxygen mask was over his face. I wanted to ask him what he thought but he was in no condition to have such a conversation.

How, in any case, does one frame the language of death? Did I have the right to make a decision about his life? What choice would he make if given the option?

The Gormans were no-nonsense pragmatists and Bruce had inherited something of that quality from his father. I believe now he was sending me a message of departure by entering another state, absenting himself from the rest of us. One minute, he was awake and could have a simple conversation; a few minutes later, his eyes would close and he would drift off or be calling to the dog as if he was rounding up the sheep. Somehow, he knew it was time. In the end, it wasn't so difficult a decision to make: let nature take its course and if nature lets him go and that ends his suffering, then that's how it should be.

I alerted family members, flew Rebecca and Henry down and brought the children out of boarding school to have their last visit. Father John Hosie, Stanley Hosie's younger brother who, throughout this time had been a magnificent support to me, came to the hospital on many days to see me and Bruce and had a few long talks with us both. Towards the end, John gave Bruce the last rites.

At 10 pm on 2 March 1973, I was sitting in the chair beside Bruce's bed, where I had been sitting most of the day every day for the last few weeks. I got up to adjust Bruce's bedclothes and, with that, he opened his eyes and said, 'Oh, you're going, darling. Goodbye.' We kissed and within minutes he lapsed back into his world of fantasies.

I had no intention of going. I had been thinking I would be there all night. The night sister-in-charge poked her head in the door and I went into the corridor to ask her what she thought.

'Well, he won't go tonight,' she said. 'All his vital signs are strong. If I were you, I'd go home to get some sleep and come back early tomorrow morning. It could be a few days yet.'

'I don't want to leave him without someone here,' I said. 'Can we get a special nurse from one of the agencies to sit with him till I get back in the morning?'

She agreed, and about an hour later a nurse arrived. I gave her my number and said if there was any change to call me immediately. My friend Shirley was staying with Joan and came in to pick me up. About midnight, we both returned to Joan's home and climbed straight into our beds.

At 4.15 am, the phone rang in the hall. I must have been on the edge of sleep and leapt out of bed to answer it. It was the sister-in-charge.

'Mrs Gorman,' she said, 'your husband passed away a few minutes before four. He slipped away peacefully.'

Regret is something I know a thing or two about: I know I did my best but was my best good enough? Could I have done more? Could I have saved my husband? But right at this moment, I regretted going home that night. Later, I would also regret not going immediately to the hospital to see my husband in death that last time. Instead, I got into bed with Joan and cried.

At 8 am, I did go in and spoke with Miles and my brother-in-law Neil. We sat on a hard mahogany bench in the echoing foyer of Royal Prince Alfred Hospital. Yet I still didn't ask to see Bruce's body, which, by then, had been moved to the hospital mortuary. I felt numb and disembodied. In my early twenties, as a white-garbed medical social worker, I had walked through this same foyer many times, little realising that eighteen years later, I would be here, not to console or counsel others but in need of consolation myself.

It was all so weird, so unreal. In the pit of my stomach, a small throbbing pulse reminded me I was still alive but worst of all that I was guilty. Guilty of not being there during his last moments. Guilty of allowing him to die in the first place. Guilty of being the one still alive.

I collected Bruce's few belongings. His battered wallet, his watch, a small transistor radio and a few other bits and pieces; what was left of a person's fifty-one years. All the knowledge he carried, all the potential to guide his children into adulthood gone, just like that.

Goodness knows what I did all that day; it's a blur. My first memory was of the next day sitting on a Fokker Friendship as I took off back to Wagga with my sisters and my three eldest children on board.

I knew it must be terrible for the children, but I was struggling so hard with my own feelings that I found it difficult to focus on much else. Henry was angry that no one had told him that his father was actually dying this time. They were older than I had been when my own father died, and I know now that is what I should have done.

For a good while, I carried the regret of not being with Bruce when he died. That changed when I went to hear Dr Elisabeth Kübler-Ross speak on the subject of death and dying. At the end of her presentation, one of the people in the audience asked her, 'Why is it that so many people die when their loved ones are no longer with them? Maybe they have even just left the room to make a cup of tea.'

She told the audience that many dying people find it hard to leave their bodies while the people they love are still around. While their loved ones are away from their side, they are free to go. I have no doubt that is why Bruce went that night and not at any other time. He knew he was going when he said, 'Oh, you're going, darling. Goodbye.'

I thought I was in charge, but it was really Bruce, or some other force, calling the shots until the very end.

35

the release

While I flew home for the funeral, Bruce's body made its way by hearse from Sydney along the Hume Highway, on which we had travelled so often before, always to the full symphony of children's complaints and laughter. As the plane sped on its way, I could not help thinking of him travelling those miles by himself. But I knew I needed to be with the living, my children.

Many people admired the way Bruce had endured his long illness. Some regarded him as a saint. I knew these people would want to attend the funeral. Most of the village would want to come, as well as friends from Wagga and the Riverina. Friends would also be coming from Sydney, Melbourne and Canberra, and the little Yerong Creek Catholic church could not accommodate them all.

The solution was to have an open-air funeral service at the Yerong Creek cemetery, a few miles west of the village – a magnificent setting, under the ancient Murray pines, with The Rock Hill as its majestic backdrop. Parishioners from the local Church of England would take their portable organ to the cemetery and the Hall Committee would transport chairs from the hall. All I had to do was get the bishop to agree. The new bishop, Frank Carroll, was a young man who had grown up in the district and, it was said, had more liberal views than the previous incumbent, Bishop Henschke.

The bishop did take some persuading, though. It was an unusual request. At first he was extremely dubious and said 'no'. I launched into a description of the numbers expected from Melbourne, Sydney and the district; the lack of accommodation in the very small church; and the willingness for people to help set it up properly. At no point did I consider having the funeral in the cathedral in Wagga, where Bruce's father's funeral had been held. Yerong Creek was Bruce's territory, a town to which he had given so much service. I knew he would have wanted his farewells to be said there.

Mercifully, the day was cool and overcast. Protestants and Catholics alike enthusiastically joined in the singing, as if we were part of the same congregation.

As I arrived at the cemetery, I saw Frankie with four of her children and their husbands and wives. They stood around her in a phalanx of solidarity to the memory of her son and their brother. I went up to kiss her and she grabbed me and held me close in a strong embrace. Both of us had tears in our eyes – two women united in our grief – the ones who loved Bruce the most.

Judy and Kerry were standing nearby. They had been involved in planning the funeral and I had a lot to thank them for. As I passed by, I squeezed Judy's hand and then it was time for us to take our own places and the Mass to begin.

The children and I, our arms around each other, stood beside the grave, each of us offering a flower as the coffin was quietly lowered into its place. The RSL sounded the 'Last Post' and then everyone else filed past to pay their respects, the pine trees whispering quietly to themselves and the congregation.

People moved silently among the old tombstones. Graves telling the story of families long since gone, of lives cut short by childbirth, epidemics taking whole families in their wake and district identities who had lived well beyond their three score years and ten.

The visitors then climbed into their cars and drove through the village, past the post office and store, both of which had closed for the afternoon out of respect. The procession moved across the railway line and onto Fairfield, where it was greeted by a group of local women led by the school principal's wife, busy preparing afternoon tea.

There was room for everyone on the lawn below the back verandah – the lawn I had so painstakingly levelled and planted with ornamental trees, which now shaded the crowd from the late afternoon sun. People were wonderfully kind as I wandered through in a dreamlike state, thanking individuals, kissing cheeks and shaking hands. *Bruce would have loved this*, I thought. He would have moved with ease, laughing with his old school friends, some of his air force mates and our mutual friends and family. The women came out of the kitchen carrying sandwiches and tea and then a full array of cakes and scones was set out on tables, brought from I know not where. Another one of those magnificent services provided with love by a local community.

Even though I had anticipated Bruce's death over so many years, it was only when it actually happened that the full reality of being alone hit me. The old house seemed strange without his presence. I had to keep reminding myself he wasn't there and would never be there again. To be honest, part of me was grateful. Grateful that his long suffering was over and grateful that I was freed from the burden of supporting him through this dreadful journey. I missed him terribly and allowed myself to weep again.

My sisters Joan, Christine, Phil and Carmel returned home to their lives in Sydney a few days after the funeral. Then a week later, Alex, Austin and Vanessa flew back to boarding school, leaving me at home with Henry and Rebecca.

One night soon after everyone had returned to Sydney, I was dreaming in the old brass bed Frankie had given us as a wedding present. The bed that had done so much excellent service since that first night after coming home from our honeymoon. In the dream, I found myself standing on a beach, looking at nature's artwork of spectacular cliff-face patterns of ochre, cream and brown. Suddenly, a stone rolled back to reveal a cave. It reminded me of pictures of the tomb where Jesus had been laid after the crucifixion.

Feeling immense trepidation, I was unwillingly propelled inside the cave. I was terrified but I couldn't stop myself going forward. Then I saw him. Bruce was lying on a marble slab. He sat up and greeted me lovingly. Straightaway, I saw that there was no trace of sickness; his arms and legs were plump and his cheeks were rosy. Smiling, he beckoned me to come closer. I was still being pushed towards him by the unknown force. What was I afraid of? I didn't know, but felt completely out of control. Wordlessly, Bruce pointed to his abdomen. There was no swelling.

'You see? It's all gone, darling. It's all right. Really. You don't have to worry any more. You see? I'm okay.' With that said, he lay down and very peacefully closed his eyes.

In that instant, I was awake and sitting bolt upright in bed. It seemed to be so real, so very real. My heart was beating wildly, my breathing was fast and shallow and I had broken out in a cold sweat.

Still shaking and awash in the dream, I got up and went to the kitchen for that age-old panacea in moments of crisis, a cup of tea. The kitchen clock said two in the morning but there was no way I was going back to bed. For the rest of the chilly night, I sat there and wrote about the events of the last weeks.

It was so like Bruce to want to relieve my mind. Relieve my guilt. Relieve my grief. Though it had been terrifying at the time, over the next few days I came to see that that was what the dream had done. His pain and suffering of the last almost ten years was over and his message was clear: I was free to put the anxiety, uncertainties and grief behind me and to get on with my life.

Not long before Bruce died, I had turned thirty-nine. There were challenges waiting out there for me. I didn't know what they were, yet I looked forward to them. I wasn't sure what they would mean for the children or whether I would be up to what might transpire.

In my naivety, I could never have imagined the possibilities that lay ahead or the risks of going solo into Shakespeare's 'naughty world' without the steadying and consoling hand of a loving partner and a bolthole to hide in when things went wrong.

36

catalysts

It was 1973, nine months after Bruce's death, the college had finished for the year and the harvesting had been halted because of heavy rain the night before. As the machines stood silent, the cicadas' incessant call from beneath the earth took up the sound of summer. It was a bumper year and the race would soon be on to get the crops off quickly, in case it rained again. Rain meant a huge drop in wheat quality and lower prices from the Wheat Board.

Rebecca and I were taking a break from cooking Christmas cakes, sipping morning tea on the back verandah. Suddenly, the dogs started barking and my brother-in-law Kerry, who owned the adjoining property, came through the gate at the end of the verandah, stepping onto the boards where the grapevine ended. Hard on his heels, like a small pack of sheep dogs, came Austin, Henry and Vanessa.

Kerry sat down beside me and after a few pleasantries told me he had some bad news. My first thought was that Alex might have been injured water skiing on the north coast, where she was staying with a school friend.

'No, Annie, it's not anything like that,' he said. 'To cut a long story short, Phillip is stealing from you.'

Early that morning, Austin, now fourteen, had seen Phillip driving the ute off the property, loaded with a bale of wool.

'We checked in the woolshed, Mum. There were two bales of wool there yesterday; now there's only one.'

Austin had also rung the wool buyer in Wagga. Sure enough, they had records of wool sold to them by Phillip, giving his address as Yerong Creek, over a ten-month period.

An incident from a few days before sprang to mind: I'd been travelling the thirteen miles south to Henty. Hurtling towards me in the opposite direction came our Bedford truck, driven by Phillip. I remembered thinking the truck would not last much longer if it was driven like that. And then I wondered what Phillip had been doing in Henty. My understanding was that he'd set out to put it over the Yerong Creek weighbridge.

Kerry's advice was to dismiss Phillip and leave it be – not to make waves. I didn't agree. To my way of thinking, if Phillip could get away with this and men around the district knew, I would be fair game. So we agreed that I should call the local policeman and tell him the story.

I was very proud of my children. They had wisdom and initiative beyond their years. Together, the five of us took a trip to Wagga and collected copies of the wool dockets with Phillip's name on them. The following day, Austin and I made the drive to Henty and spoke to the grain merchant.

'Yes,' said the merchant, 'Phillip has been here, and yes, I did buy a load of wheat from him.' But somehow he didn't have the dockets. 'It had all been a cash transaction. No records kept.'

Two days later, a couple of well-built plain-clothes rural police officers arrived on our doorstep. They had arranged to camp out in an old woolshed so their presence would not raise suspicion around the district. They didn't have much to do, really, because by the time they arrived, we'd gathered most of the evidence.

Kerry came over again to support me when I ended Phillip's employment: 'Phillip, I'm afraid I am giving you your notice.'

His face went bright red and he looked stunned. 'Why! Why!' he said. 'I thought I've been doing a good job.'

'Phillip, you will be hearing from the rural police today. They have all the evidence. We know you have sold wool to the wool merchants in Wagga and I know you've sold at least one load of wheat in Henty, so let's get this over with. Here is your cheque paid up until the end of the month. You can stay in the house in the village until a week after Christmas. Drive off the property now and don't come back under any circumstance.'

At that, he leapt to his feet and the kitchen chair fell over. He marched out of the kitchen, slamming the fly-screen door as hard as he could, and angrily stomped down the length of the verandah.

Kerry said quietly, 'Well done, Annie,' and soon afterwards we watched as Phillip's car took off in a cloud of dust.

A few days later, Phillip's father came over from Condobolin unannounced. He was the smoothest of talkers and started the conversation by telling me that I should be standing for the senate, and 'We need a woman like you in the parliament. I spoke to my friend Al Grassby about you. We could get up a lot of support for you to stand for a local seat.'

It was obvious that all this buttering up had a strong motivation. He wanted to keep his son out of gaol or at least without a legal blemish on his character. I held my tongue, only nodding from time to time so he eventually got to the point.

He apologised for his son and then offered to pay me any monies that might be owed. 'Phillip is my youngest, you know, and still has a thing or two to learn.'

But I only nodded and he filled the silence. 'I'm willing to reimburse you for your losses, so when you know what they are I will send you a cheque.'

Without waiting for my calculations, he did his own. A week later, a long letter arrived, telling me what a wonderful woman I was and how respected I was, etc., etc. It was accompanied by a cheque for $3000 to compensate me.

The whole business had left me in a highly vulnerable situation. Kerry I knew I could rely on, but he had his own property to deal with and had his own children at boarding school in Sydney to find fees for. I needed another manager, someone I could rely on. Now that people knew Phillip had left, was I even safe out here?

A few days after Phillip's departure, I received a visit from a member of our church, John, whom I had known for some years. He had been working at one of the biggest properties in the area and wondered if I might require a new manager. This was a godsend and John started to work for me the following week.

After Bruce's death, I'd employed a housekeeper – a mature woman, who was a good cook, competent and reliable to be in charge of the children. One night, when she had taken leave over the Christmas break, I was woken by a loud banging on the front door. Half asleep, I pulled on a dressing gown over my nightdress and threw the bolt. Standing on the other side of the fly-screen door stood the two rural policemen, all six foot three and sixteen stone of them.

It was clear that they wanted to come in. I opened the flyscreen door and led them down the wide black and white tiled hall, across the polished floor of the middle verandah, still sporting a decorated Christmas tree, and into the formality of the carpeted living room. Slightly dazed for a few moments, I sat there looking at them. Hurriedly and, it seemed to me, with some embarrassment, the pair offered an explanation.

'We wanted you to know that we've charged Phillip formally,' the younger of the two offered.

'Oh, good,' I said, although I thought they had already done that.

'Who else is here in the house with you?' enquired the older guy.

'Just me and the children.' Passing my bedroom, they would have seen there was no one else in the double bed.

'Do you normally live here on your own?'

'Well, yes and no. Since my husband died, it's just me and the children, and during the week a housekeeper as well. I have a number of city friends and family; they often come to stay with their children during school holidays. Some friends from Wagga were here today but went home around seven.'

Then came the lecture. 'It's not safe to be here on your own. Who lives in that cottage over there?'

'No one,' I answered. 'It's derelict but it belongs to my brother-in-law. He lives just a mile up the road. I know if I needed him, he would come immediately.'

I put some emphasis on the words 'my brother-in-law', thinking it might make them go away rather more quickly than they seemed inclined to do.

'There is a small cottage I've been looking at. I know it's for sale and it could easily be moved somewhere into that front paddock and I could have someone move in there.'

'Good,' they chimed in unison.

'Do it then,' said the bulkier one.

'I'll take your advice,' I said. *Anything to get these guys out of my living room.*

I knew from past experience that having someone living on the property wouldn't necessarily make me safer. Kerry had had the occasional oddball living in his cottage and one had become a worry during Bruce's life. Besides, I had just employed a new manager who had his own home in the village.

'I've never had any worries but if you think I should ...' my voice trailed away and I was beginning to become acutely aware of my bare feet and light dressing gown. They, too, had begun to look sheepish, if not downright embarrassed. They rose to their feet; thankfully, the awkward conversation was drawing to a close.

Down the hallway they strode, once more pointedly glancing into my bedroom as they went, leaving me to ponder what had triggered this unusual visit. One thing I had never felt at Fairfield was fear of any unknown threat. In general, I wasn't a fearful person and wasn't about to embrace their concerns. Did they know something they weren't telling me? What had they really come for?

Later it emerged that, having been found out as a thief, Phillip had been spreading stories around the pub about me. And in that gossipy environment, some of the mud must have stuck. I was an attractive widow. I had male friends. That very day, I'd had some of my colleagues from the college out for lunch. We'd eaten well and drunk wine under the grapevines and we'd been swimming in the new pool I'd had built. Their children and my children had cavorted around the place, played tennis, swum and rode the ponies. It was altogether a successful day. To the best of my knowledge, everyone drove home sober.

Compared to the rural folk of the village, my guests might have seemed a little out of the ordinary. An American lecturer in psychology and his wife; members of the Wagga Wagga branch of the Labor Party; a lesbian social-work student and her girlfriend, who were not averse to swimming topless in the pool; likewise a couple of openly gay male friends, including a bursar from the college. Once, I invited some of my college students out to an end-of-term barbecue, some of whom looked like long-haired hippies. They came with their guitars and sang the revolutionary songs of the day by Bob Dylan and Joan Baez, while Helen Reddy's 'I am woman, hear me roar', sounded my favourite clarion call.

Maybe the rural constables were genuinely worried about the possibility of an unwanted visit from one of the pub drinkers. Perhaps they were checking me out. It was also possible they felt they deserved a piece of the action. If so, all they got was a darkened building, a semi-comatose woman in her night dress and a house full of sleeping children. What a disappointment!

These episodes seeded a thought: I was in a vulnerable situation but I also knew I was free. Free to do whatever I wanted to do. Free even to sell up and move on. It would be a difficult choice because I was attached to the farm and to the house as well. What would the children say? What would the Gorman clan say or think, too? It was their childhood home and some might still be emotionally attached to the old place.

I started walking around the 1000-acre property – something I had never done before. Mostly, I had seen it through the window of a ute. One of the places I loved to visit on foot was a small grove of trees in the corner of a paddock. Bruce had told me this spot had been left as shelter for stock and as a reminder of how things had been before white men arrived to clear the paddocks for cropping. Huge logs lay around the little grove, once mighty gums, victims of earlier attempts at subjugation. Most of the space was protected by the enormous box gum survivors, their trunks adorned with hanging bark, like sad celebratory streamers at the end of a party.

Surrounded by so much majesty, I would take my place among the fallen logs, listening to the birds and the whispering gums, thinking of the Indigenous people who might have once lived or passed by here. On a hot day, the little grove was cool and in winter it was warmly protected from the cold west wind. A place to inspire poetry, to meditate or just imbibe the wonder of a natural environment, left untouched by agriculture.

At those moments, I sensed I was in the presence of something sacred – of an ancient culture. I also knew I was now the sole custodian of this land and that made me even more humble in its presence. Letting it go seemed unthinkable. But sitting there one day, it came to me, as if a voice had whispered it in my ear. No one could ever own this land. It belonged and had always belonged to itself. It would be here long after I was dead and gone and those coming after me as well. Then I asked its spirit for guidance to do whatever was best for my family and for me. That is when I knew it would soon be time to let it go.

Epilogue

Bruce hated elaborate shows of masonry in cemeteries and I knew he would have wanted something simple and elegant. The plain grey piece of polished marble over his grave carries this simple inscription:

> James Bruce Gorman
> 1922–1973
> Beloved husband of Anne and loving father of
> Alexandra, Austin, Vanessa, Henry and Rebecca.
> 'The virtuous man, though he die before his time,
> will find rest.'
> The Book of Wisdom (4:7-15)

Bruce was a virtuous man and I was the lucky one to have made the choice to marry him. It was unfair that he did not live to watch his children grow up nor had the choices that opened up for me.

The Whitlam Government had come to power in 1972, just four months before Bruce died. Whitlam jumped right into a raft of radical reforms. Troops were withdrawn from Vietnam and military conscription abolished. Free tertiary education was introduced and mature-aged women stormed the universities to take advantage of opportunities never offered them before. It was as though the country had woken from a long, long sleep.

Only weeks after Bruce's death, I received an invitation to stand for preselection for an upcoming vacancy in the senate. This invitation was a result of my work with the Labor party in the federal seat of Farrar. During that campaign, I had met politicians such as Tom Uren and Senator Arthur Gietzelt from the Left faction of the Labor party. And so, with a reliable housekeeper to look after the children, I went to Sydney and began to meet with delegates who would vote for one or other of the two candidates. In no time, I had the numbers and this upset the right-wing faction, who had lined up their own candidate. The head office officials targeted me and my supporters with a dirty tricks campaign to pressure us to withdraw from the ballot. We succumbed, but not without a struggle.

This event brought me my five minutes of fame – my name and photo were displayed all over the front pages of *The Sydney Morning Herald*, the afternoon newspapers and even the *Wagga Daily Advertiser* – a legacy, even though a losing one. People wanted to meet me. I had emerged as a visible presence at a time when the women's movement under Whitlam's national feminist agenda was in full flight.

Consequently, when Tom Uren, the Minister for Urban and Regional Development, was looking for a woman to go on the Board of the Cities Commission, I was the one he thought of. And about six months later, out of the blue, I was offered the job of Social Planner at the Albury-Wodonga Development Corporation, one of several growth centres, as part of the new government's decentralisation agenda.

I felt I was part of an opportunity to forge a new Australia. I moved to Albury with Rebecca, the only child still at home, taking her from the eighty-pupil school at Yerong Creek and enrolling her in the Albury primary school, which had more than a thousand students. Amazingly, this kid from a bush school distinguished herself the following year by becoming its head girl and a champion netballer.

Nearly two years later, and following the drama of the Whitlam Dismissal of 1975, Rebecca and I were driving home to Yerong Creek for the weekend, having spent most of the day in the autumn sunshine handing out how-to-vote cards at polling booths for the state election. As we drove home along the Olympic Highway, listening to the radio commentators, we cottoned on that history was being made. Even though a federal Labor government had been voted out a mere six months earlier, a bemused Neville Wran was accepting his party's unexpected victory.

On the heels of that poll result, six months later, another offer would be coming my way. An offer to implement the childcare policies that had been part of Labor's election promises.

Rebecca and I moved to Sydney. There Rebecca would become a day student at Kincoppal-Rose Bay. Having sold Hills Park, I had the money to buy a house with a swimming pool at Manning Road, Double Bay. We needed plenty of room for the children to have their country friends to visit and enjoy each other's company. Once they no longer needed to go to boarding school, they all moved back home.

Alex had got a very high mark in her final exams, allowing her to pick any course she wanted at any university. She was awarded a Rotary Scholarship and flew off with Qantas to have a wonderful year in Washington state near Seattle. There she experienced living with several different American families and wrote home to tell us what a marvellous family she had grown up with ... her own.

When the home front was settled, I started my job implementing the most far-reaching childcare policies the state had ever seen. New South Wales was far behind every other state in its allocation of funds for childcare and one of the biggest election promises Neville Wran had made during his election campaign was to establish a network of childcare facilities.

One night, I was sitting next to a Treasury official at a state dinner when he started to share his opinions on childcare with me.

'I know for sure from my work with the Scout Movement,' he said, 'that children who attend childcare before they're five, turn out to be delinquents.'

'You really believe that!' I said.

Missing the nuance in my response, he replied, 'Yes, yes, I do.' Warming to his subject, he plunged on. 'When I was in charge of oversighting your department's budget,' he said, 'I made sure I never approved funds for childcare services.'

He'd done me a favour: now I knew who to bypass and why New South Wales spent almost nothing on childcare.

Eventually, with the support of the Labor Women's group and their lobbying skills, we developed a raft of new policies and services, and got around Treasury to secure New South Wales's proper share of the federal childcare budget.

In 1979, I was invited to take on the extra responsibilities of the United Nations' International Year of the Child campaign in Australia. That year, I led a delegation to Moscow for an IYC conference and twelve months later, I accepted an offer of a travelling fellowship from the US Children's Defense Fund to study childcare policies in America. Leaving my children with Joan, who moved into our Double Bay home while I was away, I set off on a study trip of a lifetime, a highlight being lunch at the White House and a Washington reception where President Jimmy Carter gave the dinner address. To view my special interests in a broader landscape, to meet such important people and to bask in the admiration of what Australia had done during IYC were some of the most affirming experiences of my life.

Ten years after Bruce died, I sold Fairfield. Ever since his death, it had remained as a refuge to come back to. It took a year of terrible dust storms, drought, a locust plague and the threat of bushfires for me to make the final break and sell the property. Sold with all its friendly ghosts and memories – my sanctuary from the stress and busyness of my professional life in Sydney and a magnificent playground for the children. Letting it go was both a terrible wrench and a blessed release. Even so, it will always be a big part of our family identity.

In those days, I was moving fast, performing a high-level job in government while juggling my responsibilities as a single parent with five children in various stages of education. Up in the morning by five, out into the park for a run, breakfast on the table and school lunches prepared by seven, beds made and house tidied, then everyone on their respective school bus before eight, leaving me to drive to work by 8.30. I was working with a state government minister as a policy adviser. Before the days of legislation making it illegal, one of the senior politicians I had to deal with was prone to sexually harassing female staff, including me. Of course I was trying, as all good feminists were doing in this era of the 'superwoman', to handle it all. And wondering why trying to do it all left me falling asleep over dinner and speechless with exhaustion.

I found the courage to resign my position with the harassing minister after five years. It was a risk. I had school fees to meet but I started a consultancy practice in organisational development and later in executive coaching. Later, I was betrayed by a business partner, lost money, ended up in court to retrieve what I had lost, and won with the help of my son-in-law John – Alex's husband, who is a very able senior barrister – and a wise and just judge. Luck and good will were often on my side and I never quite knew why I deserved so much of them.

My children, those precious beings, helped me juggle work and domesticity and were in many ways as disciplined as I had to be. One unexpected bonus of having five children was the 'alert' system they developed for when they knew one of them needed my special attention. Typically, I would have a visit from one of them as I was sitting up in bed reading. They would say, 'Mum, did you know … had a problem with … at school. I think it might be a good idea if you talk to her/him about it.' We were all in this together, after all. I describe my solo parenting as 'benign neglect': intervene when necessary, say 'yes' most of the time and 'no' when you really mean it and are prepared to make it stick.

Sure, I made mistakes as a parent, and my children would be the first to tell you what they were. But I do know this: my preoccupations gave the children freedoms most of their friends envied, and it built in them a lifelong sense of resilience and responsibility. To my eternal gratitude, they grew up to be my best friends.

As I look back on saying 'yes' on Shelly Beach to the question 'Annie, will you marry me?', I'm glad I did, even amid the pain that came with loving and losing such a dear man – a perfect husband and father.

He was an unusual bushie and ahead of the times. In the face of criticism, he supported me in every way and was not afraid of putting this into words, as evidenced in this letter.

Annie Darling,
Times were when we put Mother on that early morning train she would have been heading off to a doctor's appointment or a social engagement in Melbourne. But this morning, by contrast, it was my wife going off to make her mark in a bigger world. How wonderful that is.

I wanted you to know how proud I am of you and all you do. Keep doing it. I'm sure you'll make a magnificent contribution at that conference. You bring joy to my life at every moment in all your enterprises and I wouldn't have it otherwise.

Your greatest admirer and loving husband
Bruce

As for Bruce's wish that I should marry after his death, I didn't manage to fulfil it. One or two people said they loved me, and I said I loved them back. For some time, I looked around at people with partners and felt deprived, then had one disastrous relationship. After that, somehow it never seemed possible to chance a stepfather or embark on the fantasy of a Brady Bunch. My children came first, second, third, fourth and fifth. Even after they had all left home, we were a happy family. No need to tamper with that.

Sometimes I wonder whether I could have, or should have, loved my mother more. Here she is again in my consciousness after all those years, a woman who always felt railing against life or blaming God or even dwelling on regrets were fruitless exercises and I must have inherited that from her.

As for Frankie, she was badly affected by Bruce's death and began to decline in health. Within a year or so, she packed up her house in the village and moved to live in a granny flat close to her daughter Fran on her property near The Rock. She died in Calvary Hospital in October 1978 and was buried in the Wagga cemetery next to her husband.

There is so much to be grateful for – a home, an apple pie man, a supportive family and a fulfilling occupation. Every spiritual principle is important but gratitude, I have come to realise, underpins all the rest because without it, there is nothing to join us together. Most of all, I am grateful for the gift of forgiveness – for the ability to forgive others and for the gift of self-forgiveness for those times I might have wittingly or unwittingly wronged others during this rich and fruitful life.

I am happy in the knowledge that I have done my best, even among the mistakes I've made and that more of the best is still to come.

Acknowledgements

When people ask how long it took me to write this memoir, I have to tell them the truth: it took me years. But starting it was the hardest part, and for that I have to thank Bridget Brandon for her Storyworks courses. Thanks to her, the contents of many notebooks filled during that time became the genesis of *The Country Wife*. I also thank her filmmaker son Brandon for the important part he played in this.

At a time when my energy to complete the book began to flag, rescue came from my dear friend and fellow writer Julie Bail, who introduced me to the Varuna Writers' Centre, where I wrote large chunks of this story. I gratefully acknowledge Peter Bishop (Varuna's founding creative director) and his encouragement during those periods and beyond.

My daughter Vanessa Gorman, whose own memoir *Layla's Story*, was my inspiration, painstakingly polished drafts of the manuscript, cutting and moving passages around until we both thought it good enough to take to an agent, Lyn Tranter. Thank you, Lyn, for your faith in me, and for finding the wonderful Fiona Henderson at Random House to take it on. Her faith in this book sprang from her own experience of rural life; she saw a tale that needed to be told to a wider audience, lest earlier days be forgotten. Fiona's team included structural editor Vanessa Mickan, who brought great artistry to shaping this work and taught me much about structure and focus, while Anne Reilly's copy-editing and other assistance brought grace and precision to the task.

What would history be without family? I am indebted to my sisters Philomena Skurrie (deceased) and Joan Wales for Austin family stories and anecdotes from a time before I was born. I am also indebted to my sisters-in-law Barbara Parnell and Fran Morton for their generous contributions covering the life of their parents before I became part of their family.

I owe a similar debt to my nephew Terry Austin for his invaluable research into my parents' ancestry. Thanks to my sister Christine Chaseling for her contributions to this history and to my niece Judy King for sharing difficult memories of things past, also to Robbie and his wife, Vicky King, for sharing their home for many large family gatherings. I am most grateful to my godchild and niece, Angela Wales Kirgo. Without her professional contacts, I might never have met Lyn Tranter.

To my children, Alexandra, Austin, Vanessa, Henry (especially for his help with photography) and Rebecca, thank you for bringing life to these pages. My heartfelt thanks go to my sons-in-law the two Johns – John Fernon and John Sevior – whose generous support at a difficult time gave me the peace of mind to continue with this venture.

Thanks also must go my friends Elspeth Browne, who read and edited an early manuscript, fellow writers Suzanne Marks, Shirley Ryan (now Elizabeth Crennan), Kayt Raymond, filmmaker Cathy Henkel for their support and assistance and Neelima George who when I came for a visit, gave me space to write a whole chapter in her home by the ocean. To Mehul

Joshi, thank you for your kind feedback and suggestions and to that believer in miracles, Michael McKinley, thank you for your insights about so very much.

Finally, I am grateful to many members of various incarnations of our writing group, especially for your good grace and feedback, even when it might not have been entirely deserved. In this regard, the kindness of Karen Prout, Deidre Ferguson and Desmond Edwards' humour, who kept me laughing at all times.

To all those living and dead, whose presence is brought to life within these pages, thank you for being part of this story. And to writers, readers and publishers everywhere, may we grow and thrive.

About the Author

Anne Gorman was born in Mudgee, the eleventh child in her family. After graduating from Sydney University with a BA and a postgraduate degree in Medical Social Work, her career plans hadn't factored in her decision to marry a farmer and move to a sheep and wheat property in the Riverina. When her husband became gravely ill, Anne had to take up the reins to keep the property afloat and bring up their five children alone. She later went on to have a long and highly successful professional career, including serving as head of the Australian government's task force for International Year of the Child to the United Nations. In 2003 she established The Institute of Executive Coaching with an American partner. Her clients included Telstra, BHP, ANZ and state and federal government departments. This is her first book.

Loved the book?

Join thousands of other readers online at

AUSTRALIAN READERS:

randomhouse.com.au/talk

NEW ZEALAND READERS:

randomhouse.co.nz/talk